# Human Aggression

# PERSPECTIVES IN SOCIAL PSYCHOLOGY
*A Series of Texts and Monographs* • Edited by Elliot Aronson

INTRINSIC MOTIVATION
   By Edward L. Deci

SCHOOL DESEGREGATION
   By Harold B. Gerard and Norman Miller

HUMAN AGGRESSION
   By Robert A. Baron

A Continuation Order Plan is available for this series. A continuation order will bring delivery of each new volume immediately upon publication. Volumes are billed only upon actual shipment. For further information please contact the publisher.

# Human Aggression

### ROBERT A. BARON

*Purdue University*
*West Lafayette, Indiana*

*PLENUM PRESS · NEW YORK AND LONDON*

Library of Congress Cataloging in Publication Data

Baron, Robert A
    Human aggression.

    (Perspectives in social psychology)
    Bibliography: p.
    Includes index.
    1. Aggressiveness (Psychology) I. Title.
BF575.A3B35             301.6'3             77-24567
ISBN 0-306-31050-3

© 1977 Plenum Press, New York
A Division of Plenum Publishing Corporation
227 West 17th Street, New York, N.Y. 10011

Printed in the United States of America

To The Little Red-Haired Girl,
who is the source of *my* incompatible responses,
and to my parents,
who gave me the freedom to grow.

# *Preface: A Note to My Colleagues*

An announcement appearing in a recent issue of a newsletter distributed quarterly to several thousand psychologists read, in part, as follows:

> Free. A bibliography of approximately *350 books on human aggression* is available from Prof. Gordon W. Russell. (Italics added)

Given such a wealth of existing materials on aggressive behavior, one may well wonder why, at the present time, I have chosen to add to this huge assemblage by writing still another volume on the same topic. While this is an eminently reasonable question, I hope that I can respond to it with equally reasonable answers. Basically, my decision to produce the present volume stemmed from two major sources.

First, it grew quite naturally out of my own teaching experience. Over the years, I have frequently conducted both advanced undergraduate and graduate classes on the topic of human aggression. Unfortunately, in selecting appropriate texts for these courses, I have often found myself confronting something of a dilemma. The choice, it seemed, was one between two distinct categories of books. In the first were several scholarly, comprehensive treatises, which were designed for professional audiences and which, as a result, were far "over the heads" of the students I asked to read them. In the second group, by way of contrast, were a number of briefer, simpler texts, more readily comprehended by unsophisticated readers. Disappointingly, though, these were also usually quite restricted in scope. Thus, while both groups offered certain important advantages, neither seemed quite appropriate for several of my courses.

After I had confronted this dilemma on a number of different occasions, the idea of the present volume began to take shape. Could one write a text on human aggression, I wondered, that would be both (1) comprehensible to undergraduate and beginning graduate-student readers and (2) at the same time comprehensive and up-to-date in coverage? I wasn't sure, but it seemed well worth the effort to find out. It was within this general framework that the present text developed.

As I soon learned, it is one thing to establish joint goals of comprehensibility and comprehensiveness of coverage and quite another to attain them. In order to help reach these objectives, then, I soon found it necessary to adopt several specific strategies, all of which should be made explicit here. First, with respect to comprehensibility, I attempted to write the text in a manner that would place it within the grasp of readers who had not yet completed advanced training in the behavioral sciences. This approach necessitated a reduction in the amount of detail presented at some points and the omission of certain statistical considerations. Yet it did not, I believe, require any sacrifice in scientific accuracy. Second, in contrast to most other volumes on this topic, I decided to make use of a wide range of illustrative materials. Thus, the present text contains a number of graphs and tables (all of which have been simplified from their original form in other sources or have been specially created for the present volume), as well as several photos and cartoons. My own teaching experience suggested that such materials often serve a valuable function in communicating important points and findings to readers, and they were included in the text for this reason. Finally, I attempted to hold the length of the volume to what I considered to be a manageable level. Thus, the book is long enough, I feel, to provide comprehensive coverage but not so long as to prove numbing to individuals whose interest in the topic of human violence does not quite equal our own.

With respect to my second goal, comprehensiveness of coverage, I again adopted several specific strategies. First, although the text focuses upon *human* aggression, construed within a social psychological framework, other theoretical perspectives concerning this topic are also described (see Chapter 1). Second, I have made a concerted effort to present as much information as possible and to represent as many different lines of research as feasible, given the space limitations mentioned above. As a result, both traditional areas of investigation (e.g., catharsis, the influence of frustration, the impact of punishment) and also many newer lines of research, to which I will return below, are represented in various chapters. And finally, I have included a separate unit on methods for the study of aggression—a feature that I believe to be unique to the present volume. In these ways, I have attempted to produce a text that is as broad and eclectic in coverage as I could make it.

While the present volume grew, in part, out of my desire to produce what I thought might prove to be a useful teaching aid, it also developed out of a second major motive. During the past few years, a large number of new—and to me, exciting—lines of investigation have emerged in rapid order. These have been extremely varied in scope, including, among many others, such diverse topics as the effects of sexual arousal upon aggression, the impact of environmental factors (e.g., heat, noise, crowding) upon such behavior, interracial aggression, and the influence of heightened self-awareness. Despite the fact that such topics have already generated a considerable amount of research, they were not, to my knowledge, adequately represented in any existing volume. Given this state of affairs, it seemed to me that a reasonably comprehensive summary of this newer work might prove both useful and timely. In particular, I felt that it might serve as a useful source of reference both for new researchers wishing an overview of the field and for established researchers whose harried schedules made it difficult for them to keep up with all lines of research and all new developments. The present volume, then, was written with this second goal firmly in mind. In sum, *Human Aggression* grew out of my desires to (1) provide a text suitable for use in conjunction with advanced undergraduate and beginning graduate courses on aggression and (2) provide a useful summary of recent lines of investigation as yet unincorporated into existing texts. Looking back, I can honestly say that I have spared no effort in my attempts to attain these goals. Given the imperfect nature of all human endeavors, though, I am also sure that I have fallen short of my ideal objectives in several different respects. My major hope, then, is simply that I have at least moved in the right (i.e., useful) directions. Of course, in an important sense, only you, my colleagues and readers, can tell me whether, and to what extent, this is in fact the case. Thus, I eagerly— and a bit impatiently—await your judgments and comments.

ROBERT A. BARON

*West Lafayette, Indiana*

# *Acknowledgments*

In writing this text, I have been aided immeasurably by many individuals. While I could not hope to list all of them here, I can, at the least, offer my thanks to those whose assistance has been most important.

First, I would like to thank the many colleagues who—by keeping me abreast of their own work, responding to my requests for reprints and preprints, and sharing their ideas with me—have made a substantial contribution to this volume. In a very real sense, it could not have been written without their aid.

Second, I would like to extend my sincere appreciation to my good friend Dolf Zillmann, who, through our many personal discussions, has often helped me to shape and hone my ideas. His contribution to the present volume in this and many other ways is gratefully acknowledged.

Third, I wish to extend special thanks to Ed Donnerstein, whose thoughtful and insightful reviews of the entire manuscript helped me to improve it in many different respects.

Fourth, I would like to express my gratitude to Seymour Weingarten, my editor, whose enthusiasm for the project was always high and whose expert opinions, thoughtful suggestions, and unflagging sense of humor (!) helped guide it to successful completion.

And finally, I wish to thank my wife, Sandra, who evaluated each chapter as it was completed, who prepared the entire manuscript for publication, and who, through her support and encouragement, helped me to face all those lonely and seemingly endless sessions at the typewriter. To her, to the other persons mentioned on this page, and to many others as well, a warm and heartfelt "THANKS!"

R.A.B.

# *Contents*

## 6. THE PREVENTION AND CONTROL OF HUMAN AGGRESSION

# 1

# Aggression: Definitions and Perspectives

Mylai; Bangladesh; Angola; Beirut; the Symbionese Liberation Army; terrorism in Africa and the Middle East; senseless violence on the streets of major cities; murder; kidnap; rape; assassination; child abuse—the list of human cruelty seems almost endless. Indeed, so common do instances of aggression or violence appear to be at the present time that it is virtually impossible to pick up a daily newspaper, leaf through a popular magazine, or tune in the evening news without learning of the occurrence of several new and shocking atrocities.

Given this unsettling state of affairs, it often seems as though we must be living in a period when the "dark side" of human nature is stronger and less well controlled than at any time in the past. Even a cursory examination of the events of other centuries, however, suggests that this is not the case. History reveals a long and uninterrupted record of war, invasion, torture, and destruction, stretching back to the shadowy beginnings of organized society. While the list is far too long to be examined here, a small sample of violence in other eras is provided by the following events:

—Upon the capture of Troy, in 1184 B.C., the victorious Greeks speedily executed all males over the age of 10, and sold the remaining population of women and children into slavery.

—After defeating their arch rival, Carthage, in 146 B.C., the conquering Roman legions massacred all defenders who had yielded, burned the city to the ground, and sowed the surrounding fields with salt, thus ensuring that they could never be used for agricultural production again.

—Over the course of the Mongolian invasions of central Asia and eastern Europe (1223–1241 A.D.), Genghis Khan's conquering hordes burned scores

1

of cities (including Moscow and Kiev) and massacred literally millions of
unarmed peasants and civilians.
—During the height of the Spanish Inquisition (1420–1498), several thousand
men, women, and children were burned alive at the stake for heresy and
other "crimes" against the Church or the state.

In the face of such evidence of human savagery in the past, we must
conclude that the 20th century holds no monopoly on widespread violence and brutality.

When human beings aggressed against others by means of spears,
bows and arrows, blowguns, or other primitive weapons, their assaults were destructive and led to much needless suffering. Yet, these
attacks were generally restricted to one locale and never threatened the
existence of the entire species. The power of modern weaponry, however, has radically changed all this. Today, at least two nations—and
probably soon others as well—possess the capacity to decimate all life
on earth. Moreover, we now seem to be entering a period of nuclear
proliferation, when weapons of mass destruction can be produced at
what amounts to "bargain-basement" prices and with minimal technological knowledge. These developments, unfortunately, threaten to
hasten their spread among even the poorest and least powerful nations
on earth.

In view of these unsettling trends, there can be little doubt that
the unchecked spread of violence and conflict must be numbered
among the most serious problems facing humanity today. As should
be apparent, however, recognition of this fact represents only the
first—and in some ways the simplest—step in a complex chain of inquiry. Why, we must also ask, do human beings aggress? What factors
combine to render such behavior so commonplace in human interaction? And, perhaps most important of all, what steps can be taken to
prevent or control their occurrence? Questions such as these have been
of concern to thoughtful individuals down through the ages. Moreover, they have been examined from several different perspectives,
including those of the philosopher, the poet, and the priest. It is only
during the present century, however, that they have become the subject of systematic, scientific inquiry. Indeed, the bulk of this research
has been completed only within the past two or three decades.

Given this relatively short period of orderly study, it is not surprising that answers to all of our questions concerning aggression are

not yet available. In fact, research on this intriguing topic has often yielded quite the opposite effect, raising more issues than it has resolved. Much progress *has* been made, however, and today, we already know a great deal more about the roots and nature of human aggression than we knew even a decade ago. Unfortunately, so much evidence has been gathered concerning this topic, and so much has been written about it, that it would be quite unwise—if not impossible—to consider all of this material within the scope of the present volume. Partly out of necessity and partly out of choice, then, our discussion will be restricted in two important ways.

First, it will focus primarily upon *human* aggression; similar behavior on the part of members of other species will be of only secondary interest. It is realized, of course, that many excellent studies of animal aggression have been conducted and that the findings of such research are quite instructive in many respects (see, e.g., Eleftheriou & Scott, 1971; Hutchinson, 1972; Scott, 1973). However, since aggression by men and women seems to involve many factors unique to human behavior (e.g., the desire for revenge, racial or ethnic prejudice) and since it is *this* form of behavior that threatens the continued survival of all humankind, it seems reasonable to concentrate mainly upon this topic.

Second, the present discussion will examine aggression primarily from a *social* perspective. That is, aggression will be viewed as a form of social behavior involving direct or indirect interaction between two or more persons and will be placed squarely within the tangled web of human social affairs. This will be the case for two important reasons.

First, as will become increasingly apparent in succeeding chapters of this volume, the most important determinants of aggression have generally proved to be social in nature. That is, aggression—at least in the case of human beings—seems to stem primarily from the words, deeds, presence, and even appearance of other persons. Full understanding of such behavior, then, requires knowledge of the social situations and factors that both facilitate and inhibit its occurrence. This is not to say, of course, that other factors play little part in its occurrence. On the contrary, many additional variables—ranging from changes in hormonal balance, on the one hand, through serious emotional maladjustment, on the other—also seem to exert important effects upon aggression. To a large degree, however, such behavior seems to stem from various aspects of social interaction. For this reason, then, it seems both appropriate and useful to examine it primarily from this general perspective.

Second, in the view of the present author, attempts to unravel the complex nature of human aggression conducted from a social perspective have, by and large, proved more fruitful and informative than attempts to comprehend it based upon other approaches. For example, while investigations of aggression undertaken within a biological framework have yielded important information on the common physiological and neurological mechanisms underlying aggression in many different organisms, they have generally been less successful in shedding light upon several complex factors seemingly unique to human aggression (e.g., persistent desires for revenge; the aggression-eliciting influence of racial or ethnic prejudice). And while investigations conducted from a purely clinical or psychiatric perspective have yielded much information concerning aggression by seriously disturbed individuals, they have generally told us little about the conditions under which seemingly "normal" persons will engage in dangerous assaults against others. For these reasons, too, it seems most useful to examine aggression from a social perspective.

At first glance, it might seem that restricting the scope of our discussion in the two ways noted above would prevent us from coming to grips with many interesting and important questions. In reality, nothing could be farther from the truth. Our focus upon *human* aggression, viewed mainly as a form of social behavior, will in no way prevent us from examining the most intriguing—and crucial—questions raised about such actions in recent years. On the contrary, in many cases, it will actually help to direct our attention to precisely such issues. For example, included among the questions to be considered in succeeding chapters of this volume are the following:

1. What are the effects of sexual arousal upon aggression?
2. Is punishment really an effective means of reducing or controlling such behavior?
3. What are the effects of alcohol and marijuana on aggression?
4. Do high temperatures really contribute to the occurrence of riots and civil disturbances—the so-called "long, hot summer" effect?

5. Does exposure to televised violence lead viewers to act in a similar, aggressive manner themselves?

Although it is quite tempting to turn at once to these and other intriguing topics, there are strong reasons for a temporary delay. Specifically, it seems important that we begin by addressing two preliminary tasks. First, we must formulate a precise, working definition of aggression. Only by beginning in this manner can we avoid the potential pitfalls of proceeding to discuss at some length a phenomenon whose precise meaning remains unclear. And second, we must consider several contrasting theoretical perspectives regarding the nature and origin of aggressive actions. This latter task is important because many of the ideas contained in these theories have become so well known that they are currently viewed as "common knowledge" and are accepted without reservation by scholars and the general public alike. Unfortunately, a number of these suggestions have recently been called into serious question by the findings of empirical research. Thus, it seems important that they be made explicit and that their precise sources be outlined and traced. The remainder of this initial chapter, then, will be devoted to the completion of these two preliminary tasks.

## AGGRESSION: A WORKING DEFINITION

Consider the following incidents:

1. A jealous husband, finding his wife and her lover together in bed, shoots and kills both individuals.
2. At a party, one young woman directs a string of cutting remarks to another, which embarrass their recipient so greatly that she finally flees from the room in tears.
3. A motorist who has had too much to drink at a local tavern drives her car across the highway median, thus striking an oncoming auto and killing both of its occupants. Afterwards, she expresses deep remorse over these tragic events.
4. During a battle, a soldier fires his machine gun at advancing

enemy troops. His aim is faulty, however, and the bullets sail harmlessly over the heads of these persons.
5. Despite the cries of pain uttered by his patient, a dentist seizes a seriously diseased tooth firmly in his pliers and pulls it quickly out of her mouth.

Which of these incidents listed above represent aggression? Common sense suggests that the first and probably the second as well fall readily into this category. But what about the third? Does it, too, represent an instance of aggressive behavior? At this point, common sense begins to desert us. The tipsy motorist certainly inflicted considerable harm upon others; indeed, she caused the death of two innocent victims. But given her professed remorse over this outcome, is it reasonable to describe her actions as aggressive in nature? And what of the fourth incident, in which no one was harmed, or the fifth, in which the patient was probably helped by the dentist's actions? Do either of these constitute examples of aggression?

The answers to such questions, of course, depend quite heavily upon the definition of *aggression* one chooses to adopt. And, as might well be expected, a number of contrasting formulations of this type have been offered over the years. For example, one view, proposed by Arnold Buss (1961), contends that aggression is simply any behavior that harms or injures others. According to this proposal, all of the incidents listed above, with the exception of the fourth, would qualify as aggression. This is the case because all but the fourth involve some form of harm or overt injury. In sharp contrast to this proposal, a second definition, offered by several noted researchers (e.g., Berkowitz, 1974; Feshbach, 1970), contends that in order to be classified as aggression, actions must involve the *intention* of harm or injury to others and not simply the delivery of such consequences. Thus, in accordance with this suggestion, the first, second, and fourth incidents in our list qualify as aggression, since all involve attempts—whether successful or unsuccessful—to harm or injure others. The third and fifth incidents would *not* be classified as aggression, however, since one involves accidental, unintended harm to others and the other attempts to produce beneficial rather than harmful effects. Finally, we might mention a third view, offered recently by Zillmann (1978), which restricts use of the term *aggression* to attempts to produce bodily or physical injury to others. According to this proposal, of course, only the first and fourth incidents in our list would be viewed as aggressive in nature.

The second, because it involves psychological rather than physical pain or injury, would not.

While a great deal of controversy once existed concerning these alternate definitions of aggression, recent years have witnessed at least a partial resolution of this issue. Specifically, many social scientists have now moved toward acceptance of a definition similar to the second mentioned above—that is, one involving the intention as well as the actual delivery of harm or injury to others.[1] Thus, at the present time, most—although by no means all—would find the following definition to be acceptable:

> *Aggression is any form of behavior directed toward the goal of harming or injuring another living being who is motivated to avoid such treatment.*

At first glance, this definition seems both simple and straightforward. Moreover, it appears to agree quite closely with our common-sense conception of the meaning of *aggression.* Closer examination reveals, however, that it actually involves a number of special features demanding of careful attention.

## Aggression as Behavior

First, it suggests that aggression be viewed as a form of behavior, *not* as an emotion, a motive, or an attitude. In the past (and even to some extent at present), there has been considerable confusion regarding this important point. The term *aggression* has often been applied to negative emotions such as anger, to motives such as the desire to harm or injure others, and even to negative attitudes such as racial or ethnic prejudice. While all of these factors certainly play an important role in the occurrence of harm-doing behavior, their presence is not a necessary condition for the performance of such actions. That is, as we shall soon see in more detail, it is not essential that individuals be angry toward others in order to attack them; aggression occurs in "cold blood" as well as in the heat of intense emotional arousal. Nor is it essential that aggressors hate or even dislike the persons they attack; indeed, in many cases, they attempt to inflict harm upon persons

---

[1] Despite this seeming rapprochement, a considerable amount of disagreement persists. Indeed, one group of authors (Tedeschi, Smith, & Brown, 1974) have recently contended that behaviors generally labeled or defined as "aggressive" are better viewed as instances in which one individual seeks to exert coercive power over others.

toward whom they hold positive rather than negative attitudes. In view of the fact that such emotions, motives, and attitudes may or may not accompany direct assaults against others, we will restrict the use of the term *aggression* to overt harm-doing behavior and consider these other factors separately.

## Aggression and Intention

Second, our definition limits application of the term *aggression* to acts in which the aggressor *intends* to harm the victim. Unfortunately, as may be immediately apparent, the inclusion of such a criterion of intent to harm raises a number of serious difficulties. First, there is the question of what, precisely, it means to say that one person intended to harm another. One possible meaning is that the individual in question made no effort to avoid harming others. Another, and more common interpretation, is that the aggressor *voluntarily* harmed the victim. This, of course, assigns free will to the harm doer and raises many complex issues over which philosophers in general, and philosophers of science in particular (Bergmann, 1966), continue to puzzle.

Second, as pointed out by several noted researchers (Buss, 1971; Bandura, 1973), intentions are private, hidden events not open to direct observation. As a result, they must be inferred from conditions that both precede and follow alleged acts of aggression. In some cases, establishing the presence of intention to harm seems relatively simple. Aggressors often admit their desire to injure their victims and even express regret if their attacks have failed to produce the intended effects. Similarly, the social context within which harm-producing behaviors take place often provides strong evidence for the existence of such intentions on the part of aggressors. For example, imagine a scene in which one individual in a bar is taunted verbally by another until, unable to stand further verbal abuse, he picks up an empty beer bottle and beats his tormentor senseless. Here, there would be little reason to doubt that the person administering such attacks fully intended to harm or injure the recipient or that his actions should be labeled as aggressive.

In other situations, however, it is much more difficult to establish the presence or absence of aggressive intent. For example, consider an incident in which, while cleaning a gun, one individual shoots and kills another. If the person involved expressed deep remorse and proclaimed over and over again that his friend's death was purely accidental, it might at first appear that intention to harm was lacking and that his behavior—while extremely careless—did not represent an instance of interpersonal aggression. If further evidence revealed that the victim had just attained an important promotion that both individuals had been seeking and that the so-called "accident" occurred immediately after a heated argument concerning the tactics used to win this prize, we might begin to suspect that perhaps an intention to harm was not entirely absent.

It should be noted at this point that our legal system often wrestles with precisely such problems. Moreover, varying degrees of punishment are exacted for the same actions, depending upon whether, in the opinion of judge and jury, harm-doing was accidental, partly intentional, or totally premeditated. And the length of many trials, as well as the high frequency of hung juries, attests to the complexity of reaching firm decisions regarding the intentionality of human actions.

Despite the many difficulties involved in a determination of the presence or absence of aggressive intent, however, there are several compelling reasons for retaining such a criterion in our definition of aggression. First, if all reference to such intention were eliminated, it would be necessary to classify *accidental harm* or *injury* to others, such as that described in the third incident on p. 5 as aggression. Given the fact that people do sometimes hurt each others' feelings, slam doors on each others' fingers, and even strike one another with their automobiles quite by accident, it seems important to distinguish such actions from aggression—and this can only be accomplished through reference to the intentions behind such behavior.

Second, if the notion of intention to harm were excluded from our definition of aggression, it would be necessary to describe the actions of surgeons, dentists, and even parents when disciplining their children as aggressive in nature. In view of the fact that the acts performed by these individuals are carried out with at least the ostensible purpose of helping rather than harming the persons involved, it seems unreasonable to term them aggression. Of course, in some instances, aggressors may seek to cloak a true desire to inflict pain or suffering on others behind a mask of prosocial intentions. Some dentists, no doubt, enjoy hurting their patients to a degree, and some parents spank their children partly to teach them to avoid dangerous actions and partly to cause them discomfort. To the extent that such actions are carried out for prosocial, beneficial ends, however, it makes little sense to classify them as aggression.

Finally, if the notion of intent were excluded from our definition, instances in which attempts to harm or injure others are made but fail (as in the fourth example on p. 5), would not be labeled as aggression, despite the fact that the availability of better weapons, more accurate aim, or greater skill on the part of the aggressor would have resulted in serious injury to the victim. For example, imagine a situation in which a hired professional assassin fires a high-powered rifle at a political leader but misses his target. It seems necessary to view such instances of accidental *noninjury* as aggression, even though they fail to produce the intended harm to the victim. For all of these reasons, then, it is essential to define aggression not simply as behavior that inflicts harm or injury on others but as any actions that are *directed toward the goal* of producing such negative aversive consequences.

### Aggression as Harm or Injury

A third aspect of our definition deserving of some comment is the suggestion that aggression involves either harm or injury to the victim. This implies that physical damage to the recipient is not essential. As long as this person has experienced *some* type of aversive consequences, aggression may be said to have occurred. Thus, in addition to direct, physical assaults, such actions as causing others to "lose face" or experience public embarrassment, depriving them of needed objects, and even withholding love or affection can, under appropriate circumstances, all be aggressive in nature.

While the variety of specific aggressive acts available to human beings is virtually endless, a framework for conceptualizing such behaviors proposed by Buss (1961) has often proved useful. Basically, Buss suggests that aggressive acts can be dichotomized along three dimensions: *physical—verbal, active—passive,* and *direct—indirect.* In combination, these dimensions yield eight possible categories into which most, if not all, aggressive actions can be divided. For example, actions such as shooting, stabbing, or punching, in which one person physically assaults another, would be classified as physical, active, and direct. In contrast, actions such as spreading malicious rumors about other people, or disparaging them to others would be described as verbal, active, and indirect. The eight categories of aggressive actions proposed by Buss, as well as examples of each type, are summarized in Table 1.

## Aggression Involves Living Beings

Fourth, the definition presented above suggests that only actions that harm or injure living beings may be viewed as aggressive in nature. While it is obvious that individuals often strike, kick, or hit various kinds of inanimate objects (e.g., furniture, dishes, walls), such behavior will not be considered to represent aggression *unless* it causes some form of harm or injury to another living organism. In many instances, of course, this is actually the case. For example, the proud owner of a priceless antique or a beautiful new automobile is certainly harmed when an aggressor destroys her loved possession. Similarly, the child who willfully seeks to demolish his playmates' favorite toys is clearly acting in an aggressive manner.

In many other cases, however, attacks against inanimate objects cause no harm or injury to other persons (e.g., kicking a tin can down an empty street, hurling rocks against a brick wall, repeatedly punch-

TABLE 1

*The Different Types or Categories of Aggression Proposed by Buss (1961)*

| Type of aggression | Examples |
| --- | --- |
| Physical–active–direct | Stabbing, punching, or shooting another person. |
| Physical–active–indirect | Setting a booby trap for another person; hiring an assassin to kill an enemy. |
| Physical–passive–direct | Physically preventing another person from obtaining a desired goal or performing a desired act (as in a sit-in demonstration). |
| Physical–passive–indirect | Refusing to perform necessary tasks (e.g., refusal to move during a sit-in). |
| Verbal–active–direct | Insulting or derogating another person. |
| Verbal–active–indirect | Spreading malicious rumors or gossip about another individual. |
| Verbal–passive–direct | Refusing to speak to another person, to answer questions, etc. |
| Verbal–passive–indirect | Failing to make specific verbal comments (e.g., failing to speak up in another person's defense when he or she is unfairly criticized). |

ing one's pillow). Although such actions may often resemble aggressive behaviors closely in physical form, it is suggested that they are best viewed as merely emotional or expressive in nature and do not constitute instances of aggression.

### Aggression Involves an Avoidance-Motivated Recipient

Finally, our definition notes that aggression may be said to have occurred only when the recipient or victim is motivated to avoid such treatment at the hands of the aggressor. In many cases, of course, this is true: the victims of injurious physical assaults or harmful verbal attacks generally wish to avoid such unpleasant experiences. In some instances, however, the victims of harm or injury-inducing actions are *not* motivated to avoid these consequences. Perhaps this is seen most clearly in certain forms of lovemaking encompassing overtones of sadomasochism. In such cases, the individuals involved seem to enjoy being hurt by their lovers or, at the very least, make no effort to avoid or escape from such treatment. According to our definition, such interactions do not involve aggression, for there is no apparent motivation on the part of the victim to avoid the pain inflicted.

Suicide represents a related case. Here, the aggressor serves as his or her own victim and, by definition, actively *seeks* the injuries produced. Such actions, then, cannot be classified as aggression. Even if the perpetrator's ultimate goal is not death but the dissemination of a desperate cry for help, he or she still seeks the harm experienced. Thus, such actions do not represent instances of aggression.

### Aggression Defined: A Recapitulation

In sum, throughout the remainder of this volume, aggression will be defined as any form of behavior directed toward the goal of harming or injuring another living being who is motivated to avoid such treatment. While many forms of behavior embody one or more of these criteria, only those meeting all will be viewed as instances of aggression.

By way of conclusion, let us apply this working definition to the list of instances on p. 5. According to our definition, it should be immediately apparent that the first and second incidents qualify as aggression: one person inflicted voluntary harm or injury upon another who clearly wished to avoid such consequences. In addition, the fourth also seems to meet our criteria. Although no one was harmed, the behavior enacted was certainly directed toward this final goal. The third instance, however, does not qualify as aggression for an important reason: the harm inflicted was not intentional—the harm doer did not wish to produce the serious injuries sustained by the victims. Similarly, the fifth instance, too, fails to fulfill the requirements of our definition, since the ultimate goal sought was almost certainly that of help rather than harm to the recipient (i.e., the patient). In short, if we apply the criteria contained in our working definition to varied instances of behavior, we should be able to determine whether they represent instances of aggression. It is hoped that this ability to separate aggressive from nonaggressive actions—to recognize aggression when we see it, so to speak—will constitute a useful first step toward the full understanding of this complex phenomenon.

## Hostile versus Instrumental Aggression

As may be recalled, we have already noted that aggression can be dichotomized along several different dimensions (e.g., physical—verbal, active—passive, direct—indirect). Before this discussion is concluded, one final distinction of this type—that between *hostile* and *instrumental aggression* (cf. Feshbach, 1964, 1970; Buss, 1961, 1971)—should also be considered.

Basically, the first of these terms has been applied to instances of aggression in which the primary or major goal sought by aggressors is that of causing the victim to suffer. Individuals engaging in hostile aggression, then, are seeking harm or injury to the persons they attack, and often little else. In contrast, the second term (*instrumental aggression*) has generally been applied to instances in which aggressors assault other persons not out of a strong desire to see them suffer but primarily as a means of attaining other goals. That is, individuals engaging in instrumental aggression are not seeking harm to other persons as an end in itself; rather, they employ aggressive actions as a technique for obtaining various incentives (see Figure 1).

For example, consider the case of a young executive whose promotion is threatened by the existence of a competitor. Such an individual may spread malicious rumors about his rival (and so seek to sabotage her career) not out of any animosity toward this particular

FIGURE 1. An example of instrumental aggression. In the incident shown, one person (the plumber) employed aggression as a means of terminating annoyance from another. (Source: King Features Syndicate, Inc.)

person but simply because he wishes to eliminate her as a credible rival. A second, and more dramatic example of instrumental aggression is provided by the behavior of bands of teen-aged youths who roam the streets of Detroit, New York, and other large cities, searching for opportunities to snatch a purse, steal a wallet, or seize a piece of valuable jewelry from unsuspecting passersby. In many cases, they find it necessary to resort to violence in order to accomplish these thefts, as for example, when the victims resist. As indicated by the following passage, though, their major motivation for engaging in such acts is clearly economic gain—*not* the infliction of pain and suffering upon their quarry (Stevens, 1971):

> Sometimes assault is involved. If they hurt the victim, that's his grief. Or hers. But they're not looking to hurt anybody. "We ain't into the kill thing. Anybody on that junk is workin' out of a fruit and nuts bag. We just want the money, like anybody else."

While the distinction between hostile and instrumental aggression has attained widespread acceptance, it has recently been severely criticized by Bandura (1973), who noted that both types are actually directed toward the attainment of specific goals and in this sense might both be labeled as *instrumental*. The only difference between them, Bandura has contended, lies in the contrasting nature of the goals sought.

In response to such criticism, Zillmann (1978) has recently proposed that the term *hostile* and *instrumental aggression* be replaced by the more specific *annoyance-motivated* and *incentive-motivated aggression*. The first refers to aggressive actions undertaken primarily to terminate or reduce noxious conditions (e.g., intense anger, mistreatment at the hands of others), while the second refers to aggressive actions performed mainly to attain various extrinsic incentives. Throughout the remainder of this volume, then, we will use these labels to identify instances of aggression that are primarily directed toward one or the other of these differing classes of goals.

## CONTRASTING THEORETICAL PERSPECTIVES ON AGGRESSION: INSTINCT, DRIVE, OR SOCIAL LEARNING?

That human beings frequently engage in dangerous acts of aggression is hardly open to question—the record of recent history leaves little room for doubt on this particular score. The question of *why* they engage in such activities, however, has long been the subject of serious dispute. Over the years, sharply contrasting views concerning the nature of aggression, the factors influencing its occurrence, and the forces from which it stems have repeatedly been proposed. While these opposing theoretical perspectives have taken many different forms, most seem to fall into one of three distinct categories, in which aggression is attributed primarily to (1) innate urges or dispositions, (2) externally elicited drives, or (3) present social conditions combined with previous social learning. Each of these contrasting views will now be examined.

## Aggression as Instinctive Behavior: Innate Urges toward Death and Destruction

The oldest and probably best-known theoretical perspective concerning aggression is the view that such behavior is largely instinctive in nature. That is, according to this general approach, aggression occurs because human beings are genetically or constitutionally "programmed" for such actions. While many scholars have supported such suggestions, the most influential proponents of this general position have been Sigmund Freud and Konrad Lorenz.

### Aggression as Instinctive Behavior: The Psychoanalytic Approach

In his early writings, Freud held that all human behavior stems either directly or indirectly from *eros*—the life instinct—whose energy (known as *libido*) is directed toward the enhancement, prolongation, and reproduction of life. Within this general context, then, aggression was viewed simply as a reaction to the blocking or thwarting of libidinal impulses. As such, it was neither an automatic nor a continuously inevitable part of life.

Following the violent events of World War I, however, Freud (1920) gradually came to adopt a somewhat gloomier position regarding both the nature and the origin of aggression. Basically, he proposed the existence of a second major instinct—*thanatos,* the death force—whose energy is directed toward the destruction and termination of life. All human behavior, he held, stemmed from the complex interplay of this instinct with *eros* and the constant tension between them.

Since the death instinct would, if unrestrained, result in the rapid termination of life, he further reasoned that through other mechanisms (e.g., displacement), the energy of *thanatos* comes to be directed outward and, in this manner, serves as the basis of aggression toward others. In Freud's view, then, aggression stems primarily from the redirection of the self-destructive death instinct away from the individual and outward toward others (see Figure 2).

At this point, we should call attention to the fact that the notion of a self-directed death instinct is one of the most controversial in all of psychoanalytic theory. Indeed, it was soon rejected by many scholars who shared Freud's views concerning many other issues (e.g., Hartmann, Kris, & Loewenstein, 1949). The view that aggression stems primarily from innate, instinctive forces, however, was generally retained even by these critics.

As can be readily seen, Freud's suggestions regarding the origins and nature of aggression are pessimistic in the extreme. Not only is such behavior innate, stemming from the "built-in" death instinct, it is also inevitable, for if *thanatos* is not turned outward upon others, it will soon result in the destruction of the individual himself. The only ray of hope provided centers on the suggestion that the expression of aggression-related emotions, primarily hostility and anger, may bring about a discharge of destructive energy and in this manner lessen the likelihood of more dangerous acts. This aspect of Freud's theory (the notion of *catharsis*) has often been interpreted as suggesting that the performance of expressive, nondestructive acts may generally be an effective means of preventing more dangerous ones. Close examination of Freud's writings, however, argues against such conclusions. Although he was quite ambiguous concerning both the magnitude and the duration of any cathartic effects, he generally seemed to be-

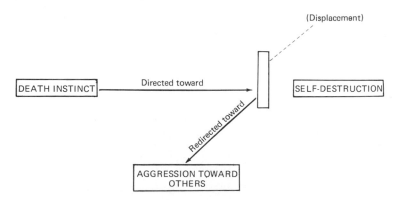

FIGURE 2. Freud believed that aggression stems from the redirection (through displacement) of a self-destructive death instinct.

lieve that they would be quite minimal and short-lived in nature. Thus, Freud actually seems to have been less optimistic on this score than later theorists have often assumed.

In sum, Freud held that aggression stems from a death instinct whose primary goal is the destruction of life, coupled with the redirection of this force outward toward others. Within his theory, then, human beings are essentially left facing a choice between continuing assaults against others on the one hand and ultimate self-destruction on the other—two bleak and gloomy options, to say the least!

*Aggression as Instinctive Behavior: The Ethological Approach*

A second and in some ways surprisingly similar view regarding the nature of human aggression has been proposed in recent years by the Nobel-prize-winning ethologist Konrad Lorenz (1966, 1974). According to Lorenz, aggression springs primarily from an innate fighting instinct that human beings share with many other organisms. Presumably, such an instinct developed during the long course of evolution because it yielded many benefits. For example, fighting often serves to disperse animal populations over a wide geographic area, thus ensuring maximal utilization of available food resources. Similarly, since it is often closely related to mating, such behavior frequently helps to strengthen the genetic makeup of various species by guaranteeing that only the strongest and most vigorous individuals will manage to reproduce.

Whereas Freud was somewhat ambiguous regarding both the generation and the release of instinctive, aggressive energy, Lorenz has been quite specific concerning these issues. Basically, he has proposed that aggressive energy (stemming from the fighting instinct) is spontaneously generated within the organism in a continuous manner and at a constant rate. Moreover, it accumulates regularly with the passage of time. The elicitation of overt aggressive actions, then, is primarily a joint function of (1) the amount of accumulated aggressive energy and (2) the presence and strength of special aggression-releasing stimuli in the immediate environment. More specifically, the greater the amount of aggressive energy present, the weaker the stimulus that will "release" overt aggression. Indeed, if sufficient time has elapsed since the performance of the last aggressive act, such behavior may occur in a spontaneous manner, in the total absence of releasing stimuli. As Lorenz himself has remarked in a recent interview (Evans, 1974), "in certain animals, aggressivity follows all the rules of threshold lowering and appetitive behavior. You can see an animal looking for trouble, and a man can do that too" (p. 90). These suggestions regarding the interplay between releasing stimuli and amount of accumulated, aggressive energy are summarized in Figure 3.

One especially intriguing extension of Lorenz's theory involves its use in accounting for the fact that human beings, unlike virtually every other form of life on earth, engage in widespread, fatal assaults

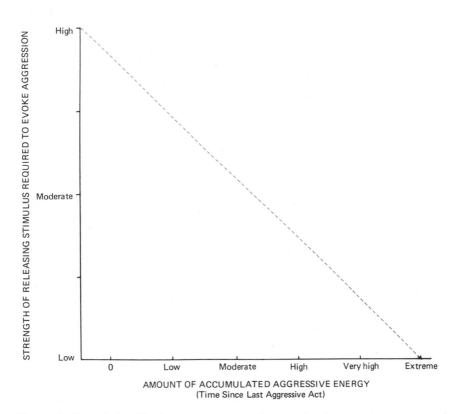

FIGURE 3. The relationship between amount of accumulated aggressive energy and strength of releasing stimulus required to evoke aggression, as proposed by Lorenz. Immediately after aggression has occurred, an extremely strong stimulus would be required to evoke such behavior again. With the passage of time (and the accumulation of aggressive energy), however, the magnitude of stimulation required to "release" such behavior decreases. Indeed, if aggressive energy has risen to extremely high levels, aggression may occur spontaneously, in the total absence of a releasing stimulus.

against members of their own species. In particular, Lorenz has suggested that in addition to an innate fighting instinct, all organisms possess inhibitions against attacking others of their kind, with the strength of those inhibitions varying directly with their capacity to inflict serious harm on their victims. Thus, dangerous predators such as lions and tigers, which are amply equipped with natural means for killing other creatures, possess very strong inhibitions against attacking members of their own species, while less dangerous organisms, such as human beings, possess much weaker inhibitions of this type. When, early in their history, men and women aggressed against others primarily by means of teeth and fists, the lack of such restraints was not very harmful; the probability that they would inflict serious injury was, after all, relatively low. As technological progress placed increasingly devastating weapons in their hands, however, the absence of such inhibitions became increasingly dangerous, until, at the present time, humanity threatens its own continued survival as a species. In short, Lorenz has explained our present perilous position near the brink of self-annihilation in terms of the fact that our capacity for violence has quickly outrun our innate, natural restraints against aggressive actions.

While Lorenz, like Freud, holds that aggression is inevitable, stemming largely from innate forces, he is somewhat more optimistic regarding the possibility of reducing or controlling such behavior. In particular, he has suggested that participation in many minor, noninjurious aggressive actions may prevent aggressive energy from accumulating to dangerous levels and so lessen the likelihood of harmful outbursts of violence. Further, he has suggested that greater feelings of love and friendship for others may prove incompatible with the expression of overt aggression and may thus tend to block its occurrence. Through appropriate steps, then, aggression can be rechanneled and so controlled.

*Aggression as Instinctive Behavior: Summary and Implications*

The views of Freud, Lorenz, and many others suggest that aggression stems primarily from innate forces within the individual. According to such perspectives, hostile impulses or tendencies are constantly generated as an integral part of basic life processes and will soon rise to dangerous levels unless continuously released.

While various instinct theories of aggression differ sharply in terms of specific detail, all encompass similar implications. In particular, the suggestion—central to each—that aggression arises largely from instinctive, innate factors leads logically to the conclusion that it is probably impossible to eliminate such reactions entirely. Neither the satisfaction of all material needs, the elimination of all social injustice, nor any other positive changes in the structure of human society will succeed in preventing the generation and expression of aggressive impulses. The most that can be attained is the temporary prevention of such behavior or a reduction in its intensity when it occurs. According to such theories, then, aggression—in one form or another—will always be with us. Indeed, it is an integral part of our basic human nature.

### Aggression as an Elicited Drive: Motivation to Harm or Injure Others

Given the essentially pessimistic implications of instinct views of aggression, it is not surprising that they have never attained widespread acceptance among psychologists. Indeed, the notion of spontaneously generated aggressive energy has been largely dismissed by the great majority of researchers in this field. The more general suggestion that aggression stems from an *aggressive motive* or *drive* (i.e., a heightened state of arousal that can be reduced through overt acts of aggression) has enjoyed a much more favorable reception. In fact, it is currently represented in several *drive theories of aggression*, which continue to enjoy considerable support at the present time (cf. Berkowitz, 1969, 1974; Feshbach, 1970). Basically, such theories hold that human aggression stems mainly from the arousal of a drive to harm or injure others, which is itself elicited by various environmental conditions. By far the most famous statement of this general perspective was elaborated several decades ago by Dollard, Doob, Miller, Mowrer, and Sears (1939) in their well-known volume *Frustration and Aggression*. Because the theory outlined by these scientists has exerted a profound impact upon both subsequent thought and subsequent research concerning aggression, it will be considered in some detail. In addition, a recent influential revision of this general framework proposed by Leonard Berkowitz (1969, 1971, 1974) will also be examined.

*Frustration and Aggression*

If you were to stop 50 individuals at random on the street and ask them to identify the most important determinant of human aggression, it is quite likely that the majority would reply with a single term: *frustration*. While the broad acceptance of this belief obviously stems from several different sources, including personal experience, it is traceable, in large measure, to a pair of suggestions that lie at the core of the theory of aggression outlined by Dollard *et al*. (1939). Together, these proposals are known as the *frustration–aggression hypothesis*. In slightly paraphrased form, they read as follows:

1. Frustration always leads to some form of aggression.
2. Aggression always stems from frustration.

Please note that in both proposals, frustration is defined as the blocking or thwarting of some form of ongoing, goal-directed behavior. Further, it should be added that in both cases, frustration is not assumed to induce aggression directly; rather, it is assumed to induce an *instigation toward aggression* (an aggressive drive), which then facilitates or encourages such behavior.

As pointed out recently by Bandura (1973), these assertions are highly appealing, partly because of their boldness and partly because of their simplicity. After all, if they are accepted, a highly complex form of behavior, human aggression, is largely explained in one daring stroke. In view of this fact, it is not at all surprising that these proposals soon gained widespread acceptance among scholars and the general public alike. Nor is it surprising that they continue to play an influential role even at the present time. Unfortunately, though, a careful analysis of each of these suggestions indicates that both are probably far too sweeping in scope.

First, it is quite apparent that frustrated individuals do not *always* engage in verbal or physical assaults against others. Rather, they often demonstrate a wide variety of reactions to such treatment, ranging from resignation and despair, on the one hand, to active attempts to overcome the obstacles in their paths, on the other. For example, consider the case of a student who has applied to several different medical, law, or graduate schools, only to be rejected by all. Such a person is probably more likely to experience discouragement and dejection than anger or rage. Similarly, an individual whose amorous advances toward a member of the opposite sex are repeatedly spurned and who, as a result, experiences strong and bitter frustration is probably more likely to weep, feel depressed, and crawl into bed and sleep than to aggress against the would-be lover or other persons.

More direct support for the conclusion that frustration does not always lead to aggression is provided by the results of many empirical studies (see, e.g., Berkowitz, 1969; Geen & O'Neal, 1976). Together, the findings of such investigations suggest that while frustration *sometimes* facilitates aggression, it by no means always—or even usually— produces such effects. Since we will return to detailed consideration of this evidence in Chapter 3 (see pp. 79–92), it will not be examined here. Suffice it to say, however, that after dozens of studies on the impact of frustration upon aggression, most psychologists believe that the link between these factors is far less certain or strong than that initially proposed by Dollard and his colleagues.

In the face of such considerations, Neal Miller (1941), one of the original formulators of the frustration–aggression hypothesis, quickly amended the first proposal listed above to read as follows:

> Frustration produces instigations to a number of different types of responses, one of which is an instigation to some form of aggression. (p. 338)

In short, he suggested that frustration leads to many forms of behavior, only one of which is aggression. Thus, the strong and sweeping proposal that frustration always leads to aggression was quickly abandoned even by one of its originators. Despite this fact, however, the initial, strong assertion continues to enjoy a surprising degree of acceptance even at present and may often be encountered in the mass media, popularized discussions of aggression, or casual conversations.

Turning to the second proposal, that aggression always results from frustration, it is clear once again that the formulators of this view went too far. As we will see in more detail in Chapters 3, 4, and 5, there can be little doubt that aggression often stems from many factors other than frustration. Indeed, it can, and often does, occur in the total absence of such conditions. For example, consider the actions of a hired professional assassin, who murders many persons he has never seen before and who have had no opportunity to frustrate him. It makes more sense to attribute the aggressive actions of this person to the rewards they provide (money, increased status, the satisfaction of sadistic tendencies) than to any previous or present frustration. Similarly, consider the actions of a pilot who, although in the best of spirits and having experienced no major frustrations on the day in question, bombs and strafes an enemy position, killing a number of innocent civilians as well as opposing troops. Here, such factors as direct orders from his superiors, the promise of various rewards for successfully completing his mission, and perhaps a sense of duty or patriotism seem to play a greater role in influencing the occurrence of highly aggressive actions than frustration. In sum, the suggestion that all acts of violence result from the blocking or thwarting of goal-directed behavior does not bear up well under close examination.

*Frustration and Aggression Theory: Some Additional Aspects*

While the two proposals of the frustration–aggression hypothesis lie at the core of the theory outlined by Dollard and his colleagues, they represent only a portion of this general framework. Thus, several additional aspects of this influential theory should also be examined.

First, with respect to the *strength of the instigation to aggression* (i.e., the strength of the aggressive drive or motive), Dollard *et al.* suggested that three factors were crucial: (1) the reinforcement value or importance of the frustrated goal response; (2) the degree of frustration of this response; and (3) the number of frustrated response sequences. More specifically, the greater the degree to which this response has been thwarted and the greater the number of responses blocked, the greater the instigation to aggressive behavior. Going further, Dollard and his colleagues suggested that the effects of successive frustrations may summate over time, so that several minor experiences of this type can combine to induce a stronger aggressive reaction than any one alone. This proposal implies that the effects of frustrating events persist—an assumption that plays an important role in several different aspects of the theory.

Since it is clear that individuals do not always aggress following frustration, Dollard *et al.* also turned their attention to factors serving to *inhibit* overt aggression. Bascially, they concluded that such behavior is primarily inhibited by the threat of punishment. In their own words, "The strength of inhibition for any act of aggression varies positively with the amount of punishment anticipated to be a consequence of that act" (p. 33). While threatened punishment was assumed to inhibit overt aggressive actions, however, it was not viewed as reducing the actual instigation to aggression. Thus, if an individual were prevented from attacking the person who had frustrated him by the fear of some type of punishment, he would still be motivated to aggress. The result might then be assaults against persons other than the frustrater who are associated with weaker threats of punishment— a phenomenon generally known as *displacement*. We will return to a more detailed discussion of this topic below.

If, as noted above, threats of punishment serve merely to block the performance of aggressive actions and leave the instigation toward such behavior largely unchanged, what factor or factors operate to reduce aggressive motivation? According to Dollard and his associates, the answer centers on the process of *catharsis*. Essentially, they proposed that all acts of aggression—even those that are covert, indirect, and noninjurious—serve as a form of catharsis, lowering the instigation to further aggression. Within the context of their theory, then, it is not necessary for a frustrated individual to harm another person in order to lessen or eliminate his aggressive drive; even such actions as aggressive fantasies, mild expressions of annoyance, or pounding one's fist on a table might be expected to produce such effects. In short, Dollard *et al.* were much more optimistic with respect to the possible benefits of catharsis than Freud. Like their predecessor, however, they left the question of the duration of such effects largely unanswered. That is, following catharsis, does the instigation to aggression remain low for a relatively long period of time, or does it quickly return to its former high levels? Dollard and his colleagues had little or nothing to say on this issue. And, somewhat unsettlingly, it has continued to be neglected in the intervening years.

## Frustration and Aggression: An Extension to Displacement

One aspect of frustration–aggression theory that has been the subject of considerable attention involves the general suggestion that when frustrated individuals are prevented, by strong fear of punishment, from attacking the person who has thwarted them, they may shift their attacks to other targets. As noted by Dollard *et al.* (1939):

> The strongest instigation, aroused by a frustration, is to acts of aggression directed against the agent perceived to be the source of frustration and progressively weaker instigations are aroused to progressively less direct acts of aggression. (p. 39)

This statement has generally been interpreted as meaning that the most appropriate or desirable target of aggression for a frustrated individual is the person who has blocked his or her goal-directed behavior, but that other persons may also serve as targets of aggression to the extent that they resemble the frustrating agent.

Extending and refining this suggestion, Miller (1948) proposed a specific model to account for the occurrence of *displaced aggression*—instances in which individuals aggress against persons other than their frustraters. Briefly, he suggested that an aggressor's choice of victims in such cases is largely determined by three factors: (1) the strength of the instigation to aggression; (2) the strength of the inhibitions against such behavior; and (3) the stimulus similarity of each potential victim to the frustrating agent. In addition, for reasons we will soon consider, Miller further assumed that the strength of inhibitions against aggression decreases more rapidly than the instigation to such behavior, with decreasing similarity to the frustrating agent. Displaced aggression, then, is predicted to be most likely against targets for which the strength of inhibitions is negligible but for whom stimulus similarity to the frustrater is still relatively high. Perhaps a specific example will help clarify the nature of these suggestions.

Consider the case of a child who is severely frustrated by his mother (e.g., she will not allow him to eat chocolate ice cream for breakfast). Since the strength of the child's inhibitions against attacking the frustrater are probably quite strong, direct assaults against her are unlikely, and displacement may well occur. Assume, then, that three potential targets of aggression are present: his mother's sister, who resembles her quite closely; his younger sister, who resembles her to a somewhat lesser degree; and a male friend from down the street. Against which of these individuals is the child most likely to aggress? While it is difficult to make precise predictions in this instance, Miller's theory might be interpreted as suggesting that attacks will be most probable against the younger sister. This would be the case because this individual resembles the frustrater in several respects (e.g., sex, physical appearance) but is associated with much weaker inhibitions against overt assaults. These predictions, as well as the general form of Miller's conflict theory of displacement, are presented in Figure 4.

Several of the suggestions contained in Miller's theory are quite intriguing and, over the years, have stimulated a considerable amount

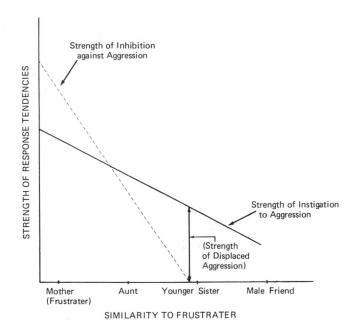

FIGURE 4. According to Miller's conflict theory of displacement, an individual who is prevented from aggressing directly against a frustrater by stronger fear of punishment will *displace* his assaults to other targets resembling this person but associated with weaker inhibitions. Thus, in the specific example shown, a child frustrated by his mother might be most likely to aggress against his younger sister, who resembles the frustrating agent but has much less capacity to punish such actions.

of empirical research (see, e.g., Berkowitz, 1969; Fenigstein & Buss, 1974; Thibaut & Coules, 1952). However, as may already be quite apparent, they involve certain ambiguities that should not be neglected. First, as pointed out recently by Zillmann (1978), the entire model hinges on the assumption that inhibitions against aggression generalize to a lesser degree than the instigation toward such behavior. Miller derived this suggestion directly from experimental studies of conflict, conducted primarily with animal subjects. In particular, he based it upon the finding that when a hungry organism is first trained to expect food at the end of an alley and is then shocked at the same location, the strength of its tendency to avoid this spot decreases more sharply with increasing distance than the strength of its tendency to approach. Thus, for example, if the subject is placed in the alley near the crucial spot, it will, initially, flee. This is the case because close to the location where it was both fed and shocked, its tendency to avoid is stronger than its tendency to approach. As the organism moves further and further away from this point, however, its tendency to avoid decreases more quickly than its tendency to approach. As a result, it will gradually stop running and, at some determinable point, actually turn toward the goal once more. Presumably, this is the case because at this point, the strength of its tendency to approach actually exceeds the strength of its tendency to flee.

Obviously, it is a very major logical leap from such findings to the suggestion that inhibitions against aggression drop off more sharply than the instigation toward such behavior as one proceeds outward along a dimension of decreasing similarity to the frustrater. Yet, surprisingly, no attempt to verify this assertion directly is known to the present author.

A second source of ambiguity in Miller's model of displacement concerns the meaning of the phrase *stimulus similarity*. The most straightforward interpretation, and one consistent with the usage of this term in the literature upon which Miller based his model, would involve physical or perceptual similarity to the source of frustration. Most research concerned with the theory, however, has varied the degree of similarity between potential targets of aggression and the initial frustrater in terms of semantic rather than physical characteristics. For example, similarity has been varied along such dimensions as kinship (Murray & Berkun, 1955), academic rank (Ferson, 1959), and acquaintance (Fenigstein & Buss, 1974; Fitz, 1976). Unfortunately, there is no indication in Miller's model as to which of these, and many other possible dimensions, are most relevant to the phenomenon of displacement. Until systematic research directed to this question is conducted, therefore, some degree of ambiguity will persist.

*Frustration and Aggression Revisited: Berkowitz's Aggressive-Cue Theory*

Since its formulation nearly 40 years ago, frustration–aggression theory has undoubtedly been the subject of a greater amount of attention within psychology than any competing formulation regarding the nature of aggressive behavior. As a result of this continuing, careful scrutiny, a number of different revisions of the theory have been suggested. We have already noted, for example, that at the present time, few, if any, researchers continue to believe that frustration always leads to aggression or that aggression always stems from frustration. Similarly, it is now realized that other factors aside from fear of punishment may serve to inhibit aggression (cf. Bandura, 1973; Donnerstein & Donnerstein, 1976). Perhaps the most influential—and in some ways the most controversial—revisions of frustration–aggression theory, however, have been offered by Leonard Berkowitz (1965a, 1969, 1971, 1973). While this prominent investigator has proposed a number of such alterations, we will focus here on only two. First, and perhaps of greatest importance, Berkowitz has suggested that contrary to the theory as initially proposed by Dollard *et al.*, frustration is *not* a sufficient condition for the elicitation of aggression. In addition to such treatment, he believes, another factor—the presence of *aggressive cues*—is generally required. More specifically, Berkowitz has proposed that frustration induces an emotional reaction, anger, which creates only a *readiness* for overt aggressive acts. Such behavior will then actually follow only if suitable aggressive cues—stimuli associated with the present or previous anger instigators or with aggression generally—are present.

While the process through which such stimuli acquire their aggression-evoking properties has not been outlined in great detail, Berkowitz's writings seem to suggest that this process probably resembles classical conditioning in its essential nature. That is, he has suggested that stimuli that are regularly associated with anger instigators or aggression may gradually acquire the capacity to elicit aggressive actions from individuals who have previously been provoked or frustrated. Since a wide range of stimuli might well meet these requirements, it would be expected that many will acquire aggressive cue-value. This, in fact, is precisely what Berkowitz has suggested. Persons, certain of their characteristics, and even physical objects (e.g., weapons) can all acquire aggressive cue-value under appropriate conditions. And once these properties have been acquired, such stimuli can act to elicit aggressive behavior from angry, frustrated persons.

In order to examine the accuracy of these suggestions, Berkowitz and his colleagues have conducted a long and systematic series of investigations (see Berkowitz, 1974; Geen, 1976). For example, in several of these studies (e.g., Berkowitz & Geen, 1966; Geen & Berkowitz, 1966), male subjects were provided with an opportunity to aggress (by means of electric shock) against a confederate whose first name either did or did not associate him with a character in a violent movie. In accordance with Berkowitz's suggestions, results indicated that angry (but not nonangry) subjects generally directed stronger attacks against the confederate when he was associated with the violent film than when he was not (see Table 2). We shall return to more detailed consideration of these and related experiments in Chapter 4. For the present, suffice it to say that in general, the results obtained lend support to the suggestion that aggressive cues—if not essential for the occurrence of overt aggressive actions—may often tend to facilitate their performance.

A second major revision of frustration–aggression theory proposed by Berkowitz (1965a, 1969) concerns the conditions required for the reduction of aggressive drive. As will be recalled, Dollard *et al.* held that the instigation to aggression could be reduced through assaults against targets other than the original frustrater and through virtually any form of aggressive act, including noninjurious forms. In contrast to these suggestions, Berkowitz has contended that strongly frustrated individuals can reduce their aggressive drive only through the infliction of harm upon the frustrater. Such persons, he has suggested, experience a strong *completion tendency* and "will not attain completion until the goal object (the frustrater) has been aggressively injured" (1965a, p. 342). Indeed, going still further, Berkowitz has reasoned that since attempts to harm the agent of frustration that fail are themselves frustrating, they may actually *enhance* rather than re-

TABLE 2

*Evidence for the Aggression-Enhancing Effects of Aggressive Cues*[a]

|  | Experimental condition[b] | |
|---|---|---|
| Anger arousal | Confederate's name did not associate him with the violent film | Confederate's name associated him with the violent film |
| Nonangry subjects | 1.45 | 1.73 |
| Angry subjects | 4.55 | 6.09 |

[a] Based on data from Berkowitz & Geen, 1966.
[b] As shown above, angry (but not nonangry) subjects behaved more aggressively toward a male confederate when his name associated him with a previously witnessed violent movie than when his name did not involve such an association. The numbers shown represent the number of shocks directed by subjects toward the confederate.

duce the tendency to aggress. Only successful, harm-inducing assaults will serve to reduce or eliminate aggressive drive.

These proposals, of course, rule out the possibility of catharsis through displaced aggression or through the performance of expressive, noninjurious acts. Only aggression against the frustrater himself—and aggression that succeeds—is assumed to be drive reducing. As might be anticipated, these proposals are quite controversial. Indeed, many researchers currently reject the notion that aggressive drive can be reduced only through injury to the source of frustration (cf. Feshbach, 1964, 1970; Zillmann, 1978). Moreover, in recent years, there has been an increasing tendency among psychologists to perceive the drive induced by frustration as quite diffuse in nature. That is, it is now often seen as a form of *general arousal* rather than as a specific motive that can be satisfied only through the infliction of harm upon the frustrater. This alternative view suggests that frustration-induced arousal may be reduced through many different activities, including ones that are nonaggressive in nature (see Zillmann, 1978). Because we will return to a more detailed consideration of the role of arousal in aggression in Chapter 4, we will not comment further upon this topic here. For the present, however, it seems reasonable to conclude that while Berkowitz's suggestions concerning the impact of aggressive cues have proved quite influential, his proposals regarding the conditions necessary for the reduction of aggressive drive have won far less widespread acceptance.

### Frustration and Aggression: A Concluding Comment

Because drive theories of aggression such as the ones proposed by Dollard *et al.*, Berkowitz, and others attribute such behavior to the presence of specific environmental conditions (i.e., frustrating events) rather than to innate tendencies toward violence, they are somewhat more optimistic with respect to the prevention or control of such behavior than instinct theories. That is, they seem to suggest that the removal of all external sources of frustration from the environment would go a long way toward eliminating dangerous instances of human aggression. Unfortunately, though, frustration—in one form or another—is probably such a frequent and commonplace occurrence for most individuals that its total elimination seems quite unfeasible. For this reason, drive theories, too, seem to leave human beings burdened with a continuous and largely unavoidable source of aggressive impulses. In this case, such urges stem mainly from external rather than internal sources. However, they still seem far too prevalent and common to allow much room for optimistic conclusions.

## Aggression as Learned Social Behavior: Direct and Vicarious Training for Violence

In recent years, a third distinctive theoretical perspective regarding the nature of aggression has received increasing attention and support. Basically, this point of view regards aggression primarily as a specific form of social behavior, which is both acquired and maintained in much the same manner as many other forms of activity. Although this general position has been supported by several noted authorities on aggression (e.g., Buss, 1971; Zillmann, 1978), perhaps its most outspoken proponent has been Albert Bandura (1973).

According to Bandura, a comprehensive analysis of aggressive behavior requires careful attention to three issues: (1) the manner in which such actions are acquired; (2) the factors that instigate their occurrence; and (3) the conditions that maintain their performance. In short, a thorough understanding of aggression entails knowledge of the same factors and conditions that would be required for a similar analysis of many other forms of behavior. Since we will turn to a detailed examination of the social, environmental, and individual antecedents of aggression in Chapters 3, 4, and 5, we will focus here upon the acquisition and maintenance of such actions. It should be noted, however, that in sharp contrast to the instinct or drive views of aggression, which suggest that this dangerous form of behavior stems from one or a small number of crucial factors, the social-learning framework holds that it may actually be elicited by a large and varied range of conditions. Thus, included among the factors we will consider in this regard in later discussions are direct provocation from others; exposure to live or filmed aggressive models; heightened physiological arousal; environmental stressors such as heat, noise, or crowding; and lasting attitudes and values. Within the social-learning perspective, these—and many other variables as well—may reasonably be expected to exert important effects upon overt aggressive actions.

*Acquisition of Aggressive Behavior: The Role of Instrumental Learning*

One important way in which individuals may acquire a wide variety of aggressive responses is through experiences in which they are directly rewarded for such behavior. Consistent with general principles of instrumental learning, it would be expected that if acts of aggression are followed by various forms of positive reinforcement, the tendency to engage in such behaviors will be strengthened. Thus, the probability that they will be repeated on later occasions will increase.

Evidence for the occurrence of such effects has been obtained in many experiments conducted with animals (e.g., Hutchinson, 1972; Scott, 1973). In these studies, organisms provided with various forms of reinforcement (e.g., food, water, escape from electric shock) for aggressing against others quickly acquire strong tendencies to engage in such behavior. For example, in one well-known investigation, Ulrich, Johnston, Richardson, and Wolff (1963) found that initially docile rats quickly learned to attack their cage mates when they were deprived of water and could obtain a drink only through such behavior.

That human beings, too, acquire at least some forms of aggression through the process of instrumental conditioning is now widely accepted (e.g., Bandura, 1973; Zillmann, 1978). As is the case in many other forms of human learning, however, a much wider variety of positive reinforcers appear to play a role in this process than is the case with various animal species. For example, among the positive outcomes that have been found to markedly increase the tendency of both children and adults to engage in aggression against others are the following: acquisition of various material incentives, such as money, desired objects, toys, and candy (Buss, 1971; Gaebelein, 1973; Walters & Brown, 1963); social approval or increased status (Geen & Stonner, 1971; Gentry, 1970a); and the alleviation of aversion treatment at the hands of others (Patterson, Littman, & Bricker, 1967). In addition, there is some indication that signs of pain and suffering on the part of the victim may serve as a form of reinforcement for strongly provoked individuals (Baron, 1974a, 1977; Feshbach, Stiles, & Bitter, 1967; Hartmann, 1969), thus strengthening their tendency to engage in such behavior on later occasions. In sum, there seems to be little reason to doubt the general proposition that human beings acquire at least some forms of aggression because, quite simply, they are rewarded for engaging in such behavior.

*Acquisition of Aggressive Behavior: The Role of Social Modeling*

While instrumental learning appears to play an important role in the acquisition of aggressive responses, Bandura (1973) has suggested that another process—*social modeling*—is probably even more crucial. Specifically, he has called attention to the fact that human beings frequently acquire many new forms of behavior, including patterns of aggression, through observation of the actions and outcomes of others. A very large body of experimental findings lends support to this conclusion. In these investigations, both children and adults have been found to readily acquire novel aggressive responses not previously at their disposal simply by observing the behavior of other persons (see Bandura, 1973; Goranson, 1970). Moreover, additional findings indicate that it is not necessary for the social models demonstrating such actions to be physically present on the scene; their symbolic representation in films, television shows, or even stories is quite sufficient for the occurrence of considerable amounts of learning among observers (see Bandura, 1973; Geen, 1976). And perhaps of even greater importance, when youngsters, or even adults, witness aggressive models receiving reinforcement—or merely avoiding punishment—for engaging in such behavior, they are often encouraged to adopt these actions themselves. Dramatic and often tragic illustrations of this latter fact are provided by incidents in which unusual forms of violence given heavy play by the mass media are soon repeated in geographic settings far removed from their original location. In such cases, viewers (or readers) presumably master new aggressive techniques in a vicarious manner and are then encouraged by the violent episodes they have witnessed to put these techniques into actual practice in their dealings with others. Since we will return to the impact of social models upon aggression in Chapter 3, further discussion of this topic will be reserved until that point. For the present, we simply wish to note that there is currently little doubt that exposure to the actions of aggressive social models often serve to equip both children and adults with new aggressive responses not previously represented in their behavior hierarchies.

*Conditions Serving to Maintain Aggressive Behavior*

Once aggressive responses have been acquired, a number of different factors operate to ensure that they will be maintained and perhaps strengthened even further. Not surprisingly, many of these are similar to the factors that facilitate their initial acquisition.

First, it is often the case that successful aggression against others continues to provide aggressors with important tangible rewards. For example, children who successfully assault their playmates may repeatedly claim the most desirable toys and privileges available. Similarly, as noted by Buss (1971), aggression frequently "pays" quite handsomely for adults as well. The rulers of organized crime, for example, continue to reap huge fortunes from the expert use of violence, and despots who successfully employ terror and violence against their political opponents often greatly prolong their time in power.

Second, aggression is also frequently maintained by continued social reward and approval. During time of war, soldiers often receive medals and gain special privileges for killing a large number of enemy troops. And the toughest teen-ager in any neighborhood continues to receive a considerable amount of status and prestige, in addition to various tangible rewards, as a result of successful attacks against others. A particularly grizzly illustration of the ability of social reinforcers to maintain and encourage a high level of aggression is provided by the records of Nazi concentration camps during World War II. Here, medals, promotions, and many other benefits were distributed to those most successful in the mass murder of innocent prisoners, and the commanders and staffs of different camps often competed vigorously for such rewards (Bandura, 1973).

Third, but by no means last, patterns of overt aggression are frequently maintained by the process of *self-reinforcement*, in which aggressors more or less "pat themselves on the back" for successful assaults against others, self-administering praise and approval for the completion of such actions (Bandura, 1973). Many highly aggressive individuals often take great pride in their abilities to harm or injure others (Toch, 1969), and even less violent persons may occasionally take satisfaction in having restored lost pride or "face" by repaying affronts from others (Feshbach, 1970). In these and several other ways, aggressive actions—once acquired—are maintained as an active part of individuals' behavior hierarchies.

*The Social Learning View: Some Important Implications*

Before concluding this discussion of the social-learning perspective, we should call attention to the fact that it is much more optimistic with respect to the possibilities of preventing or controlling human aggression than either the drive or the instinct views considered previously. This is the case for two important reasons. First, according to this general perspective, aggression is a learned form of social behavior. As such, it is open to direct modification and can be readily reduced through many procedures. For example, removal of those conditions tending to maintain its occurrence, where feasible, should be quite effective in this respect. Aggressive behaviors would still be present in individuals' hierarchies, but there would be little reason for their direct translation into actual performance.

Second, in contrast to the drive and instinct theories, the social-learning approach does not view human beings as constantly driven or impelled toward violence by built-in internal forces or ever-present external stimuli (i.e., frustrating events). Rather, it suggests that individuals aggress only under appropriate social conditions that tend to facilitate such behavior. Alter these conditions, it is argued, and aggression may be readily prevented or reduced. Not surprisingly, this basic optimism of the social-learning approach has led many psychologists to examine it very carefully. And as we shall soon see, their efforts in this respect have yielded growing empirical support for its basic accuracy. Thus, in recent years, theoretical perspectives that view aggression as a learned form of social behavior have gained increasing acceptance as the most sophisticated—and perhaps most accurate—framework within which to comprehend the nature of human violence.

## SUMMARY

Aggression may be defined as any form of behavior directed toward the goal of harming or injuring another living being who is motivated to avoid such treatment. At first glance, this definition seems quite simple and straightforward. Closer examination reveals, however, that it actually encompasses a number of complex issues, including the assumptions (1) that aggression must involve voluntary or intentional harm to the victim; (2) that only behavior meant to harm or injure living organisms can be viewed as aggression; and (3) that victims must be motivated to avoid such treatment.

Over the years, several contrasting theoretical perspectives regarding the nature and the origins of aggression have been proposed. The oldest, and perhaps best known, suggests that such behavior is largely innate or instinctive in nature. Freud, one famous proponent of this general view, held that aggression stems from an innate, self-directed death instinct that is turned outward against others. Lorenz, a more recent supporter of this position, holds that such behavior stems from an innate fighting instinct possessed by all animals, including human beings.

A second major perspective concerning aggression suggests that it stems primarily from an externally elicited drive or motive to harm others. By far the most influential statement of this general framework is the famous *frustration–aggression theory* proposed several decades ago by Dollard and his colleagues. According to this theory, frustration elicits a persistent instigation (i.e., drive) toward aggression. Such behavior can then be blocked or inhibited by fear of punishment. However, in such cases, the instigation remains and may lead to assaults against targets other than the frustrater who are associated with lower degrees of inhibition. This general notion of *displaced aggression* was extended and refined by Miller (1948), who devised a systematic model to account for its occurrence. While Miller's theory of displacement has remained influential and is supported by some recent findings, it suffers from certain ambiguities that limit its applicability.

A third and final theoretical perspective regarding the nature of aggression suggests that it be viewed primarily as a learned form of social behavior. According to Bandura (1973), perhaps the most outspoken proponent of this general view, a thorough understanding of aggression may be obtained only through careful attention to (1) the manner in which it is acquired; (2) the factors that instigate its occurrence; and (3) the conditions that maintain its performance. With respect to the acquisition of aggression, it is generally accepted that *instrumental conditioning* and *social modeling* are of crucial importance. Similarly, many different factors are assumed to instigate its occurrence, and several different conditions (e.g., the attainment of material and social reinforcers) are assumed to maintain its strength within individuals' behavior hierarchies. In contrast to instinct and drive views of aggression, which perceive individuals as continually impelled toward violence either by internal forces or pervasive external stimuli (e.g., frustration), the social-learning view suggests that aggression will occur only under appropriate social conditions. Thus, it is considerably more optimistic with respect to the possibility of preventing or controlling such behavior than the other perspectives.

# 2

# *Aggression: Methods for Systematic Study*

Down through the ages, philosophers, poets, theologians, novelists, and others have grappled repeatedly with the puzzle of human violence. What is its nature? Why does it occur? What factors influence its form and direction? These and many related questions have been the subject of continued, careful attention. Unfortunately, attempts by such scholars to unravel the nature of aggressive behavior were based largely upon informal observation and rational speculation. As a result, they often made intriguing reading but failed to provide anything remotely approaching definitive answers to the important questions discussed.

In the 20th century, all this has radically altered. At the present time—and for the past several decades—aggression has been the subject of careful scientific inquiry. Largely as a result of this shift in methods, "hard" empirical data have come to replace opinion, and systematic knowledge has gradually emerged in place of speculation. Despite the fact that this change in general approach is far from new, however; it is still the subject of considerable confusion. Indeed, even psychologists sometimes admit to bewilderment regarding this specific issue. In a sense, this is hardly surprising. How, after all, does one go about gaining scientific knowledge regarding such a dangerous form of behavior as aggression? The answer, unfortunately, is far from obvious. And precisely for this reason, it seems important that it be supplied before we proceed to a consideration of the information presented in remaining portions of this volume. That is, it seems crucial that a detailed account of the manner in which knowledge regarding aggression has been acquired be provided prior to the presentation of this knowledge itself. For this reason, then, the present chapter will focus on the various techniques employed by active researchers in the systematic study of human aggression.

Not surprisingly, the first method adopted by psychologists and others in their attempts to examine the origins and nature of aggression centered on the use of *systematic observation*. That is, actual instances of aggression were observed—either directly or indirectly—and on the basis of such information, attempts were made to explain the occurrence, the direction, and the form of such actions. Freud, for example, based much of his theorizing about aggression on careful observation of his many patients. And ethologists have long employed approaches based largely on systematic observation in their ingenious studies of various forms of animal behavior—including aggression—in natural settings.

Such techniques have often proved useful and made substantial contributions to our understanding of certain forms of aggression. Indeed, in some cases, they have been the only procedures that could be safely or ethically adopted. For example, attempts to determine the nature of events serving to trigger dangerous riots have, of necessity, relied mainly upon direct or secondhand reports of such occurrences. Similarly, efforts to explicate the factors responsible for dangerous forms of child abuse have, for equally obvious reasons, been restricted to the collection of information concerning parental personality, socioeconomic background, and parents' own child-rearing experiences. In these and many other cases, research methods based upon the general principle of systematic observation have been, and continue to be, of considerable use.

Despite the many advantages offered by such procedures, however, they suffer from one major shortcoming that sharply lessens their overall appeal: the findings they provide are somewhat ambiguous with respect to cause-and-effect relationships. That is, it is generally impossible, on the basis of investigations employing such methods, to determine which specific factors lead to, direct, or inhibit overt acts of aggression. To see why this is so, let us consider a specific example.

In recent years, it has often been reported that the incidence of riots and other forms of civil disorder increases during periods when uncomfortably high temperatures prevail. Such findings have often been interpreted as suggesting that unpleasant environmental warmth causes individuals to feel irritable and so increases the likelihood that they will aggress against others. While such conclusions seem quite plausible, they may actually be unjustified. High temperatures are accompanied by several other conditions that may also underlie the apparently direct relationship between aggression and heat. For example, more people are generally out on the street during "heat waves" than at other times (especially in central-city areas, where air-conditioning is rare) and are therefore more readily available to participate in any growing quarrel. Similarly, most heat waves occur during the summer months, a time when an especially volatile group of individuals—teen-agers—are home from school. And finally, such environmental conditions also tend to develop at times of the year when there are simply more hours of daylight and thus more opportunities for the occurrence of various provocative incidents. In view of such considerations, the relationship between uncomfortably warm temperatures and aggression remains problematic: Is it unpleasant heat itself or these other factors that account for the occurrence of "long, hot summers"? On the basis of purely observational data, it is quite impossible to tell.

Largely because of such difficulties, psychologists have generally concluded that the most effective means of studying aggressive behavior is that of direct experimentation. Thus, they have sought to obtain more definitive information concerning such behavior through investigations in which factors believed to influence aggression are varied in a direct and systematic manner. That is, one or more variables assumed to elicit or inhibit overt aggression are manipulated, and the effects of such procedures are then assessed.

As is probably quite apparent, attempts to investigate aggressive behavior in this manner raise a number of perplexing questions. How, after all, can one hope to study such a dangerous form of activity in a systematic manner without any risk of serious harm—psychological or physical—to research participants? At first glance, this dilemma seems virtually insoluble. Yet, as the existence of the present volume attests, such is not the case. Psychologists have responded to this challenge by devising a number of different techniques for investigating aggression in a safe, yet rigorous manner. While the varied research methods devised for this purpose can be divided in several different ways, we will consider them under two major headings: those employed in *laboratory experiments* and those employed in *field investigations*. Within each of these major divisions, several contrasting methods for the study of aggression will be described, and questions concerning the validity and the generalizability of the findings yielded by each will be considered.

## LABORATORY METHODS FOR THE STUDY OF AGGRESSION: HURTING WITHIN THE CONTEXT OF A CONTROLLED PSYCHOLOGICAL ENVIRONMENT

Recent investigations of aggression have been conducted in a wide range of contexts. The great majority, however, have been performed within laboratory settings (cf. Geen & O'Neal, 1976; Zillmann, 1978). Several different factors have contributed to this recent emphasis upon laboratory research. First, in the opinion of most investigators, precise, systematic manipulation of independent variables of interest can be more readily attained in this context than in any other. More specifically, since experimenters can carefully control the nature of the events occurring in their laboratories, as well as the conditions prevailing within them, systematic variations of factors assumed to affect aggression can often be readily produced.

Second, the psychological laboratory affords what many researchers believe to be the safest and the most ethical context within which to conduct research on aggression. All possibility of harm to participants can be eliminated, and individuals taking part in such research can be fully advised, in advance, of the nature of the activities they will be asked to perform. Further, subjects can be readily provided with a full and detailed explanation of all portions of the investigation, as well as its major implications, upon completion of the experimental session. Many psychologists currently believe that together, these techniques of *informed consent* and thorough *debriefing* of participants go a long way toward resolving the ethical issues raised by systematic research on aggression and other complex forms of social behavior (American Psychological Association, 1973). And since such procedures cannot be followed in other, more naturalistic settings, these psychologists favor the use of laboratory research for this important reason.

Finally, laboratory investigations often prove to be far more efficient in terms of time and effort than other, contrasting approaches.

Subjects can be scheduled at regular intervals, and instances of aggression can be elicited from participants with a relatively high degree of frequency. This circumstance contrasts sharply with conditions prevailing in natural settings, where acts of aggression are often widely separated in terms of both time and location.

For these and several related reasons, most psychologists have preferred to conduct their investigations of aggression in laboratory settings. This preference does not imply that the adoption of such procedures represents a totally unmixed blessing. On the contrary, laboratory research raises a number of potential problems that must be faced by the investigators choosing to pursue it. For example, it has often been noted that individuals participating in laboratory studies of aggression know quite well that they are taking part in a psychological experiment. As a result, their reactions may be far from natural and quite different from those that would occur in other settings. Similarly, the participants in such research often engage in active attempts to "second-guess" the experimenter, seeking to determine the major hypotheses under investigation. And once they form some notion of the investigator's expectations, they may, on an individual basis, seek to confirm, refute, or ignore these predictions (cf. Chaikin, Sigler, & Derlega, 1974; Sigall, Aronson, & Van Hoose, 1970). Fortunately, sophisticated techniques for counteracting the influence of such reactions exist and have commonly been adopted in recent investigations of aggression. However, such problems are always present to trap unwary researchers and invalidate the findings of their studies. In this regard, these problems represent potential drawbacks to laboratory research.

While many different methods for investigating aggression in laboratory settings have been devised, most seem to fall into one of four major categories, involving (1) verbal assaults against others; (2) attacks against inanimate objects; (3) "safe," noninjurious assaults against live victims; and (4) ostensibly harmful attacks against such persons. Each of these procedures will now be considered in turn.

### Verbal Measures of Aggression: When Words (or Evaluations) Harm

Virtually all early studies of aggression (e.g., Cohen, 1955; Davitz, 1952; Doob & Sears, 1939; McClelland & Apicella, 1945) focused primarily upon verbal rather than physical forms of such behavior. In these investigations, participants were generally frustrated or exposed to some other form of instigation and then provided with an opportunity to retaliate against their tormenter through verbal statements, written comments, or more formal evaluations. While such procedures no longer constitute the most common approach in laboratory studies of aggression, they are still very much in use and are therefore worthy of careful attention (e.g., Ebbesen, Duncan, & Konečni, 1975). Basically, two major variants of such procedures have been employed.

In the first and less commonly used technique, subjects are provided with an opportunity to aggress against the source of their frustration in a direct, overt manner (e.g., DeCharms & Wilkins, 1963; Rosenbaum & DeCharms, 1960). A clear example of the use of such procedures is provided by an interesting study conducted by Wheeler and Caggiula (1966).

In this investigation, male subjects (naval recruits) first listened to another individual (actually a confederate of the investigators) express extreme and socially undesirable opinions on several different issues. For example, with respect to religion, he stated, "I think my religion is best, and I don't think the others are worth a damn . . . If I had my way, all other religions would be illegal." Next, they heard a second individual (also a confederate), evaluate this person in either a hostile or a less provocative manner. And finally, they themselves were given an opportunity to evaluate both of these persons by commenting upon their previous statements. Since the two confederates could, presumably, overhear the subjects' statements, it was possible for the participants to launch direct, verbal assaults against these individuals if they so desired.

Recordings of their actual comments were made, and these data were then scored in terms of the degree of hostility they expressed toward the obnoxious confederate. Specifically, evaluations in which subjects used such terms as *idiot, queer, crazy, nuts,* and *insane* or in which they suggested that this person be shot, locked up, or deported were scored as extremely aggressive in nature, while less provocative statements were assigned lower ratings. (That subjects often expressed considerable verbal aggression against the confederate is indicated by the fact that in some experimental groups, more than 60% made extremely aggressive comments.) With minor variations, procedures resembling those employed by Wheeler and Caggiula (1966) have also been employed in several other studies (e.g., DeCharms & Wilkins, 1963; Rosenbaum & DeCharms, 1960).

A second and more commonly used technique for investigating verbal aggression involves less direct expressions of hostility toward the victim. In experiments employing such procedures, subjects are first frustrated or otherwise instigated to aggression and then asked to complete a questionnaire on which they evaluate the frustrater in some manner (e.g., Berkowitz, 1970; Berkowitz, & Knurek, 1969; Ebbesen, Duncan, & Konečni, 1975). Further, these evaluations are generally made in a context that suggests that negative ratings will harm the victim in some important way. An illustration of the effective use of such procedures is provided by a recent investigation conducted by Zillmann and Cantor (1976).

In this study, male subjects were first angered by an obnoxious experimenter, who unfairly accused them of failing to cooperate, and were then asked to respond to the questionnaire shown in Table 3. As can be readily seen, the first three items concerned their treatment in the experiment, while the last three related directly to their feelings toward the unpleasant experimenter. These latter questions were introduced by a statement indicating that subjects' responses would be used to determine whether this individual would continue to receive financial support for his graduate studies. Thus, negative ratings could, potentially, cause the experimenter considerable harm. Ratings on the items relating directly to this person were made on a scale ranging from −100 to +100, with negative numbers reflecting harsh evaluations and positive numbers indicating favorable reactions. That subjects were willing to express considerable verbal aggression against this individual is indicated by the fact that in some experimental conditions, mean ratings as low as −86 were obtained.

Procedures such as the ones described above offer several important advantages. First, because they involve only the interchange of verbal comments or ratings on questionnaires, they are quite safe and generally eliminate the possibility of any serious harm to participants. Indeed, since the victim is generally either a confederate of the experimenter (e.g., Zillmann & Cantor, 1976) or totally nonexistent (e.g., Berkowitz, 1970), no harm is actually inflicted on any individual. Second, since verbal aggression is quite common in everyday life, such procedures provide subjects with an opportunity to aggress against the victim in a familiar and well-practiced manner. Third, question-

TABLE 3

*The Questionnaire Employed by Zillmann and Cantor (1976) to Investigate Verbal Aggression against an Obnoxious Experimenter[a]*

---

1. Are you in any way dissatisfied with the way you were treated in this experiment?

   Not at all dissatisfied[b]                                    Extremely dissatisfied

   0 ------------------------------------------------------------------------- 100

2. Do you think the demands made upon you in this experiment were in any way excessive?

   Not at all excessive                                          Extremely excessive

   0 ------------------------------------------------------------------------- 100

3. Were you in any way mistreated by the experimenter conducting this experiment?

   Not mistreated at all                               Mistreated to a great extent

   0 ------------------------------------------------------------------------- 100

4. How well did the above-named graduate student perform in his role as an experimenter?

   Poorly                                                               Excellently

   −100 --------------------------------------------------------------------+ 100

5. How would you rate his manner of interacting with others?

   Extremely unpleasant and discourteous     Extremely pleasant and courteous

   −100 -------------------------------------------------------------------- +100

6. In your opinion, should this student be reappointed as a research assistant?

   Definitely not                                                    Definitely yes

   −100 -------------------------------------------------------------------- +100

---

[a] Adapted from Zillmann & Cantor, 1976.
[b] Subjects responded to each item by placing a mark at any point they wished along the appropriate line.

naire responses can be readily quantified and, as a result, yield convenient and readily gathered dependent measures. And finally, since, in general, verbal aggression involves indirect rather than direct assaults against the victim (i.e., paper-and-pencil evaluations of this person rather than direct, face-to-face confrontations with him), such behaviors are less subject to the influence of strong restraints or inhibitions than other forms of aggression. As a result, they can be readily elicited and studied in laboratory settings.

Given these advantages, it is not surprising that verbal measures of aggression have been employed in many different investigations. One important point regarding their use, however, should not be overlooked: unless there is the potential for some type of harm to the victim, negative evaluations of this person or negative comments about him cannot be interpreted as instances of aggression. Instead, it seems more appropriate to view such actions as expressions of sub-jects' current emotional arousal, liking for the victim, or general affec-tive state. In view of such considerations, it is important to distin-guish between investigations in which subjects' evaluations of another person can potentially inflict negative consequences upon this individual (e.g., Berkowitz, 1970; Ebbesen, Duncan, & Konečni, 1975; Zillman *et al.*, 1975) and those in which they cannot (e.g., Berkowitz & Knurek, 1969; Landy & Mettee, 1969). Further, it is essential to deter-mine whether, and to what extent, subjects actually accept the sugges-tion that their verbal comments or evaluations can harm the victim in some manner. Only to the degree that they attach credence to such statements can it be argued that aggression has occurred. Unfortu-nately, information regarding this issue has not been gathered in many past investigations. Thus, it is difficult to determine the extent to which such studies have yielded valid measures of harm-doing be-havior. Provided that careful attention is directed to this and related issues, however, it seems reasonable to conclude that verbal measures of aggression can often provide a useful and efficient means of ex-amining the nature of such behavior under safe, laboratory condi-tions.

### "Play" Measures of Aggression: Assaults against Inanimate Objects

A second major method frequently employed in the investigation of aggressive behavior centers on assaults by individuals against various types of inanimate objects. Within the context of such proce-dures, participants are typically first instigated to aggression in some manner—often through exposure to the actions of an aggressive model—and then provided with an opportunity to kick, punch, or otherwise attack some inanimate object. Aggression is then assessed in terms of the frequency with which they direct such actions against the target.

By far the best-known application of such procedures is found in the famous "Bobo doll" studies, first conducted by Albert Bandura and his colleagues (e.g., Bandura, Ross, & Ross, 1963a,b; Grusec, 1972). In these investigations, young children were first exposed or not exposed to the actions of a social model—sometimes another child, sometimes an adult, and sometimes a cartoon character—who demon-

strated unusual assaults against a large inflated plastic toy. For example, in one investigation (Bandura, Ross, & Ross, 1963a), the model
performed such unusual acts as sitting on the doll, punching it repeatedly in the nose, pommeling it on the head with a toy mallet, kicking
it around the room, and making such statements as "Sock him in the
nose . . . ," "Hit him down . . . ," "Throw him in the air. . . ." Following exposure to such actions, the children were placed in a room
containing a variety of toys, several of which had been used by the
model in his novel assaults, and were allowed to play freely for a brief
period of time (generally 10–20 minutes), during which their behavior
was carefully observed. The major question under study in such investigations was whether subjects would acquire—and later perform—
the model's novel actions. Not surprisingly, they generally did. Indeed, frequently, they seemed to become veritable carbon copies of
the model they observed (see Figure 5).

In other studies, children have observed attacks against different
forms of inanimate objects. For example, in one experiment conducted
by Grusec (1972), the children observed the following sequence, involving assaults against a stuffed bear, a plastic doll, and several other
objects:

> As soon as the experimenter left the room, the model proceeded to play.
> He punched the doll and then kicked it across the room, shot arrows at the
> panda, whipped it with the rope, and stabbed it in the stomach with the
> mallet. Then he pounded the bottle on the table, jumped on the boat,
> ripped a page from the book, and broke two balloons. (p. 144)

Following these procedures, the children were provided with an opportunity to assault these objects themselves.

While such procedures have been employed in a number of different studies, they have been the subject of severe criticism by several investigators (e.g., Klapper, 1968). In particular, such critics have
argued that since no living being is harmed by such actions, it is not
appropriate to describe them as involving instances of aggressive behavior. Rather, they may best be interpreted as a form of play—
especially in cases where the objects attacked (e.g., an inflated Bobo
doll)—are specifically designed for this purpose.

In response to such comments, Bandura (1973, pp. 82–83) has
called attention to the important distinction between the *learning* and
the *performance* of aggressive responses. Procedures based upon attacks against inanimate objects, he argues, are quite useful with re-

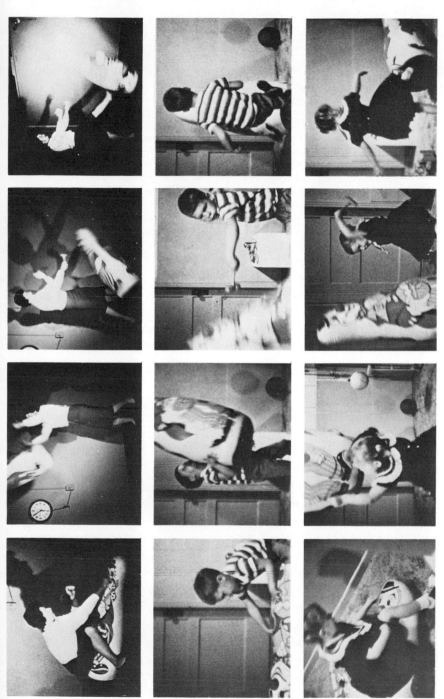

FIGURE 5. Adult models and young children attacking a large, inflated Bobo doll. Such assaults against inanimate objects form the basis of one popular method for investigating human aggression. (Photo courtesy Dr. Albert Bandura.)

spect to an understanding of the manner in which such behaviors are learned. This is the case, he has suggested, because aggressive responses are often acquired in contexts far removed from actual harm to others. In Bandura's own words:

> Behavior that has dangerous or costly consequences is typically acquired and perfected in simulated learning situations. Airline pilots, for example, develop basic flying skills in simulators . . . that reproduce the motion of actual airplanes. Similarly, aggressive behavior is largely learned under nonfrustrating conditions in the absence of injurious intent and often with inanimate objects. . . . Boxers develop pugilistic skills by using punching bags . . . ; hunters acquire the basic rudiments of hunting by shooting at inanimate targets . . . ; and parents rarely follow their children around to teach them how to fight in the context of actual battles. (p. 82)

In view of such considerations, Bandura believes that studies involving assaults against inanimate objects can be quite useful from the point of view of examining the origins of aggressive behavior. After all, a youngster (or an adult) who has acquired new techniques for assaulting and harming others can as readily demonstrate the mastery of such behavior in his or her actions toward plastic dolls as in assaults against other human beings. Such "play" measures of aggression, however, are viewed by Bandura as being far less useful with respect to the task of specifying those conditions under which aggressive responses already in an individual's behavior hierarchy will be put to actual use. In order to gain information on this important issue, he contends, procedures involving the infliction of real or imagined harm upon others are essential. In short, while "play" measures such as those used in the early Bobo doll studies shed light upon the manner in which new forms of aggression are mastered, they tell us little about the conditions under which such actions will be directed toward live human victims.

Unfortunately, despite the clarity with which these restrictions have been stated, they have not been uniformly heeded. Instead, assaults against inanimate objects—including toys specifically designed for such treatment—have frequently been interpreted as providing information about the performance as well as the learning of aggressive responses. For example, the findings, in a number of early studies, that exposure to filmed or televised violence encourages viewers to attack inanimate objects such as inflated plastic clowns in precisely the manner demonstrated by the model have frequently been construed as indicating that such materials facilitate the occurrence of overt assaults against other persons. Consistent with Bandura's suggestions, however, it seems more reasonable to adopt a less provocative interpretation, assuming only that such results underscore the fact that individuals can acquire new aggressive responses by observing others. While additional investigations employing other methodologies suggest that exposure to filmed or televised violence may in fact sometimes facilitate interpersonal aggression (see Comstock, 1975), such conclusions do *not* seem warranted solely on the basis of Bobo doll and related studies.

Before concluding the present discussion, it should be noted that the findings of a recent study (Johnston *et al.*, 1977) offer support for the view that children's behavior in such play situations may in fact be related to their aggression toward other human beings. Specifically, these researchers found that the amount of play aggression demonstrated by nursery school children toward a Bobo doll and other toys was significantly related to ratings of their general aggressiveness by peers ($r = .76$) and teachers ($r = .57$). Although suggestive, these findings are, of course, far from conclusive. For example, to mention only one possible complication, high ratings of aggressiveness and a high incidence of "attacks" against Bobo dolls or similar toys may both be underlain by a high level of motor activity, and have little relation to intentions to harm or injure others. Further, since the Johnston *et al*. study is the only one conducted to date which has specifically examined the validity of play measures of aggression, it must be replicated before its findings can be accepted with confidence. For the present, then, it appears most prudent to interpret measures of aggression based upon attacks against toys or other inanimate objects with a considerable degree of caution.

## *"Safe" Attacks against a Live Victim: Noninjurious Physical Aggression*

A third approach to the laboratory study of aggression, developed only within the past few years, involves procedures in which subjects are provided with an opportunity to launch vigorous—but noninjurious—physical assaults against a passive, live victim (Diener, 1976; Diener, Dineen, & Endresen, 1975). In studies employing this technique, subjects are instructed to behave in any manner they wish toward another person they find sitting on the floor of a dimly lit room. In reality, this individual is a confederate of the experimenter, specifically trained to remain passive regardless of the subjects' actions. Various objects—including a toy gun that shoots Ping-Pong balls, sponge-rubber bricks, styrofoam swords, and a large bowl of rubber bands—are also present in the room and can be used in assaults against the passive victim. Subjects' behavior during a two-minute period is then carefully recorded by observers who watch through special one-way mirrors. Aggression scores for each participant are then obtained by the multiplication of all aggressive acts they have directed toward the confederate by the previously obtained value of such behaviors along a scale of aggressivity (see Table 4). For example, hitting the confederate lightly with a styrofoam sword receives a rating of 3.3. Thus, if a subject strikes the victim in this manner 10 times during the two-minute session and performs no other aggressive actions, he or she receives an overall score of 33.

Results obtained with such procedures indicate that under some conditions, subjects emit a very high level of aggressive behavior. Indeed, in some cases, average scores of 600 or more have been obtained. Some indication of the nature of subjects' actions in these cases is provided by the fact that in order to achieve a score of 603 (the average obtained by one group in a recent investigation by Diener), it would be necessary for subjects to hit the victim sharply with the toy swords 83 times during the two-minute period or to shoot rubber

TABLE 4

*Aggressivity-Scale Scores for Various Behaviors Directed by Subjects against a Passive Confederate in Diener's Procedures for Investigating Aggression*[a]

| Behavior | Aggressivity score |
| --- | --- |
| Hitting confederate lightly with toy sword | 3.3 |
| Throwing newspaper balls at confederate | 4.6 |
| Shooting rubber bands at confederate | 5.0 |
| Shooting toy gun at confederate | 5.6 |
| Hitting confederate sharply with toy sword | 6.9 |
| Shoving confederate | 7.5 |
| Kicking confederate lightly | 7.5 |
| Dragging confederate around the room | 7.6 |

[a] Adapted from Diener, Dineen, & Endresen, 1975.

bands at him 141 times during this brief interval. As noted recently by Diener (1976, p. 505), such behavior by research participants can only be described as quite frantic in nature.

Procedures based on noninjurious physical assaults against a passive victim offer several important advantages. First, they provide a degree of realism lacking in the other techniques we have discussed up to this point. Subjects aggress directly against a live victim, and the actions they perform—hitting with a sword, shooting with a toy gun, dragging the victim about the room—are quite similar in nature to those that are enacted in more dangerous instances of aggressive behavior. Second, participants have complete freedom of choice with respect to their actions toward the victim; they can treat him in an aggressive or in a totally nonaggressive manner.

While such advantages enhance the appeal of the procedures devised by Diener and his colleagues, certain disadvantages or potential problems should not be overlooked. First, it seems possible that subjects perceive their behavior in this context primarily as part of a game in which no one can possibly be hurt. To the extent that this is true, it seems inappropriate to view their actions as instances of aggression. And second, such procedures involve the possibility of actual physical harm to the victim, despite the many precautions taken to avert such consequences. Indeed, in some of the investigations conducted to date (Diener, 1976), it has been necessary to halt the session in a number of cases because the actions directed by subjects against the confederate threatened to get out of hand. Thus, the methodology devised by Diener, ingenious though it is, seems to involve negative as well as positive features.

Some evidence for the overall validity of Diener's procedures is provided by the repeated finding that factors which would be expected—on the basis of both theory and previous investigations—to exert important effects upon aggression do strongly affect subjects' behavior in this general setting. For example, participants have been found to direct more aggressive actions toward the confederate after witnessing the actions of an aggressive model and being informed that they will not be responsible for their actions than they are in the absence of such a model and after learning that they will be directly responsible for their actions (Diener, Dineen, & Endresen, 1975). Moreover, findings obtained with postexperimental questionnaires suggest that participants are not generally successful in guessing the hypothesis under study and express relatively low levels of suspicion concerning the true purposes of the investigation (Diener, 1976). Together, such evidence suggests that procedures involving noninjurious physical assaults against a live victim may provide a useful—and intriguing—means of studying human aggression under safe laboratory conditions. However, additional evidence regarding the validity of this approach is necessary before it can be accepted without reservation.

## Direct Physical Aggression: Hurt without Harm

A fourth and by far the most commonly used technique for the laboratory study of aggression involves direct physical assaults against a live victim. Briefly, such procedures rest upon a crucial deception, in which research participants are led to believe that they can physically harm another person in some manner, when in fact they cannot. In this fashion, it is reasoned, subjects' intentions or desires to inflict pain or suffering upon the victim can be assessed without any risk of actual physical injury to this person. In short, as supporters of this general approach argue, it becomes possible to investigate intentions to hurt without the possibility of any accompanying physical harm (cf. Buss, 1961).

Because they permit the direct investigation of physical assaults—the form of aggressive behavior viewed as most dangerous by many researchers—such procedures have attained widespread use in recent years (cf. Geen & O'Neal, 1976; Zillmann, 1978). Indeed, several variations on this basic theme have been developed and put to use in different lines of investigation. We will now consider each of these approaches in some detail.

### The Buss Technique: Hurting via the "Aggression Machine"

The first and perhaps the most popular technique for the direct investigation of physical aggression was devised some years in the past by Arnold Buss (1961). In summary form, the method he developed proceeds as follows.

When subjects arrive for their experimental appointment, they are informed that they will be participating, along with another individual (actually a confederate of the investigator), in a study concerned with the effects of punishment on learning. It is further explained that in order for this topic to be examined, one of the two persons present will serve as a *teacher* and the other as a *learner*. The teacher's task is then described as that of presenting various materials to the learner, who will attempt to master them. (In the original procedures devised by Buss, these materials consisted of patterns of lights; in subsequent studies, however, they have taken many different forms.)

It is further explained that on each occasion when the learner makes a correct response, the teacher will reward him by illuminating a light indicating that he has responded appropriately. Whenever he makes an error, however, the teacher will punish him by means of electric shock. Both rewards and punishments are to be administered by means of a device such as the one shown in Figure 6A, an apparatus that has generally come to be known in psychology as the *aggression machine*. As can be readily seen, this equipment contains ten buttons, and it is explained to subjects that on each occasion when the learner makes an error, the teacher will choose one of these switches and deliver an electric shock to the person by depressing it. The first button is described as delivering very mild shock, the second as delivering somewhat stronger punishment, and so on, up to the tenth, which presumably delivers extremely powerful jolts.[1]

At this point, the actual subject is always chosen to serve as the teacher, and the confederate is chosen to serve as the learner. In order to convince the subject that the apparatus actually works in the manner described, sample shocks are then delivered from several of the buttons. Following this procedure, the learning session proceeds. During this portion of the study, the confederate makes a prearranged series of errors, thus providing subjects with several opportunities on which to shock him. (In the original procedures outlined by Buss, 36 shocks were delivered to the victim; however, in subsequent studies, this number has usually varied between 10 and 20.)

The strength of subjects' tendencies to aggress against the confederate is then assessed by recording both the intensity and the duration of the shocks he or she chooses to deliver. Thus, two basic measures of

[1]In the original procedures devised by Buss, the aversive stimuli delivered by the aggression machine were electric shocks, and this has also been the case in many subsequent studies. However, more recent investigations have sometimes involved other types of unpleasant consequences, such as irritating noise (Fitz, 1976) or varying degrees of excessive heat (Liebert & Baron, 1972).

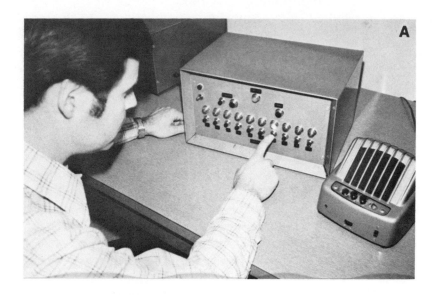

FIGURE 6. (A) An aggression machine similar to the one devised by Buss (1961). Note that the individual shown is pushing button 7 and is, therefore, behaving in a highly aggressive manner. (B) An experimenter recording the two measures of aggression obtained with such an apparatus: shock intensity and shock duration.

aggression—*shock intensity* and *shock duration*—are obtained (see Figure 6B). In addition, a third measure based upon the total amount of aversive stimulation directed by the subject against the confederate (shock intensity × shock duration) can also be readily generated. Of course, it should be noted once again that these measures reflect the amount of painful stimuli the victim *would* receive if he were actually the recipient of the subject's assaults. In reality, he is not connected to the apparatus in the manner described by the experimenter and never receives any of the shocks directed to him by the participants.

Because they seemed to offer an ingenious method for investigating physical aggression under safe, laboratory conditions, the procedures devised by Buss quickly attained widespread adoption. Indeed, with minor modifications of the type mentioned in passing above, these procedures have been employed in literally hundreds of different experiments during the past 10–15 years (cf., Bandura, 1973; Geen & O'Neal, 1976). Given their sweeping acceptance, it seems reasonable to assume that the validity of these procedures has been clearly established by extensive research. Surprisingly, however, this is not the case. Only a few investigations have been conducted to determine whether they actually yield valid measures of overt physical aggression—a far smaller number than might be desired (e.g., Cherry, Mitchell, & Nelson, 1973; Shemberg, Leventhal, & Allman, 1968; Wolfe & Baron, 1971). Fortunately, though, the results of several of these studies indicate that the Buss procedures do yield valid and useful measures of physical aggression.

For example, in an experiment conducted by Shemberg, Leventhal, and Allman (1968), both male and female teen-agers rated as highly aggressive by their counselors in an "Upward Bound" program directed significantly higher levels of aggression against a male confederate via the aggression machine than teen-agers rated as low in aggressivity (see Table 5). Similarly, in another, related study, Hartmann (1969) found that male adolescents with a history of violent behavior selected stronger shocks on the aggression machine than those without such a history. Further, individuals above the median in terms of the number and severity of their past offenses demonstrated higher levels of aggression than those below the median in this respect. Additional—and in some ways even more convincing—support for the validity of the Buss procedures is provided by an investigation conducted by Wolfe and Baron (1971).

Table 5

*Mean Intensity of the Shocks Directed against a Male*
*Confederate by Male and Female Subjects Rated by Their*
*Counselors as Being High or Low in Aggressiveness[a]*

|         | Subjects' rated aggressiveness[b] | |
|---------|------|------|
|         | Low  | High |
| Males   | 4.62 | 6.54 |
| Females | 4.77 | 7.01 |

[a] Adapted from Shemberg, Leventhal, & Allman, 1968.
[b] As expected, highly aggressive individuals chose to deliver significantly stronger shocks. Note also that females were *not* less aggressive than males—a finding to which we will return in Chapter 5.

In this study, it was reasoned by the investigators that if the aggression machine actually measures subjects' willingness to harm another person, individuals whose past behavior is indicative of strong and persistent aggressive tendencies will tend to push higher buttons on this apparatus than persons whose past behavior has not been similarly aggressive. In order to test this straightforward prediction, the behavior on the aggression machine of two sharply contrasting groups of individuals was compared. The first group consisted of 20 randomly chosen male college students ages 18–20, while the second was made up of an equal number of male prisoners of the same age who were currently incarcerated in the maximum-security division of a state prison. These latter individuals possessed a history of highly aggressive acts and had been convicted of such violent crimes as murder, manslaughter, and assault with a deadly weapon. It was predicted, of course, that they would direct stronger shocks against the victim than the college-student sample.

Before aggressing, individuals in both groups were either exposed or not exposed to the actions of a highly aggressive model (an individual who pushed only buttons 8, 9, or 10 on the apparatus), in order to determine whether they would be differentially affected by such experience. It was tentatively predicted that exposure to the model's behavior would increase subsequent aggression by both groups of subjects.

As can be seen in Figure 7, both major predictions were confirmed. Aggression by the students as well as the prisoners was enhanced by exposure to the actions of the model, and the prisoners did in fact select and use significantly higher shock buttons than the students. While it is possible that this difference between the two groups stemmed from factors other than their contrasting tendencies to

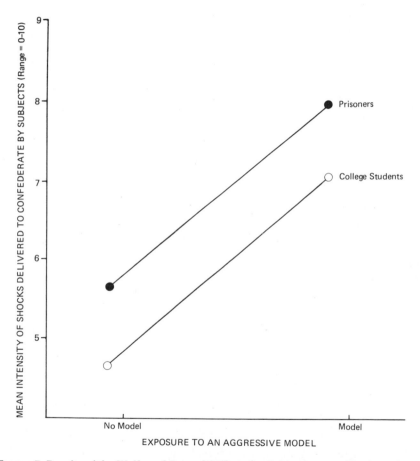

FIGURE 7. Results of the Wolfe and Baron (1971) study. Subjects exposed to the actions of an aggressive model directed stronger shocks against the confederate than those not exposed to the model, and prisoners employed stronger shocks than did college students. (Based on data from Wolfe & Baron, 1971.)

engage in overt aggression, these findings provide at least suggestive evidence for the view that assaults on the aggression machine parallel those under more naturalistic conditions. More specifically, they point to the conclusion that behavior on this apparatus does indeed provide some indication of the strength of subjects' tendencies to attack and harm others.

Although the findings reported by Wolfe and Baron (1971), Shemberg, Leventhal, and Allman (1968), Hartmann (1969), and others are encouraging with respect to the validity of the Buss paradigm, they fail to address a related and potentially important issue. Specifically, several investigators (e.g., Rule & Hewitt, 1971; Weiss, 1969) have called attention to the fact that in some cases, at least, subjects may employ high-numbered buttons on the aggression machine not out of a desire to inflict pain and suffering on the victim but rather out of a precisely opposite motive. That is, they may make use of such stimuli in an attempt to help the victim master the experimental materials rapidly and so avoid any future punishment for errors.[2] To the extent that this is true, of course, performance on the aggression machine may reflect the strength of subjects' motivation to help as well as their motivation to harm the victim.

Evidence relating to this possibility has actually been reported in an investigation conducted by Baron and Eggleston (1972). In this study, male college students were first either angered or not angered by a confederate of the experimenter and then provided with an opportunity to aggress against this individual by means of electric shock in one of two different contexts. In one, procedures closely resembling those devised by Buss were employed. That is, subjects were informed that the purpose of the investigation was that of examining the effects of punishment upon learning and were instructed to shock the victim each time he made an error on the learning task (memorizing several pairs of nonsense syllables). In a second, in contrast, subjects were informed that the purpose of the study was that of examining the effects of shock upon physiological reactions. Thus, no mention of any learning task was included, and participants shocked the confederate on a number of supposedly randomly chosen occasions.

Following the last shock trial, subjects completed a postex-

[2] It should be noted that Buss himself was aware of this potential problem. As a result, he recommended that only shocks of an intensity above the minimum needed to inform the learner of his errors be considered aggressive in nature.

perimental questionnaire on which they rated (on 7-point scales) the extent to which their choice of shocks was influenced by a desire to help the victim, a desire to hurt him, or a desire to help the experiment succeed. It was reasoned that to the extent that subjects' use of highly numbered shock buttons reflected a desire on their part to help the confederate master the experimental materials, a positive correlation would exist between the strength of the shocks they employed and the strength of their reported desire to help this person. As can be seen in Table 6, this prediction was confirmed: under the standard learning instructions, shock magnitude and reported desire to help the confederate were in fact positively related. Further, and also consistent with the suggestion that subjects' behavior within this paradigm is related to altruistic as well as aggressive motives, shock magnitude and reported desire to help the experiment succeed were also positively related. In contrast, under the more neutral physiological instructions, where strong shocks could in no way be perceived as helpful to the victim, similar positive relationships failed to emerge. Indeed, under these conditions, the magnitude of the shocks employed by subjects and the strength of their stated desire to help the confederate correlated negatively. Thus, in this case, the weaker the participants' desire to help the victim, the stronger the shocks they employed.

Together, these findings suggest that in the context of the stan-

TABLE 6

*Correlations between the Magnitude of Shocks Employed by Subjects and Their Stated Desires to Help the Confederate or to Help the Experiment Succeed[a]*

| | Questionnaire item[b] | |
| --- | --- | --- |
| Type of instructions | Desire to help the confederate | Desire to help the experiment succeed |
| Learning (standard Buss procedures) | +.45[c] | +.74[d] |
| Physiological reactions | −.55[c] | +.01 |

[a] Adapted from Baron & Eggleston, 1972.
[b] As can be seen, shock magnitude and the strength of these "altruistic" motives were positively related only under the standard Buss procedures.
[c] $p < 0.05$.
[d] $p < 0.01$.

dard "teacher–learner" paradigm devised by Buss (1961), performance on the aggression machine may indeed reflect desires on the part of some subjects to help the victim and to make the experiment a success, as well as motives to harm this person and inflict painful suffering upon him. In an attempt to lessen this source of potential contamination, the present author has recently adopted the more neutral physiological instructions outlined earlier, in which subjects are informed that the purpose of the study is simply to examine the impact of unpleasant stimuli such as electric shock upon physiological reactions (e.g., Baron & Bell, 1975, 1976). With the use of such procedures, it is hoped, the advantages conferred by the basic Buss paradigm may be retained, while the contribution of altruistic motives to subjects' choice of shock buttons is lessened. To date, investigations employing this modified form of Buss's methodology have indicated that it is readily accepted by subjects and succeeds in eliminating the belief among participants that they can help the confederate by using strong shocks. Thus, initial findings have been quite promising. Further information regarding the validity of these procedures is essential, however, before final conclusions regarding their ultimate value in the laboratory study of aggression can be reached.

## The Berkowitz Paradigm: Aggression as a Form of Negative Evaluation

A second and related technique for the direct laboratory study of physical aggression was first devised by Leonard Berkowitz (1962, 1964). In this procedure, too, subjects direct aversive stimulation (electric shock) to another person within the general framework of a learning task. Both the rationale for delivering these shocks and the method of their administration, however, are somewhat different than in the Buss paradigm.

Briefly, when subjects report to the laboratory for their appointment, they are informed that they will participate with another individual (actually a confederate of the experimenter) in a study concerned with the effects of stress upon problem-solving ability. Their task within this context is then described as that of offering a written solution to a problem posed by the experimenter (e.g., how a department store can improve labor–management relations). The investigator further explains that stress will be introduced into the situation by virtue of the fact that the subject's solution will be evaluated by the other participant, who will express his reaction to it by delivering anywhere from 1 to 10 electric shocks. That is, if he finds a solution to be quite excellent, he will deliver only 1 shock. If he judges it to be somewhat less satisfactory, he will administer 2 shocks, and so on, up to 10 shocks for a very poor solution.

Following these instructions, subjects work on the problem for five minutes, after which their solution is collected and ostensibly given to the confederate for evaluation. In reality, this individual delivers a predetermined number of shocks to the subject (usually either 1 or 7), depending upon whether he or she is to be provoked or not provoked during the session.

Following receipt of the confederate's evaluation, various experimental treatments are enacted (e.g., subjects witness either a violent or a nonviolent film). Finally, in a third phase of the study, they receive *their* turn to evaluate the confederate's work, also by means of electric shock. Aggression is then measured in terms of the number—and sometimes the duration—of shocks delivered by subjects to this individual. Note that in contrast to the Buss procedures, the intensity of the shocks delivered to the victim is *not* directly under the subjects' control; only the number, and sometimes the duration, of these jolts can be varied by participants.

As might be expected, several variations on this general aggression-as-a-form-of-evaluation theme have been devised. For example, Konečni (1975a) and Konečni and Doob (1972) have employed procedures in which subjects deliver electric shocks to a confederate as a means of evaluating the creativity of his responses in a free-association task. Regardless of the specific rationale employed, however, the basic methodology remains the same: subjects are provided with an opportunity to deliver noxious stimuli to another individual, ostensibly as a means of evaluating some form of work he or she has completed.

Some evidence for the validity of these procedures is provided by the fact that while the confederate's problem solution or other performance is held constant across experimental conditions, subjects who have been angered by this person (i.e., those receiving a negative and painful evaluation of their work) generally administer a greater number of shocks to him than participants who have not been so angered (i.e., those receiving a more positive evaluation). However, some question concerning the validity of the Berkowitz paradigm has recently been raised by the findings of an experiment conducted by Schuck and Pisor (1974).

In this investigation, male college students wrote an essay concerning means for dealing with campus violence and then received an evaluation of their work from a confederate of the experimenter. In one experimental condition, electrodes were attached to their forearms, and they actually received either one or seven shocks from the confederate, while in a second condition, the electrodes were not attached, and they merely learned how many shocks this person had planned to administer. Following these procedures, subjects in both groups were given an opportunity to evaluate the confederate's work, also by means of electric shock. Schuck and Pisor reasoned that if subjects' behavior in this situation was determined largely by *demand characteristics*—their belief that the experimenter wanted them to behave in a particular fashion—those who actually received shocks from the confederate and those who did not would act in a highly similar manner. Presumably, this would be the case because individuals in both groups would simply be responding to their belief that the experimenter wanted them to return the same number of shocks they received and would not be responding to the actual experimental treatments themselves. As can be seen in Figure 8, such findings were actually obtained; subjects receiving the shocks and those merely learning how many shocks the confederate had intended to deliver behaved in a very similar manner.

Although this pattern of results can be interpreted as pointing to the role of demand characteristics in the Berkowitz paradigm, it may also be viewed from another perspective. Specifically, additional research (Greenwell & Dengerink, 1973) suggests that the indication of hostile intent on the part of another person is often as provocative as the receipt of direct attacks from this individual. That is, knowing that another person intends to attack us is frequently as anger-provoking as actually receiving his or her assaults. In view of this fact, it seems possible that similar behavior on the part of subjects receiving and not receiving shocks in the Schuck and Pisor (1974) study stemmed at least in part from this factor and not solely from the influence of demand characteristics. That is, having learned that the confederate intended to deliver only one or fully seven shocks, subjects not actually receiving these jolts may have reacted with the same low or high degrees of anger, respectively, as participants actually receiving these painful stimuli. In short, the fact that the two groups behaved in a similar fashion does not in any sense guarantee that demand characteristics played a major role in the obtained findings.

Given such ambiguity regarding the interpretation of the findings reported by Schuck and Pisor, it seems premature to discard the Berkowitz paradigm as failing to yield a valid measure of aggression. Rather, a more conservative course of action seems to be that of deferring final judgments regarding the usefulness of these procedures until additional evidence has been obtained.

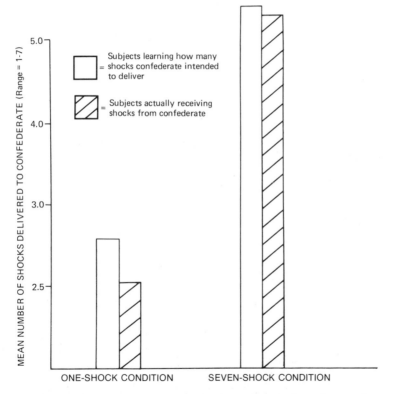

FIGURE 8. Mean number of shocks directed to the confederate by subjects who actually received one or seven shocks from this person and those who merely learned how many shocks the confederate intended to deliver to them. The behavior of those receiving and not receiving shocks was highly similar in both the one- and seven-shock conditions. (Based on data from Schuck & Pisor, 1974.)

*The Taylor Procedure: Aggression in a Competitive Setting*

A final method for the laboratory study of physical aggression, and one that differs markedly in several respects from the two we have already considered, has been devised by Stuart Taylor (1967). In an initial phase of these procedures, subjects' "unpleasantness" threshold for electric shock—the level of shock they rate as definitely unpleasant—is obtained in a systematic manner. (The purpose of this step will soon be made apparent.) Following the completion of this preliminary task, both the subject and a second individual who is also present (a confederate of the experimenter) are informed that they will be competing on a reaction-time task, under conditions where the slower player on each trial receives an electric shock. It is further explained that the magnitude of these shocks will be set in advance by both players, who will use a series of switches on the apparatus shown in Figure 9 for this purpose. Thus, on each occasion, the slower of the

FIGURE 9. The apparatus devised by Taylor (1967) to investigate physical aggression under safe, laboratory conditions. (Photo courtesy Dr. Stuart P. Taylor.)

two competitors will receive the shock set for him by his or her opponent.

Following these instructions, a number of reaction-time trials (usually 20–28) are actually conducted. The subject is then made to "lose" on a predetermined proportion of these trials and, as a result, receives a prearranged series of electric shocks from the confederate. The intensity of these stimuli varies but it is adjusted in terms of the "unpleasantness" threshold established earlier. Thus, the shocks delivered to the subject by button #10 on the confederate's apparatus are equal to this threshold, those delivered to the subject by button #9 are set at 95% of this value, those delivered by button #8 are set at 90%, and so on. Aggression is then measured in terms of the strength of the shocks subjects set for their opponent on each trial.

As is probably already apparent, these procedures offer several important advantages. First, as is often the case in actual instances of physical aggression, the victim is not entirely helpless; rather, he or she can retaliate in kind for strong attacks (i.e., high shock settings). This is in sharp contrast to conditions prevailing in both the Buss and the Berkowitz paradigms, where the victim is entirely at the subjects' mercy and cannot retaliate in any manner. Second, since the opponent is actually a confederate, his behavior during the session can be systematically varied in any desired manner, so that the effects of such variations upon subjects' reactions can be determined. For example, the opponent can be made to act in a progressively provocative manner, raising the strength of his shock settings over trials (e.g., Borden, Bowen, & Taylor, 1971; O'Leary & Dengerink, 1973), or he can be made to behave in a consistently conciliatory manner, employing only low shock magnitudes throughout the session (Pisano & Taylor, 1971). Finally, the influence upon the subjects' behavior of a wide variety of variables—anything from alcohol (Taylor, Gammon, & Capasso, 1976) through the presence of an audience (Borden, 1975)—can be readily examined. Together, such advantages make the Taylor paradigm an attractive one in several major respects.

Along with these important advantages, however, come several potential problems or drawbacks. First, participants in the Taylor paradigm actually receive a series of painful electric shocks during the course of the session—an outcome that raises complex ethical issues. Similarly, since the entire study is conducted within the context of a competitive reaction-time task, the possibility exists that subjects' behavior should be viewed primarily as competitive rather than aggressive in nature.

Unfortunately, direct evidence for the validity of the procedures devised by Taylor corresponding to that available with respect to the Buss paradigm has not yet been reported. Indirect evidence regarding this issue, however, is provided by the fact that variables that would be expected to influence the subjects' level of aggression against their opponent do in fact influence their actions within this setting in the predicted manner. For example, participants generally set higher shocks for their opponent when he has strongly attacked them (e.g., Borden, Bowen, & Taylor, 1971; O'Leary & Dengerink, 1973) than when he has acted in a less provocative fashion. Similarly, they are restrained from setting high levels of shock by the presence of an audience that seems to disapprove of such actions (Borden, 1975). These and other findings suggest that the Taylor procedures do in fact yield a useful and valid measure of physical aggression. However, pending the acquisition of more definitive evidence regarding this issue, such conclusions must be accepted only with some degree of caution.

*Methods for the Study of Physical Aggression: A Concluding Comment*

The procedures devised by Buss (1961), Berkowitz (1964), and Taylor (1967) have all received widespread use in the laboratory study of physical aggression. Indeed, one or another of these procedures has been employed in the great bulk of recent investigations of this important topic. In view of this fact, it is surprising—and somewhat unsettling—that there has been so little research specifically concerned with the validity of these methods. At the present time, evidence concerning this crucial issue appears to exist only with respect to the Buss approach. And as noted earlier, the findings of these experiments suggest the need for certain modifications in this technique. Fortunately, there are several grounds for assuming that all three methods provide essentially valid means for studying physical aggression. For example, factors that would be expected to influence overt aggression, such as strong provocation, have been found to alter subjects' behavior in the expected directions in all three settings. However, it seems unwise to base conclusions regarding the validity of these approaches solely upon such informal foundations. Instead, it is strongly recommended that further attempts to examine—and improve—these ingenious methods of research be conducted simultaneously with further, substantive studies. Only through such efforts will it be possible to guarantee that the findings uncovered in laboratory studies of aggression are directly applicable to the occurrence of such behavior in other settings as well.

## Field Methods for the Study of Aggression: Harm-Doing Behaviors in Naturalistic Settings

At first glance, it does not seem feasible to conduct experimental studies of aggressive behavior in various field settings—the potential risks to participants and investigators alike appear to be so great as to preclude the possibility of such investigations. Yet, despite the existence of many obvious difficulties, a number of such projects have actually been completed (e.g., Deaux, 1971; Harris, 1974a; Turner, Layton, & Simons, 1975). As might be anticipated, the specific procedures employed in these ingenious studies have varied considerably, depending upon the particular context or setting in which they were performed. Generally, however, they seem to have fallen into two major categories: those involving *indirect* confrontations between individuals, such as exchanges between drivers in traffic situations, and those involving *direct,* face-to-face confrontations between the antagonists. Both of these approaches will now be considered.

### Aggression in Traffic Situations: Horn Honking at Intersections

Informal observation suggests that motorists often become angry while driving in traffic. For example, they frequently shout, gesture, or honk their horns at one another when subjected to even minor delays. The relatively high incidence of such actions suggests that traffic situations may provide a useful context within which to conduct field studies of aggressive behavior. That this is indeed the case is indicated by the fact that a number of successful experiments have already been completed in such settings. While these studies have varied greatly in both purpose and detail, most have adopted procedures in which a confederate fails to move his or her vehicle after a traffic signal turns green, thus delaying other motorists for some predetermined interval. The reactions of these individuals to such frustration are then assessed in a systematic manner.

For example, in one recent study conducted by the present author (Baron, 1976), a male confederate failed to move his vehicle for 15 seconds after the traffic signals at preselected intersections turned green. The reactions of passing motorists to this unexpected delay were then recorded by two observers seated in a second car parked near the intersection. One of these individuals operated a portable tape-recorder so as to obtain a permanent record of the frequency, duration, and latency of any horn honking by subjects, while the second noted other types of behavior (e.g., verbal comments, facial expressions, gestures) on a special form.

While the period of delay, method of data collection, and specific dependent measures collected have varied in other studies (e.g., Doob & Gross, 1968; Turner, Layton, & Simons, 1975), the basic procedure of delaying passing drivers and then observing their reactions to such frustration in some manner has been generally adopted. Further, these basic procedures have been employed to investigate the impact upon aggression of a number of different factors, including status of the frustrater (Doob & Gross, 1968), the presence of aggressive cues (Turner, Layton, & Simons, 1975), visibility of the victim (Turner, Layton, & Simons, 1975), and even ambient temperature (Baron, 1976). Thus, they have proved applicable to a wide range of topics.

The validity of some of the dependent measures of aggression collected in these investigations is hardly open to question. Hostile remarks, angry or obscene physical gestures, and related actions clearly represent instances of over aggression. The aggressive nature of horn honking, however, is more problematic. Is this a valid measure of aggressive behavior? Or is it simply an expressive act, which fails to inflict any harm upon its recipients? Fortunately, a considerable amount of evidence points to the conclusion that within the context of traffic situations, such behavior often represents a form of overt aggression against others. First, findings obtained in one of several studies conducted by Turner, Layton, and Simons (1975) indicate that drivers often become angry with and express aggression toward other motorists. For example, fully 77% of the males and 56% of the females questioned indicated that they sometimes swear under their breath at other drivers. Similarly, 58% of the males and 92% of the females reported becoming angry when another driver turns without signaling.

As noted by Turner, Layton, and Simons (1975), such anger or irritation may sometimes lead to overt aggression, and one readily available form of such behavior is horn honking at other drivers.

Additional evidence pointing to the validity of horn honking as a measure of overt aggression has also been gathered by the present author (Baron, 1976). In a questionnaire study directly concerned with this issue, 37 undergraduate students (19 males, 18 females) were asked to imagine that they found themselves stopped behind another vehicle that failed to move for 15 seconds after the light at an intersection turned green. Then, within this general context, they were asked to answer a series of questions concerning their reactions to such an incident. The crucial findings of interest may be summarized as follows. First, 67% reported that they would feel irritated or annoyed by the other driver's delay. Second, 62% indicated that they would honk under these conditions, with 41% reporting that they would do so in order to express their anger or irritation to the other driver. Third, an overwhelming majority (94%) indicated that they themselves would find being honked at by other motorists aversive and embarrassing. In sum, subjects reported that they would feel irritated when delayed in traffic by other drivers, that they would often honk at them in order to express such anger or irritation, and that they recognized such honking to be aversive or embarrassing to the recipients. To the extent that such reports are accurate, it may be concluded that horn honking is often performed with the intention of harming other drivers (by subjecting them to embarrassment or "loss of face") and often produces such effects. Thus, it seems to fulfill the major requirements of the definition of aggression outlined in Chapter 1.

Of course, this is not to suggest that all horn honking is aggressive in nature. Drivers do often honk at other motorists in order to warn them of danger or to alert them to their presence. In contexts where individuals resorting to such actions have been subjected to strong provocation, however, it seems reasonable to view honking at other drivers as a valid measure of overt aggression.

## Personal Confrontations: Direct Elicitation of Overt Aggression

While most field studies of aggressive behavior have been restricted to the relatively indirect methods described above, a markedly different approach has been adopted in a series of investigations conducted by Mary Harris and her colleagues (Harris, 1973, 1974a,b; Harris & Samerotte, 1975). In these ingenious—but somewhat un-settling—experiments, individuals who happen to be present in stores, shopping centers, restaurants, airline terminals, and many other locations have been exposed to strong and direct instigation to aggression. As might be expected, given the many different physical settings for such research, several contrasting procedures have been employed for this purpose. For example, in one technique (Harris, 1973), male and female confederates purposely bumped into other in-dividuals from the rear. Subjects' reactions to such unexpected and of-fensive treatment were then scored as being either polite, nonrespon-sive, somewhat aggressive (e.g., brief protests or glares), or very aggressive (lengthy, angry comments, or retaliatory shoves).

In several other studies (Harris, 1973, 1974a,b), male and female confederates performed a different offensive act, simply pushing into line ahead of individuals waiting their turn in stores, restaurants, and banks or in front of movie theaters or ticket windows. In some cases, the confederate said "Excuse me," while cutting in front of subjects, while in others they made no comments whatsoever. Subjects' verbal and nonverbal responses to such provocation were then recorded. Ver-bal reactions were scored as being either polite, nonresponsive, some-what aggressive (short remarks such as, "This is my place"), or very aggressive (threatening or abusive comments). Nonverbal reactions were coded as friendly (a smile), nonresponsive, glares, unfriendly or threatening gestures, and pushes or shoves.

These and other procedures have been employed by Harris to in-vestigate the influence upon aggression of a number of different fac-tors, including frustration, the presence of an aggressive model, and the status of the frustrater. In many cases, interesting and informative results have been obtained in this manner. Further, the realistic nature of Harris's procedures seem to guarantee a relatively high degree of validity with respect to the measures collected; after all, participants in these studies have no idea that they are taking part in an experiment and generally respond in a completely natural fashion. Unfortunately, however, the use of such methods raises a number of complex ethical issues.

First, it is obviously impossible to obtain subjects' written, in-formed consent to participate in such experiments. While this is also true in the less direct methods of field investigation described earlier (i.e., those relating to traffic situations), the highly provocative nature of Harris's approach emphasizes the ethical dilemma of exposing subjects to aversive experimental treatments to which they have not previously consented. Of course, it can be argued that most individuals are exposed to similar experiences at some time or other in the normal course of events and that this reduces the force of possible objections to them. Whether this affords researchers the right to expose unsuspecting subjects to unpleasant situations they would otherwise not encounter, however, remains an open question.

Second, the procedures employed by Harris appear to involve a very real danger of possible harm to participants and/or confederates. For example, consider one actual incident in which a female subject, irritated by the actions of a male confederate, sprayed him directly in the face with an aerosol can (Harris & Samerotte, 1975). Clearly, the occurrence of such events suggests the need for extreme caution in the use of these procedures.

Given such considerations, one may well ask whether it is permissible for researchers to conduct further investigations employing methods similar to those devised by Harris. Obviously, this is a complex question. On the one hand, the need for further systematic knowledge concerning human aggression suggests that such procedures may sometimes be justified. On the other, however, the obvious risks to participants, and related legal and ethical issues, argue strongly for great caution in the adoption of their use. What, then, is the answer to this puzzling dilemma? In the opinion of the present author, it lies in a thorough assessment of the *cost–benefit* ratio of such proposed research. That is, investigators proposing to employ such procedures must carefully evaluate the potential benefits of their planned research both to science and to society and then weigh these in a very careful and sober manner against the potential risks to participants. Only in cases where the resulting cost–benefit ratio is extremely favorable—where potential benefits far outweigh potential risks—can they then proceed. While assessments of this type will, of course, depend quite heavily upon the particular project under consideration, a few straightforward guidelines may be suggested.

First, such procedures should never be employed merely to replicate findings already clearly established in other contexts. In such cases, the cost–benefit ratio does not appear to be favorable enough in nature to justify their use. Second, they should be employed only in

investigations that seem to offer reasonable potential for practical social benefits. That is, in contrast to research conducted in other settings, practical rather than theoretical outcomes should be given primary consideration. And finally, it is crucial that when such
procedures are employed, investigators adopt every conceivable pre-
caution to protect the rights and well-being of participants. Provided
that appropriate cost–benefit analyses are conducted in advance, and
provided that researchers employ great caution and restraint in conducting their studies, it is the opinion of the present author that the
provocative methods devised by Harris may in fact be employed as
one additional means of extending our knowledge of human aggression.

## SUMMARY

The first methodology employed in the scientific study of aggression centered around the principle of systematic observation. While
such procedures have proved useful in a number of different contexts
and are still in use today, the findings they yield are generally somewhat ambiguous with respect to the nature of cause-and-effect relationships. Thus, they have largely been replaced within psychology by
methods of direct experimentation.

With respect to laboratory research on aggression, several different methods have been employed. The oldest and perhaps the best
known involves attempts to measure verbal aggression. Such procedures are quite safe and yield readily quantified measures of aggression. In addition, because verbal assaults represent a common and
well-practiced form of aggressive behavior and are relatively free from
the powerful restraints that inhibit other forms of harm-doing, they
can be readily elicited and studied in laboratory settings. It is important to note, however, that verbal measures of aggression are valid
only when the comments or evaluations made by subjects can harm
the recipient in some manner.

A second method for investigating aggression in laboratory settings involves attacks against various inanimate objects (e.g., inflated
plastic Bobo dolls). Such procedures appear to be quite useful in ex-
aminations of the processes through which aggression is acquired.

However, they are less valuable in determinations of those factors that influence the performance of such responses once they are acquired.

A third and recently developed technique for the laboratory study of aggression involves noninjurious attacks against a live, passive victim. Since the responses employed by subjects in such attacks closely resemble those used in more dangerous assaults, and since subjects are provided with complete freedom of choice as to whether to behave in an aggressive or a nonaggressive fashion toward the victim, such procedures offer several important advantages. However, their attraction is somewhat reduced by the possibility of actual harm to the victim and by the fact that subjects may often view their actions as part of a game in which no one can be injured.

By far the most commonly employed techniques for examining physical aggression in the laboratory are those based upon a crucial deception in which participants are led to believe that they can somehow harm another person when in fact they cannot. Several distinct variants of such procedures have been developed. In procedures devised by Buss, subjects deliver electric shocks to another person (actually a confederate) on each occasion when he makes prearranged errors in a bogus learning task. In a similar paradigm devised by Berkowitz, subjects deliver electric shocks to another person as a means of evaluating his work on some task. Finally, in procedures designed by Taylor, subjects compete with a partner on a reaction-time task in which the slower person to respond on each occasion receives a shock. Since subjects are permitted to determine the strength of the shocks their partner will receive on each trial when he loses, aggression is assessed in terms of these settings.

Although it might seem impossible to conduct systematic studies of aggression in naturalistic field settings, several procedures for performing such research have actually been devised. In one commonly used technique, passing motorists are delayed in traffic, and their reactions to such frustration—horn honking, verbal comments, gestures, etc.—are observed. In other and more unsettling procedures involving direct confrontations, confederates provoked subjects by such tactics as bumping into them from the rear or cutting into line ahead of them. Such techniques afford a great degree of realism and provide what appear to be valid measures of aggression. However, they raise important ethical issues and must be used only with great caution and restraint.

# 3

# Social Determinants of Aggression

CHICAGO (AP)—Two Chicago girls, aged 13 and 15, have been named in delinquency petitions for allegedly shooting their 60-year-old father. . . .

Authorities and the girls at first suggested that he might have been killed in a robbery attempt. Later they broke down and admitted they had planned the killing since Sunday when Thomas allegedly beat them, police said. . . .

HOUSTON (AP)— . . . Police quoted the three children, aged 9, 11, and 12, as saying "Punkin" was bad, so they pounded him with their fists and feet and whipped him with belts until he died.

"Punkin" was Robert Hillard Battles, 4. He was found dead Sunday from blows to the head, chest, and abdomen, an autopsy showed. . . .

Police quoted the three children as saying they beat Robert "for being bad," and that the Saturday night assault followed the breaking of a model car. . . .

NEW YORK (AP)—"I yelled for someone to call police—that kids were being thrown out of a window," said Jesse Blake.

He was one of the horrified tenants of a Spanish Harlem housing project who saw Celina Martinez, 7, and her half-sister, Felicia Ocacio, 5, hurled to their deaths from a 14th floor apartment Monday.

Police said the girls were thrown from the window by their mother's common-law husband. Only minutes later, he fatally stabbed her 6-year-old son, Mark Martinez, and then leaped to his own death.

The tragedy was triggered by a quarrel between Julio Delgado, 30, and the children's mother, Felicita Sanchez, 28, police said. . . .

LAFAYETTE, IND.— . . . On April 1, 1965, his estranged wife Gail, 29, was killed by a .45-caliber pistol bullet in the head, and Neal was brought to trial for murder. He testified that she had held the gun at his head as they made love, angered because he had accused her of sleeping with other men, and that she was accidentally killed as they struggled for the pistol. . . .

Incidents such as these are unsettling, to say the least. Moreover, their existence leaves us facing a puzzling question: what factors led to their occurrence? A simple answer—and one that has been quite popular for many years—focuses on characteristics of the persons involved. Briefly, it is assumed that aggression in these and similar incidents stems from the disturbed mental state or emotional imbalance of its perpetrators. In one sense, this seems to be a reasonable suggestion; after all, few individuals would engage in such actions, and the persons who perform them must be unusual in *some* respects. Further, as we shall see in Chapter 5, this idea gains support from research findings, which indicate that certain persons are indeed more prone to engage in acts of aggression than others. Yet closer examination of such occurrences suggests that this is only part of the answer. Consider the examples listed above. Would the girls in the first incident have brutally murdered their father in the absence of strong prior provocation (a beating)? It seems doubtful. Would the youngsters in the second have pounded their playmate to death if he had not acted in an irritating manner and broken a favorite toy? Again, it seems unlikely. And what of the father in the third incident? Would he have tossed innocent children out the window if there had been no heated quarrel with his wife? Once more a negative answer is suggested. Finally, what of the young woman in the fourth incident? Would she have met her untimely end if she and her lover had not traded a series of angry accusations? This, too, seems unlikely.

In sum, close examination of these and many other aggressive interchanges suggests that violence does not take place in a "social vacuum." Rather, such behavior often seems to stem from aspects of the social environment that instigate its occurrence, and influence both its form and its direction. In many cases, such factors center around the words or deeds of the victim, who may provoke, frustrate, anger, or annoy the attacker in some fashion. In others, they may involve the actions or statements of additional persons, who either order or urge destructive acts. Regardless of the specific factors involved, however, it is clear that a thorough understanding of the origins of human violence must involve careful attention to the social conditions that stimulate its occurrence, as well as to characteristics of the persons involved in its performance.

While this important fact is generally overlooked in mass-media accounts of aggressive episodes, it has been well known to psychologists for several decades. As a result, a great deal of research has been conducted to examine the social antecedents of aggression. Not surprisingly, given the great complexity of social behavior, many different factors have been implicated in this relationship. Most attention in recent years, however, has been focused upon the influence of five specific antecedents: (1) frustration; (2) direct provocation from others; (3) exposure to the actions of aggressive models; (4) orders or commands from superiors; and (5) the presence and actions of bystanders. Consistent with this past research emphasis, we will also focus upon the impact of these factors in the present discussion.

## FRUSTRATION: INTERPERSONAL THWARTING AS AN ANTECEDENT OF AGGRESSION

There can be little doubt that the social antecedent of aggression that has received the greatest amount of attention from psychologists is *frustration*—the blocking of ongoing, goal-directed responses. In short, it has frequently (and repeatedly) been assumed that the thwarting by one individual of another's goal-directed behavior is often a strong elicitor of aggressive reactions.

As we noted in Chapter 1, this emphasis upon frustration as an antecedent of aggression stems primarily from the *frustration–aggression hypothesis* (Dollard et al., 1939), which, in its initial form, suggested that:

1. Frustration always leads to some form of aggression.
2. Aggression is always the result of frustration.

We have already indicated on pp. 22–23 that both portions of this hypothesis are now generally viewed as being far too sweeping in scope (cf. Bandura, 1973; Zillmann, 1978). Frustration does *not* always lead to aggression, and such behavior frequently stems from other factors aside from thwarting—several of which we shall consider in later portions of this chapter. Thus, neither proposal currently enjoys widespread support among active researchers. Rejection of these relatively extreme suggestions, however, in no way necessitates rejection of the more moderate view that frustration is simply one of several important determinants of aggression and sometimes—if by no means always—serves to initiate such behavior. This modified version of the frustration–aggression hypothesis has recently gained a degree of popularity and is currently accepted by several noted investigators. For example, as stated by Berkowitz (1969), perhaps the most famous proponent of this view:

> Basically, I believe a frustrating event increases the probability that the thwarted organism will act aggressively soon afterward. . . . Under some conditions there *is* an increased likelihood of aggressive behavior following a frustration. (pp. 2–3)

At first glance, the suggestion that frustration is one of several important determinants of aggression and sometimes serves to facilitate such behavior seems quite reasonable. Somewhat surprisingly, though, empirical evidence regarding even this moderate position is quite mixed in nature. Since acquaintance with the nature of these conflicting findings will prove useful in our later attempts to offer a resolution to this puzzle, we will now consider a portion of this evidence in detail.

### Evidence Suggesting That Frustration Facilitates Aggression

The notion that frustration enhances aggression currently enjoys widespread support. Indeed, it is so much a part of our intellectual heritage that it has entered the realm of "common knowledge" and is frequently cited in the mass media as an established, unquestioned fact. Given the broad-based acceptance of this view, it seems only reasonable to assume that it enjoys convincing empirical support. At first glance, this appears to be the case. A large number of experiments—conducted over the course of several decades with different subject populations and sharply contrasting procedures—suggest that frustration is indeed an important antecedent of aggression. In these studies, individuals exposed to some form of frustration (e.g., failure, inability to attain some desired goal) have often demonstrated higher levels of aggression toward the source of their thwarting—and sometimes other persons as well—than individuals not exposed to such treatment (see Berkowitz, 1962, 1969). Unfortunately, however, there seems to be a very large fly in a major portion of the ointment.

As noted by Buss (1966b), Taylor and Pisano (1971), and others, close examination of the procedures employed in many of these studies—especially those conducted a number of years ago—raises important questions. In particular, it has often been the case in such investigations that frustration was accompanied by other factors or conditions that might also have influenced subjects' behavior. For example, consider a well-known study conducted by Mallick and McCandless (1966). In this experiment, children in one group (the *frustration* condition) were prevented by a confederate from completing a series of simple tasks and so obtaining monetary reward; those in a second group (the *no-frustration* condition) were not thwarted by this person. When later provided with an opportunity to aggress against the confederate, those who had been thwarted were indeed more aggressive than those who had been permitted to complete the tasks. Thus, results seemed to offer clear support for the view that frustration facilitates aggression. Unfortunately, however, interpretation of these seemingly clear-cut results is clouded by one important fact: at the same time that the confederate thwarted the subjects, he directed a number of sarcastic—and potentially anger-provoking—comments toward them. As a result of these procedures, it is impossible to determine whether subjects in the frustration condition later demonstrated greater aggression against the confederate than those in the control group primarily because of his thwarting actions, primarily because of his irritating comments, or as a result of both factors.

Regrettably, such confounding of frustration with other possible antecedents of aggression is far from rare among early investigations concerned with the impact of this factor upon aggression (see Bandura, 1973; Buss, 1961, 1963). Largely as a result of such difficulties, therefore, empirical support for the view that frustration is an important antecedent of aggression turns out to be far less overwhelming than at first meets the eye.

Fortunately for supporters of the modified frustration–aggression hypothesis, however, this is not the entire story. Even when all investigations subject to the criticisms outlined above are discounted, a number of more sophisticated experiments pointing to the conclusion that frustration sometimes enhances aggression remain (e.g., Berkowitz & Geen, 1967; Burnstein & Worchel, 1962; Geen, 1968). Perhaps the clearest evidence regarding this issue is provided by the study conducted by Geen (1968).

In this investigation, four groups of male subjects were asked, as one part of a more complex set of procedures, to work on a jigsaw puzzle. Their experience while performing this simple activity was then varied in a systematic manner so as to expose them to frustration or other potentially aggression-enhancing experiences. In one group (the *task-frustration* condition), the puzzle upon which the subjects worked was insoluble. Thus, they were unable to complete it within the time limits imposed, and they experienced frustration. In a second (the *personal-frustration* condition), the puzzle *was* soluble. However, subjects worked in the presence of a male confederate who interfered with their performance and prevented them from completing it within the allotted time. As a result, individuals in this group, too, were exposed to frustration. In a third experimental group (the *insult* condition), subjects again worked on a soluble puzzle, and in this case, the confederate permitted them to complete it without interruption. After its completion, however, he delivered a series of strong insults to each participant, accusing him of low intelligence and inadequate motivation. Finally, in a fourth (*control*) condition, subjects were exposed neither to frustration nor to direct verbal provocation.

Following this phase of the study, participants in all conditions watched a brief, violent movie (we will comment upon the importance of this procedure below) and were then provided with an opportunity to aggress against the confederate within the teacher–learner paradigm devised by Buss (see pp. 54–62). As can be seen in Figure 10, their behavior during this portion of the experiment offered strong support for the view that frustration facilitates aggression: participants in both the task-frustration and the personal-frustration groups directed stronger shocks toward the confederate than those in the control condition. In addition, and not unexpectedly, those exposed to direct verbal insult also showed greater aggression than individuals in the control group. We will return to the impact of such treatment upon aggression in a later section. For the present, however, it is most important to note that subjects in both frustration groups, who were not attacked in any manner, demonstrated higher levels of aggression than those in the control condition. These findings—and similar results reported in other studies (e.g., Berkowitz & Geen, 1967; Burnstein & Worchel, 1962; Harris, 1974a)—seem to provide clear-cut support for the view that under some conditions, at least, exposure to frustrating experiences can facilitate later aggression.

## Evidence Suggesting That Frustration Does Not Facilitate Aggression

Our discussion up to this point has left us facing a somewhat clouded—but still interpretable—picture. To recapitulate, we have seen that while many investigations seem to offer support for the view

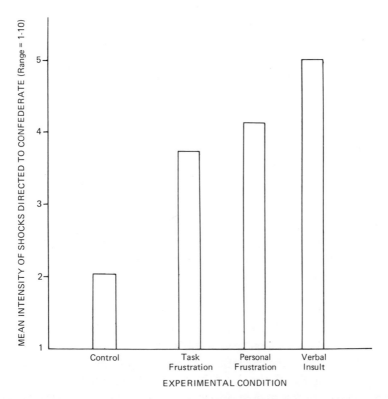

FIGURE 10. The effects of two types of frustration and verbal provocation (insult) on aggression. Both types of frustration, as well as insult, facilitated later aggression. (Based on data from Geen, 1968.)

that frustration enhances aggression, a large proportion of these are flawed and are open to serious question. When such investigations are discounted, then, we are left with a smaller number of experiments, not subject to such criticisms, that seem to suggest that frustration does indeed facilitate aggression. In short, frustration emerges from our analysis as a possible antecedent of aggression but as one resting upon a much weaker empirical foundation than is widely believed. Now, however, we must go one step further and muddy the waters still more. During the past 15 years, a number of investigations conducted by many different researchers in several independent laboratories have reported that various forms of frustration are often totally ineffective in enhancing overt aggression by research participants (e.g., Buss, 1963a, 1966; Kuhn, Madsen, & Becker, 1967; Taylor & Pisano, 1971). In short, such investigations argue strongly against the view that frustration serves as an important social antecedent of aggression. As an example of this research, let us consider an investigation conducted by Arnold Buss (1966a).

In this study, male subjects were asked to play the role of a teacher and instruct another individual (actually an accomplice) in certain materials. On each occasion when the learner made an error in mastering these items, the subjects were instructed to administer an electric shock to him that, at their discretion, could vary from very mild to quite intense. As noted in Chapter 2, the strength of their tendency to aggress against the victim was then assessed in terms of the magnitude of the shocks they chose to deliver.

In one experimental condition (the *know-how* group), the participants were told that if they did their job well, the learner would succeed in mastering the experimental materials within 30 trials. In a second group (the *grades* condition), they were provided with the same information and were also informed that their performance as a teacher would be reported to their college instructor and could, conceivably, affect their course grades. Finally, in a third (*control*) group, subjects were given no information regarding the number of trials generally required for mastery of the experimental materials and were told nothing about the possible impact of their performance on their grades. During the course of the study, the confederate followed a prearranged pattern of responses and failed to master the required items until the 70th trial. Since subjects in the know-how and grades groups expected him to complete this training within 30 trials, they were, of necessity, prevented from reaching the goal of serving as effective teachers. In short, they were frustrated by the confederate's actions. Moreover, since this apparent failure might also adversely affect their grades, subjects in the grades group experienced greater frustration than those in the know-how condition. In contrast, participants in the control group, who had no specific expectations regarding the number of trials required for successful learning, would not be expected to experience frustration during the session; as far as they knew, they *were* succeeding in their role as a teacher.

If, as is often assumed, frustration enhances overt aggression, it would be predicted that participants in the two experimental groups (grades and know-how) would direct stronger shocks to the confederate than those in the control condition. Further, assuming that the stronger the frustration experienced, the greater the level of aggression produced, participants in the grades group would be expected to deliver stronger shocks than those in the know-how condition. As shown in Figure 11, however, none of these findings materialized; subjects in the three experimental conditions delivered essentially similar levels of shock to the confederate. Frustration, in short, totally failed to influence participants' aggression against this individual. These negative findings become even more impressive when it is noted that several other factors that were also varied in the study (e.g., the confederate's sex, signs of pain on the part of this person) all exerted significant effects upon the subjects' behavior; only frustration failed to influence their choice of shocks.

FIGURE 11. Evidence suggesting that frustration has little, if any, effect upon aggression. Subjects exposed to two different magnitudes of frustration failed to demonstrate significantly higher levels of aggression than those in a control group not exposed to thwarting. Moreover, the two frustration groups failed to differ from each other. x x x = "Grades" Group (High Frustration); ● ● ● = "Know how" Group (Mild Frustration); - - - = Control Group (No Frustration). (Adapted from Buss, 1966b.)

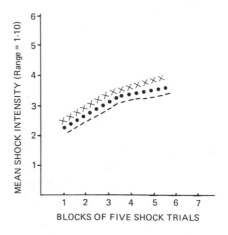

Convincing as the findings of Buss's investigation appear to be, they would remain merely suggestive in nature if they represented an isolated instance in which frustration failed to enhance aggression. As we have already noted, however, this is definitely not the case. Several additional studies, employing widely different procedures and sharply contrasting groups of subjects have also reported similar negative results. For example, in one well-known study, Kuhn, Madsen, and Becker (1967) exposed children to a situation in which they were promised candy as a reward for watching a brief movie. After the film, individuals in one group were simply told that they would not receive the promised reward, while those in a second condition were not exposed to such frustrating treatment. When the play behavior of both groups of children was then observed in a standardized setting, no significant differences emerged: the frustrated youngsters were *not* more aggressive than those in the nonfrustrated control condition. (Incidentally, as might be expected, the children in both groups were actually given the promised candy at the end of the experimental session.)

Together, the findings of these and other studies (e.g., Taylor & Pisano, 1971) cast doubt upon the suggestion that frustration generally—or even frequently—facilitates overt aggression. Perhaps even more surprising than these results, however, is the suggestion in several additional experiments (Gentry, 1970a; Rule & Hewitt, 1971) that exposure to strong frustration may sometimes serve to *reduce* rather than enhance later aggression. For example, in the investigation conducted by Gentry (1970a), male subjects who were frustrated by the experimenter (he repeatedly interfered with their attempts to complete an intelligence test and so caused them to attain a low score) later delivered *fewer* shocks to this person than those who were not exposed to such treatment.

On the basis of these and related findings, several investigators have concluded that frustration is not a strong or a major antecedent of aggression. In short, these researchers reject even the weakened, modified version of the frustration–aggression hypothesis, insisting instead that other factors are far more important as social determinants of aggression than various forms of interpersonal thwarting. In the words of Arnold Buss (1966a), "It may be concluded that frustration leads to no physical aggression . . . it is clear that . . . pure frustration is a relatively unimportant antecedent of physical aggression" (p. 161).

### Frustration and Aggression: A Tentative Resolution

At this point, of course, we find ourselves facing a confusing and contradictory set of empirical findings. On the one hand, several studies seem to suggest that frustration may indeed enhance the likelihood of aggression, while on the other, an equally convincing set of investigations points to the conclusion that it has little if any effect upon such behavior. Can this complex puzzle be resolved? Fortunately, we believe that it can. While the type of definitive evidence needed for the attainment of a final, elegant solution is as yet lacking, sufficient information does seem to be available to suggest the outlines of at least a tentative resolution. In particular, it seems reasonable, given existing evidence, to conclude that frustration does sometimes facilitate aggression. Whether it exerts this dangerous influence, however, seems to be strongly determined by several mediating factors. All of these have not as yet been brought sharply into focus. Two that seem to be of major importance, however, are (1) the *magnitude* of frustration experienced by potential aggressors and (2) the extent to which the thwarting they experience is *arbitrary* or *unexpected*.

Turning first to the magnitude of frustration, it should be noted that despite the careful attention directed to this factor by Dollard *et al.* (1939; see pp. 24–25), it has largely been neglected in research on the effects of interpersonal thwarting. Most investigations conducted to date have followed the simple procedure of exposing one group of participants to frustration and another to more neutral procedures and then comparing their level of aggression against some target person. Given the fact that each investigator in such research seems to have followed his or her own intuition in establishing conditions to induce frustration among subjects, it is clear that the magnitude of this factor has varied from study to study. Thus, it is far from surprising that the results have been mixed; indeed, it would be far more surprising if they had been otherwise! What is clearly needed, then, is parametric research in which the level of frustration is varied in a systematic manner over a wide range of values, through alterations in the attractiveness of the goal being sought, the number of response sequences

blocked, and so on. Despite the current absence of such rigorous research, however, careful examination of existing evidence points to
the conclusion that whether frustration will enhance later aggression
depends quite heavily upon the magnitude of this variable. That is,
with few exceptions, investigations that yielded negative results
regarding the aggression-enhancing influence of frustration have employed relatively mild levels of thwarting, while those which have reported positive findings have involved stronger levels of this factor.

For example, consider an ingenious field experiment conducted
by Mary Harris (1974a). In this study, male or female confederates literally cut into line in front of individuals waiting their turn outside
restaurants, at ticket windows, in grocery stores, and in several similar
locations. In one condition, they cut in front of the 2nd person in line,
while in another, they cut in front of the 12th individual. Since close-
ness to one's goal at the time of thwarting is believed to have a strong
effect on degree of frustration (see Haner & Brown, 1955; Longstreth,
1966), it seems reasonable to assume that individuals in the first group
would experience much higher levels of frustration than those in the
second. Thus, they would also be expected to demonstrate greater
aggression in response to the confederate's unusual actions. As can be
seen in Figure 12, this was actually the case. Moreover, consistent
with the suggestion that frustration must be relatively intense to induce appreciable levels of aggression, it was found that confederates
who cut into line ahead of the 12th person were the recipients of very
little aggression. This low level of aggression was in sharp contrast to
the much stronger levels received by the same individuals when they
cut ahead of the 2nd person in line.

These and similar findings in several other studies (e.g., Ebbesen,
Duncan, & Konecni, 1975; Worchel, 1974) suggest that low levels of
frustration usually induce little or no aggression. One important modification of this general conclusion, however, appears to be warranted.
As may be recalled from Chapter 2, Leonard Berkowitz (1962, 1969), a
noted authority on aggression, suggests that frustration produces only
a readiness for such behavior. In order for overt assaults actually to
occur, he contends, *aggressive cues*—stimuli associated with anger
arousal or aggression—must generally be present. Implicit in this
suggestion is the possibility that even mild levels of frustration may
facilitate overt aggression in the presence of a sufficient range of aggressive cues. Since we will return to the effect of such stimuli in more

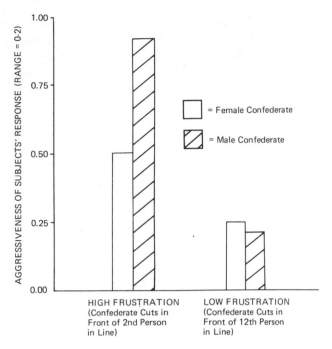

FIGURE 12. Magnitude of frustration and aggression. When subjects were close to their goal, thwarting by another person led to considerable aggression. When subjects were still quite far from their goal, however, frustration elicited relatively little aggression. Numbers refer to ratings of subjects' responses: 0 = no response or a polite response; 1 = a somewhat aggressive verbal response (e.g., "Watch it!"). (Based on data from Harris, 1974a.)

detail in Chapter 4 (see pp. 159–167), we will not pursue this topic here. It should be noted, though, that the research we have already considered seems to provide relatively convincing support for the accuracy of this general position. In particular, recall that in the study conducted by Geen (1968), it was found that even mild levels of frustration were sufficient to induce increased aggression among participants (refer to Figure 10). One reasonable explanation for these findings may lie in the fact that in that investigation, all subjects viewed a violent movie prior to their opportunity to aggress against the frustrator. As a result, aggressive cues were clearly present—and in abundance. Given such findings, it seems reasonable to conclude that in the presence of such stimuli, even relatively mild thwarting can stimulate overt aggression. In their absence, however, our initial generalization seems to hold: frustration must be relatively strong or intense to induce heightened aggression among the persons who endure it.

A second factor that appears to strongly mediate the effects of frustration upon aggression is the degree to which such thwarting appears to be *arbitrary* or *unexpected*. A large number of studies (e.g., Burnstein & Worchel, 1962; Cohen, 1955; Pastore, 1952; Zillmann & Cantor, 1976) have reported that individuals generally demonstrate much higher levels of aggression in response to arbitrary or unexpected frustration than they do in reaction to nonarbitrary or expected frustration. Indeed, there is some indication in this research that fully justified and expected frustrations often fail to induce either physiological arousal (Zillmann & Cantor, 1976) or subsequent attacks against the source of thwarting. Perhaps the clearest evidence regarding this latter point is provided by an experiment conducted by Stephen Worchel (1974).

In this interesting study, subjects were offered one of three incentives (an hour of experimental credit, $5 in cash, or a bottle of men's cologne) as payment for their participation in the experiment. In an initial portion of the experiment, all subjects rated these items in terms of their relative attractiveness. These ratings were then employed to vary the degree of frustration they later experienced. Specifically, after completing several intervening tasks, the subjects in one group were given the prize they had previously rated as most attractive. As a result, they experienced little if any frustration. Those in a second group received their second choice and so experienced a moderate degree of thwarting. Finally, those in a third condition received only their last choice and so endured the highest degree of frustration in the study. An additional aspect of the experiment involved the extent to which frustration, when it occurred, was unexpected or arbitrary in nature. So that this factor could be varied, one third of the participants within each frustration condition were led to believe that the experimenter's assistant would simply assign them any one of the three prizes he wished (the *no-expectancy* group). A second third were told that they would later receive the prize they had rated as most attractive (the *expectancy* group), while the final third were informed that they would later be able to choose any prize they wished (the *choice* group). It was reasoned that only in the latter two conditions would frustration be unexpected and that only in these groups would increasing degrees of thwarting lead to increasing amounts of aggression.

In order to assess the accuracy of these predictions, the investigators provided the subjects with an opportunity to aggress verbally against the assistant by rating his performance. As shown in Figure 13, results obtained with this measure were generally in accordance with expectations: only subjects in the expectancy and choice groups showed increments in aggression as the level of frustration rose. Thus, as expected, frustration led to such behavior only when it was either arbitrary or unexpected in nature.

To summarize: existing evidence suggests that frustration can indeed facilitate later aggression. However, it seems most likely to produce such effects when it is (1) quite intense and (2) unexpected or arbitrary in nature. In view of the fact that intense frustration is a relatively rare experience for most individuals most of the time, and given the fact that when it occurs, it is often expected or anticipated, the following general conclusion seems justified: frustration is indeed

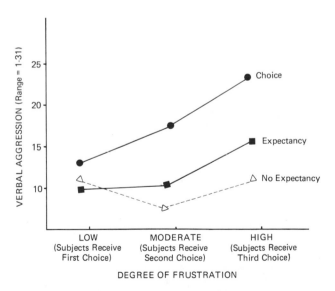

FIGURE 13. Reactions to expected and unexpected frustration. Frustration (receipt of a nonpreferred incentive) facilitated aggression only when such thwarting was unexpected (in the choice and expectancy groups). (Adapted from Worchel, 1974.)

one of the social antecedents of aggression; however, it is not a very common or important one and is probably far less crucial in this respect than has widely—and persistently—been assumed.

## VERBAL AND PHYSICAL ATTACK: DIRECT PROVOCATION FROM OTHERS AS AN ANTECEDENT OF AGGRESSION

How would you react if, for no apparent reason, a clerk in a store began to insult you, criticizing your taste and berating your judgment? In all probability, you would grow quite angry, and if this person was not too large or imposing, you might well choose to answer in kind, defending your "honor" with harsh words of your own. But now imagine that he or she stepped from behind the counter and began to push or shove you or to make a series of menacing gestures; how would you react then? Assuming that you did not turn and flee, there is a very good chance that you might again respond in a reciprocal fashion, trading push for shove and threat for threat. Indeed, the

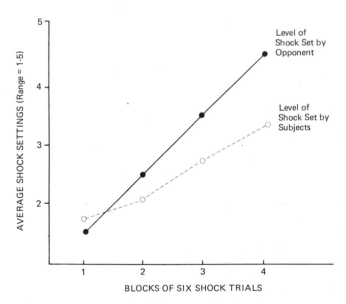

FIGURE 14. Physical attack as an elicitor of aggression. Subjects generally respond to increasing provocation from their opponent in a reciprocal fashion (i.e., by raising the strength of their own shock settings). (Based on data from Taylor & Pisano, 1971.)

whole encounter might quickly escalate, so that soon, you might find yourself exchanging kicks and punches in place of threats and gestures. The following description of "playing the dozens," a ritualized trading of provocations common among ghetto teen-agers, provides a vivid illustration of the nature of this dangerous process:

> One of the tormenters will make a mildly insulting statement, perhaps about the mother of the subject, "I saw your mother out with a man last night." Then he may follow this up with, "She was drunk as a bat." The subject, in turn, will make an insulting statement about the tormenter or some member of the tormenter's family. This exchange of insults continues . . . until they eventually include every member of the participants' families and every act of animal and man. . . . Finally, one of the participants, usually the subject . . . reaches his threshold and takes a swing at the tormenter, pulls out a knife, or picks up an object to use as a club. That is the sign for the tormenter . . . to go into action, and usually the subject ends up with the most physical injuries. (Berdie, 1947, p. 120)

Of course, not every insult or threat leads to such outcomes. Individuals often react to such treatment with attempts at reconciliation, statements of surrender, or overt flight. Informal observation indicates, however, that encounters of this type are far from rare and that direct provocation—either verbal or physical—often initiates aggressive reactions.

More formal evidence for the powerful aggression-enhancing impact of such treatment has been obtained in a number of laboratory experiments. For example, a series of investigations by Stuart Taylor and his colleagues (Borden, Bowen, & Taylor, 1971; Dengerink & Bertilson, 1974; Dengerink & Myers, 1977; Taylor, 1967) indicates that most individuals respond to physical provocation from others with strong counterattacks of their own. In these studies, a subject competes with an opponent on a reaction-time task under conditions in which the slower player on each trial receives an electric shock (see Chapter 2, pp. 66–68, for more detail). The magnitude of these shocks is set in advance by both players, so that each supposedly controls the strength of the jolts that will be received by the other, should he or she lose on a given occasion. In reality, however, subject's opponent is usually fictitious, and participants are simply made to lose on a set proportion of the trials. As shown in Figure 14, the strength of the shocks they receive on these occasions is made to rise steadily, thus suggesting that their partner is behaving in an increasingly aggressive manner. (That is, he appears to be setting stronger and stronger shocks for them as the session proceeds.) The reactions of most individuals to this situation are quite straightforward: in general, they respond to such provocation by raising the strength of their *own* shock settings, retaliating in kind rather than "turning the other cheek." Indeed, they generally seem to match their own level of aggression quite closely to that shown by their partner (refer to Figure 14). Perhaps the close reciprocal nature of these reactions is most clearly illustrated in an experiment conducted by O'Leary and Dengerink (1973).

In this study, subjects found themselves facing an opponent who adopted one of four distinct strategies during the experiment. In one condition (known as the *increasing-attack* group), he followed the pattern described previously, increasing the strength of his shock settings over trials. In a second (the *decreasing-attack* group), he followed the opposite strategy, starting with high settings and then gradually reducing these during the session. In a third (the *high-attack* group), he employed strong shocks in all cases, and in a fourth (the *low-attack* group), he set only very mild shock for the subject on each occasion. On the basis of previous research, it was expected that subjects in each group would act in a reciprocal fashion, returning very much the same level of provocation as they received from their partner. Results indicated that this was actually the case. Individuals in the high-attack group responded with strong shocks of their own, those in the low-attack group directed much weaker shocks toward their opponent, and those in the increasing- and decreasing-attack conditions altered the strength of their settings in accordance with the changes shown by their partner. In short, they behaved in a highly reciprocal manner. The major implication of such research, of course, is that direct physical provocation will often be answered in kind and serves as a very powerful elicitor of overt aggression.

The fact that most individuals seem to respond aggressively to direct physical assaults from others is hardly surprising; the notion of an "eye for an eye" is, after all, a very ancient one in the history of human society. Somewhat more unexpected, however, is evidence pointing to the conclusion that individuals often react aggressively to indications of aggressive intention on the part of others, even when they are not actually attacked by these persons. That is, the mere knowledge that another harbors hostile intentions is often sufficient to elicit overt aggression. This important fact is demonstrated quite clearly in an ingenious experiment conducted by Greenwell and Dengerink (1973).

In this study, male college students competing with a fictitious partner in the kind of reaction-time task we have already described received information from a set of lights indicating either that (1) their opponent was raising the level of his shock settings over trials or (2) he was maintaining those shocks at a constant, moderate level. For half of the subjects within each of these groups, the strength of the shocks received actually *did* increase, while for the others, it remained constant. The major question of interest, of course, was whether the subjects would be influenced by the information concerning their opponent's apparent intentions as well as by the strength of the jolts they actually received from him. Results indicated that this was definitely the case. Indeed, there was some indication that the opponent's intentions were more important in determining the subjects' own shock settings than the strength of the shocks they received from this person. In the condition in which the information lights suggested that the opponent was increasing his shock settings, the subjects raised theirs, regardless of whether the shocks they received rose or remained constant. And in the condition in which the lights suggested that the opponent was holding his shock settings constant, the subjects did not raise theirs, even when the magnitude of the jolts they received rose steadily. In commenting upon these results, Greenwell and Dengerink (1973) noted, "while attack is an important instigator of aggressive behavior, it appears that the physical discomfort experienced by a person may be subordinate to the symbolic elements that are incorporated in that attack" (p. 70). In short, the apparent motives or intentions behind another person's actions—especially when these are potentially provocative—may often be far more important in influencing our tendency to aggress against him or her than the nature of these actions themselves. (For an illustration of this fact, see Figure 15.)

Although we have concentrated, up to this point, on physical rather than verbal provocation, it is clear that this latter type of treatment also frequently serves as an important elicitor of aggressive actions. Indeed, it is almost certainly more common in this respect than assaults involving fists, feet, or weapons. As we all know from our personal experience, "cutting" comments and sarcastic remarks from

FIGURE 15. Even provocative actions may fail to elicit aggression when they are viewed by the recipients as stemming from beneficial motives. (Source: King Features Syndicate, Inc.)

other persons may often hurt as much as—and sometimes more than— actual physical attacks. Indeed, when they come from individuals whose esteem we value or when they cause us to "lose face" in front of others, they can be an extremely aversive experience. That such actions often serve to elicit strong counteraggression has been demonstrated in many laboratory studies (e.g., Baron & Bell, 1976; Donnerstein, Donnerstein, & Evans, 1975; Geen, 1968; Wilson & Rogers,

1975). In all of these investigations, direct insults, taunts, or derogatory evaluations from a confederate have been shown to facilitate later
aggression against this person. Such findings are, of course, far from
unexpected and agree closely with informal observation of natural
social interactions. These studies have also yielded two less obvious
results, however.

First, they have consistently pointed to the fact that verbal attacks
may often lead to physical retaliation. That is, after receiving taunts or
insults from another person, participants in such studies have often
demonstrated considerable willingness to direct strong electric shocks
or other kinds of aversive physical treatment to the sources of verbal
provocation. These findings suggest why incidents that begin with
verbal taunts or a trading of insults may quickly escalate into violent
brawls.

Second, the results of several of these studies provide suggestive
evidence that verbal provocation may often serve as a stronger antecedent of overt aggression than several types of frustration. We have
already considered one of these investigations—an experiment conducted by Geen (1968)—on pp. 82–83. As may be recalled, results indicated that subjects who were exposed to unprovoked verbal insult
from a confederate demonstrated higher levels of aggression toward
this person than those exposed to two kinds of frustration. While
these findings appear to be quite clear-cut, we must, unfortunately,
view them as only suggestive for one important reason: no attempt
was made to equate the magnitude of the frustrations and verbal assaults employed. As a result, it is by no means certain that the same
pattern of results would be obtained at all values of these two factors.
For example, would mild insult always be more effective in eliciting
subsequent aggression than extremely strong frustration? On the basis
of available evidence, it is impossible to tell. Needless to say, equating
the magnitude of frustration and of verbal attack is a difficult and
complex task, involving such steps as extensive preratings by judges.
However, additional research in which such procedures are followed
is necessary before any definitive conclusions regarding the relative
impact of these two variables can be reached. Given the strong aggression-enhancing influence of physical and verbal provocation and the
relatively weak influence of all but intense and arbitrary frustration,
however, we might venture what seems to be a reasonable first guess:
under conditions in which magnitude is equated, verbal provocation

may well represent a stronger antecedent of subsequent aggression than interpersonal thwarting.

## EXPOSURE TO AGGRESSIVE MODELS: THE IMPACT OF WITNESSED VIOLENCE

One of the classic findings of social psychology—perhaps *the* classic finding—is that individuals are often strongly affected by the actions or words of the others around them. A huge body of research findings gathered over several decades indicates that individuals can frequently be induced to alter their attitudes, feelings, or behavior as a result of social influence from others. For many years, it was generally assumed that such influence must be intentional in order to produce these effects; that is, only when one person overtly attempted to change the attitudes or actions of others would such changes be induced. In recent years, however, it has become increasingly clear that social influence can be unintentional as well. In particular, a growing body of evidence suggests that simple exposure to the actions and outcomes of others is often quite sufficient to produce large and important alterations in the feelings, behavior, or thoughts of observers (see Bandura, 1977).

An increasing awareness of the existence and pervasive impact of such unintentional influence—generally termed *modeling*—has led, in turn, to an interesting question relevant to the present discussion: Can aggression, too, be affected through this process? More specifically, can exposure to the behavior of others who act in a highly aggressive manner serve to elicit similar actions on the part of observers? Interest in this issue has been intense and, as we shall soon see, has sparked some of the most heated public controversies ever to involve psychologists. Basically, it has stimulated two distinct, yet closely related lines of research.

The first has sought to determine whether exposure to live aggressive models plays an important role in the occurrence and spread of collective violence, while the second has investigated the impact of mass-media portrayals of violence—especially those on television—upon the behavior of viewers. Evidence relating to both issues is now quite extensive. Since the second has been the subject of considerably more attention, however, we will examine it at somewhat greater length.

## Exposure to Live Aggressive Models: The "Contagion" of Violence

Do aggressive models play an important role in the initiation of riots, insurrections, and similar events? Eye-witness accounts by social scientists present on the scene during the initiation of such events suggest that they may. In many cases, it appears that large-scale aggression fails to develop until one or more "hot-headed" individuals commit an initial act of violence (Lieberson & Silverman, 1965; Momboisse, 1967). Prior to such events, angry muttering and a general milling about may predominate. Once the first blow is struck, the first rock hurled, or the first weapon fired, however, a destructive riot may quickly ensue. It seems reasonable to view the persons who initiate violence in such situations as aggressive models, who by their own overt acts of aggression sharply reduce the restraints of other bystanders against engaging in similar behavior. The following description of the events immediately preceding the start of one of the tragic riots of the late 1960s provides a clear illustration of such effects:

> Without conscious thought of his action he darted into the street and hurled the empty pop bottle in his hand toward the last of the departing black-and-white cars. Striking the rear fender of Sgt. Rankin's car, it shattered, and it was as if in that shattering the thousand people lining the street found their own release. It was as if in one violent contortion the bonds of restraint were snapped. Rocks, bottles, pieces of wood and iron—whatever missiles came to hand—were projected against the sides and windows of the bus and automobiles that, halted for the past 20 minutes by the jammed street, unwittingly started through the gauntlet. . . . It was 7:45 P.M. Amidst the rending sounds of tearing metal, splintering glass, cries of bewilderment and shouts of triumph, the Los Angeles uprising had begun. (Conot, 1967, p. 29)

Of course, in this and related cases, the individuals present on the scene had been made "ready" to aggress by strong prior provocation, powerful frustration, and other factors. Yet, despite these strong instigations to aggression, an initial act of violence often seems to be required before large-scale rioting erupts.

The powerful impact of aggressive models in eliciting subsequent violence among observers has also been demonstrated in a number of recent laboratory studies (e.g., Baron, 1971c; Baron & Bell, 1975; Baron & Kepner, 1970; Donnerstein & Donnerstein, 1976; Wheeler & Caggiula, 1966). For example, in the investigation conducted by Baron and Kepner (1970), male college students were first provoked through verbal insult from a confederate (he accused them of being unintelligent and incapable of performing their role in the study) and then were provided with an opportunity to aggress against this individual within the context of the teacher–learner procedures devised by Buss (1961). So that the influence of an aggressive model on the strength of subjects' attacks against the learner could be investigated, a second confederate, who played the role of another teacher, also participated in the study. In one group (the *aggressive-model* condition), this individual was chosen to serve as the first teacher and was allowed to perform on the aggression machine before the subject. He then acted in a highly aggressive manner, depressing buttons 8, 9, or 10 on each occasion when the learner appeared to make an error. As a result, subjects in this group were exposed to the actions of a highly aggressive model before being provided with their own opportunity to attack the confederate victim. In a second group (the *no-model* condition), by contrast, the subject was chosen to serve as the first teacher and performed this role before the model. In this group, then, the subject aggressed against the learner before witnessing the actions of the aggressive model. (In a third condition, the subjects were exposed to the actions of a nonaggressive model, who pushed only buttons 1, 2, and 3 on the apparatus before gaining their own opportunity to aggress. However, we will reserve discussion of this condition until Chapter 6, where techniques for the prevention and control of human violence will be considered.)

The results of the experiment were quite straightforward: as expected, subjects in the aggressive-model group delivered stronger and longer-lasting shocks to the victim than did subjects in the no-model condition (see Table 7). In short, exposure to the actions of another person who acted in a highly aggressive manner increased subjects' tendency to behave aggressively themselves. While it is certainly a long jump from the relatively artificial conditions prevailing in such research to alarming and dangerous instances of collective violence occurring in natural settings, the consistency with which such findings have been obtained in other studies and their close agreement with the eye-witness accounts mentioned above suggest that related processes may be at work in both settings. In short, there is reason to believe that violence—at least in the case of individuals who have been strongly provoked—may indeed be contagious.

TABLE 7

*Effects of Exposure to a Live Aggressive Model upon Overt Aggression*[a]

| Measure of aggression | Exposure to a live aggressive model[b] | |
|---|---|---|
| | No model | Model |
| Shock intensity | 4.74 | 6.81 |
| Shock duration (sec) | 0.72 | 0.84 |

[a] Based upon data from Baron & Kepner, 1970.
[b] Subjects exposed to the model before aggressing against a confederate delivered stronger and longer-lasting shocks to this person than subjects who aggressed prior to witnessing the model's behavior.

## Aggressive Models in the Mass Media: The Effects of Filmed and Televised Violence

While much attention has been focused on the impact of live aggressive models, an even greater amount of interest has been directed to the possible influence of portrayals of violence in the mass media (cf. Bandura, 1973; Berkowitz, 1971; Geen, 1976). The major question under investigation in such research, of course, has been whether exposure to a steady diet of violent events in movies, television shows, and other entertainment media may significantly increase the tendency of both children and adults to behave in a similar manner. Partly because of its intrinsic interest to psychologists and partly because of the important social issues it raises, this topic has been one of the most heavily researched within psychology in recent years. As a result, a very large number of relevant experiments have been conducted, and literally mountains of interesting data have been produced (see Comstock, 1975, for a useful summary of much of this work). Because of obvious space limitations, we could not hope to examine all of this evidence in detail—it would easily fill the remainder of this volume. What we can provide, however, is an outline of the major findings uncovered, and a description of important developments in the methodology of the studies conducted. Basically, research concerned with the effects of media violence may be viewed as having taken place in three distinct phases or "generations" of increasing sophistication and refinement. The procedures and findings of each of these phases will now be considered.

*Phase One: The Bobo Doll Studies*

The earliest research relating to the effects of media violence was conducted by Albert Bandura and his colleagues (e.g., Bandura, Ross, & Ross, 1963a,b; Bandura, 1965). In these studies, young children of nursery-school age were exposed to short films (often projected into the screen of a television set) in which adult models aggressed in very unusual ways against a large inflated toy clown (a Bobo doll). For example, in one particular study (Bandura, Ross, & Ross, 1963a), the model performed such unusual acts as sitting on the doll and punching it repeatedly in the nose, pommeling it on the head with a toy mallet, drop-kicking it about the room, and making such statements as "Sock him in the nose . . . ," "Hit him down . . . ," and so on. Following exposure to these scenes, the children were placed in a room containing a variety of toys, several of which had been used by the model in this aggressive behavior, and were allowed to play freely for a brief period of time (e.g., 10 or 20 minutes). During this interval, their behavior was carefully observed so that it could be determined whether and to what degree they would match the novel actions of the model. In general, the results of these studies revealed strong imitative effects. Indeed, as noted in Chapter 2, the children often appeared to become veritable carbon copies of the adult models they had observed.

Further findings revealed that, as might be expected, these basic results were mediated by several different factors. For example, it was noted that boys generally demonstrated more imitative aggression than girls, that the sex of the model exerted important effects (both boys and girls were influenced to a greater degree by male than by female models), and that the reality of the model (live, filmed, or cartoon) might determine the amount of imitation shown by observers (Bandura, Ross, & Ross, 1963a,b). Overall, however, the experiments left little doubt that young children could often acquire new aggressive responses not previously at their disposal through exposure to aggressive models.

This finding, in and of itself, was hardly surprising or controversial. The results of many other investigations suggested that individuals could acquire a wide variety of responses through exposure to the actions of social models. The facts that in this case the responses mastered were new forms of physical or verbal aggression and that they were acquired through brief exposure to filmed or televised models, however, pointed to one potential implication that soon made Bandura's studies the center of a heated controversy. In particular, it seemed possible that if children could learn new ways of harming others through such experience, mass-media portrayals of violence might be contributing, in some degree, to increased levels of violence in society. Bandura himself cautioned against such interpretations and even demonstrated that the fact that children acquire such responses through exposure to aggressive models in no way guarantees that they will put them to actual use (Bandura, 1965). The mere possibility of such effects, however, was enough to focus considerable public attention upon his research.

In behavioral science, when research is subjected to widespread, public interest, severe criticism is often close behind. With respect to the early Bobo doll studies, this was definitely the case. Several crucial questions regarding the meaning and interpretation of the results of these experiments were soon raised by other social scientists (Klapper, 1968) and by spokesmen for the television industry. First, it was noted that the subjects in these experiments aggressed against inflated plastic toys specifically designed for such treatment rather than against another human being. As a result, it is not entirely clear that their behavior may reasonably be termed aggression—after all, no one was actually hurt in any manner. Second, the films viewed by the subjects in these studies differed in several important ways from standard TV or movie fare. For example, they failed to include a plot, provided no cause or justification for the model's behavior, and showed adults engaging in actions highly unlikely to appear on TV (or anywhere else!). Finally, the children in this research were provided with an opportunity to aggress in precisely the same manner as the models they observed, whereas viewers who witness violent acts by television or film characters seldom attain similar opportunities. (How many children who witness military battles or showdowns with outlaws on TV, after all, are able to take part in such actions themselves?) For these reasons, it was argued, Bandura's studies and similar research failed to provide strong evidence for the suggestion that filmed or televised violence encourages interpersonal aggression.

*Phase Two: Laboratory Studies of Hurting*

Confronted with such criticisms, several researchers quickly began to plan and execute studies designed to eliminate these problems. Basically, these experiments sought to accomplish three major goals. First, they attempted to employ more realistic measures of aggression in which subjects' attacks would be directed against other human beings rather than against mere plastic toys. Second, they exposed the participants to more realistic violent materials—ones quite similar to or actually taken from TV shows or movies. And finally, they sought to eliminate the precise similarity present in earlier studies between the aggressive incidents watched by subjects and the context within which they themselves could aggress. Many such studies were conducted, both with children (Grusec, 1972; Hanratty, O'Neal, & Sulzer, 1972; Rice & Grusec, 1975) and with adults (Berkowitz & Alioto, 1973; Buvinic & Berkowitz, 1976; Geen & Stonner, 1972), and in general, the results pointed to the conclusion that under these conditions, exposure to filmed or televised violence tended to facilitate similar behavior by observers. As an example of this research, let us consider an investigation conducted by Liebert and Baron (1972).

In this study, children in two different age groups (5–6, 8–9 years) were exposed to one of two brief excerpts taken directly from actual television programs. In one condition (the *aggressive-program* group), they observed a three-and-a-half-minute segment taken from "The Untouchables," a crime program popular during the early 1960s and widely syndicated in recent years. This excerpt depicted such events as a chase, two fist fights, two shootings, and a knifing, arranged in a manner suggestive of a simple story. In a second condition (the *nonaggressive-program* group), the subjects witnessed an exciting track race, which also lasted for approximately three and a half minutes. This segment was taken from a nationally broadcast sports program and depicted athletes running around a track, jumping over hurdles, and demonstrating other similar behavior. The excerpt was specifically chosen so as to be as exciting as the segment viewed by the subjects in the aggressive-program condition, so that any differences in the later behavior of the two groups could not be attributed solely to contrasting levels of emotional excitement (see Rule & Nesdale, 1976a; Tannenbaum & Zillmann, 1975).

After witnessing one of these two films, the children were escorted to a second room and seated in front of a panel containing two buttons labeled, respectively, "hurt" and "help" and a white "ready" signal light (see Figure 16). They were then informed that another child in the next room would attempt to play a game and win a prize

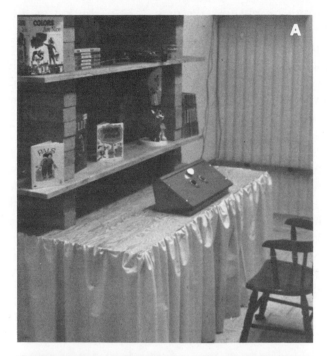

FIGURE 16. The apparatus and general setting employed by Liebert and Baron (1972) to investigate the effects of televised violence upon children's aggressive behavior (A). Subjects were informed that by pressing one of the two buttons shown (B), they could burn another child. (In reality, of course, no one was actually harmed in any manner during the experiment.)

and that each time the white signal light was illuminated, they could either help him by pushing the green "help" button or hurt him by pushing the red "hurt" button. They were further instructed that whenever they pushed the red "hurt" button, a handle being turned by the child in the next room would get hot, and he would be hurt (presumably burned). In contrast to the earlier studies described above, in which subjects "aggressed" against an inanimate toy, therefore, participants in this experiment were informed that they could inflict pain—and perhaps suffering—on another human being. In reality, of course, there was no other child in the next room, and no one was actually harmed during the study.

Following the completion of these instructions, the child was left alone in the experimental room, and the white "ready" signal was illuminated on 20 different occasions. The results of the experiment are shown in Figure 17, where it can be seen that, as expected, subjects who had witnessed the aggressive program inflicted significantly more

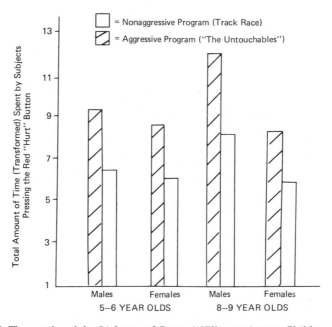

FIGURE 17. The results of the Liebert and Baron (1972) experiment. Children in two different age groups demonstrated higher levels of aggression after viewing a violent excerpt from "The Untouchables" than after viewing an equally exciting but nonviolent track race. (Based on data from Liebert & Baron, 1972.)

punishment on their nonexistent victim (as measured by use of the "hurt" button) than those who had witnessed the nonaggressive program. Moreover, this effect was obtained for girls as well as boys and for both age groups.

As we have already noted, similar findings have been reported in a large number of additional studies. Thus, it appears that exposure to even relatively brief episodes of filmed or televised violence may facilitate later aggression by children and adults. As might be expected, however, there do appear to be certain limiting conditions with respect to such effects. First, it appears that exposure to filmed or televised violence may facilitate similar actions by observers only when the aggression they witness seems to be justified. If it seems unjustified, aggression may fail to be increased (e.g., Berkowitz & Alioto, 1973). Second, it appears that such effects are relatively short-lived in nature and may fade quite quickly with the passage of time. Indeed, the aggression-enhancing impact of witnessed violence may begin to dissipate within a few minutes (Doob & Climie, 1972) and may entirely vanish within an hour (Buvinic & Berkowitz, 1976). Third, there is some indication that while actual aggressive behavior may be enhanced by exposure to scenes of violence, feelings of anger or hostility may sometimes be reduced by such experience (Manning & Taylor, 1975). This latter finding has been reported in only one recent study, however, and should be interpreted with some degree of caution.

While the studies performed in this second "generation" of research seemed to eliminate several of the problems raised concerning the earlier Bobo doll studies, they, too, were open to criticism on several grounds. First, it was noted that the measures of aggression employed in such investigations, although improved over the striking of a plastic toy, were still open to question. Human beings rarely aggress against specific persons by pushing a button to burn or shock them (although they do often push buttons to attack in more destructive ways, e.g., launching missiles or dropping bombs). As a result, there is some question as to whether the participants in such experiments always believed that they were actually hurting another person through these actions. Second, although the programs shown to subjects were quite realistic in content, they were often artificially brief— usually lasting no more than a few moments. Since most filmed or televised aggression is of a much longer duration, and since viewers are exposed to it over a period of years, it is quite possile that long-term exposure to such materials produces somewhat different effects than those observed in laboratory studies. And finally, the brief segments presented generally lacked a well-developed plot, a feature presumably present (although arguably so!) in most TV and Hollywood offerings.[1] In order to take account of such criticisms, a number of researchers have recently conducted what might be termed a series of third-generation experiments concerning the effects of witnessed violence.

*Phase Three: Long-Term Field Studies*

In these recent experiments, subjects have been exposed to full-length films, to complete television shows, or even to controlled diets of violent or nonviolent materials for several days or weeks. Then their actual aggressive behavior in naturalistic settings has been observed over similarly extended periods of time. In this manner, the major criticisms leveled against earlier research on this topic have been largely eliminated.

Despite all the differences between these sophisticated field studies and earlier laboratory experiments, however, their findings have usually pointed to the same general conclusions: exposure to filmed or televised violence increases the likelihood that viewers will themselves engage in similar behavior (e.g., Leyens *et al.*, 1975; Parke *et al.*, 1975). For example, consider a major project conducted by Leyens *et al.* (1975). In this investigation, the researchers began by observing both the aggressive and the nonaggressive behaviors of a large number of boys living at a private school in Belgium. After one week of this unobtrusive observation, subjects were divided into two groups on the basis of the particular housing units in which they lived and were then exposed to either five violent or five nonviolent movies. These films were shown one each day, in the evening, for five consecutive

[1] An additional criticism of many studies in this second category lies in their failure to include an appropriate no-film control group. As a result of the omission of such a condition, it is impossible to determine whether reported differences between the aggressive-film and neutral-film groups in such investigations derive from (1) increments in aggression stemming from exposure to the former or (2) reductions in aggression stemming from exposure to the latter. The fact that at least two experiments offer support for the second of these interpretations (Donnerstein, Donnerstein, & Barrett, 1976; Zillmann & Johnson, 1973) suggests that the findings of many such laboratory studies of hurting must be viewed with somewhat more caution than has usually been the case.

days, and those in the two categories differed sharply in the amount of aggression they contained. (For example, included among the highly aggressive films were *Bonnie and Clyde* and *The Dirty Dozen;* included among the nonaggressive films were *Lily, Daddy's Fiancée,* and similar nonviolent epics.)

In accordance with previous research, it was hypothesized that exposure to the violent movies would produce an increase in subjects' level of aggression toward their peers. In order to determine if this was indeed the case, observation of the boys' activities was continued on days when the films were shown. While not as clear-cut as might be hoped, results offered at least partial support for the major prediction: participants exposed to the violent movies did show an increase in some but not all forms of aggression. In contrast, subjects exposed to the nonviolent films failed to demonstrate any consistent changes in behavior.

Because such long-term field investigations seem to be successful in countering most of the criticisms leveled against laboratory research, many psychologists believe that their findings are more conclusive and open to generalization than those of earlier investigations. Thus, they seem to offer strong and convincing evidence for the view that exposure to media violence may indeed tend to facilitate similar behavior by observers. But why, precisely do such effects occur? What underlying psychological processes account for their existence? Perhaps we should pause here to say a few words about this issue.

Basically, the impact of witnessed violence upon observers has usually been attributed to three major factors. First, it is apparent that individuals exposed to such scenes often acquire new ways of aggressing. That is, they learn new verbal or physical responses with which they were previously unacquainted and which can be used to harm other persons in some manner. Such *observational learning* is a well-established phenomenon and has long been assigned an important role in accounting for the influence of witnessed violence (see Bandura, 1977). Second, individuals exposed to aggressive actions on the part of others may frequently experience sharp reductions in the strength of their restraints against engaging in such behavior. After all, they may reason, if other persons aggress with impunity so may they. Such *disinhibitory effects* may then increase the likelihood of aggressive actions by observers. Finally, there is growing evidence that continued exposure to scenes of violence may produce a gradual *desensitization* to both aggression and signs of pain on the part of others (Cline, Croft, & Courrier, 1973; Thomas, Horton, Lippincott, & Drabman, 1977). The end result is that observers become so inured to violence and its consequences that they cease to view it as a very significant form of behavior. The role of such a casual attitude toward aggression in facilitating its occurrence should be obvious. Acting together, then, these three processes seem to account quite adequately for the aggression-enhancing effect of witnessed violence.

Before concluding, we should hasten to add that although most findings reported to date support the conclusion that exposure to media violence may facilitate subsequent aggression, there have been two notable exceptions to this pattern. First, in a highly controversial project, Feshbach and Singer (1971) found that boys exposed to a steady diet of aggressive TV programs over a six-week period actually demonstrated lower levels of aggression in their interactions with others than boys exposed to nonaggressive shows for a comparable period. Similarly, Milgram and Shotland (1973) reported neither an increase nor a decrease in various antisocial behaviors (e.g., stealing, making abusive phone calls) as a result of viewing or not viewing such actions on an actual television program.

Because both of these studies (and especially the project conducted by Feshbach and Singer) have been criticized on methodological grounds, it is my impression that the weight of existing evidence strongly favors the view that exposure to scenes of violence in the mass media does increase the likelihood that observers will behave in a similar manner themselves. But please note: this does *not* mean that after watching their favorite action-packed (and aggression-packed) program, adults or children are likely to rush out and launch blind assaults against any individual unfortunate enough to land in their paths. Judging from the magnitude of the effects reported in most investigations, the increase in aggressive tendencies produced by exposure to such materials is probably slight. Moreover, as will become increasingly apparent in the present and later chapters, the number of different factors influencing the occurrence of aggressive actions is legion, and as a result, the impact of any one upon the behavior of a large number of individuals is probably quite small. In sum, while existing evidence does indeed suggest that the high level of violence prevalent in current television and movie offerings probably contributes, along with other variables, to the occurrence of some aggressive encounters, care must be taken to avoid overstating or emphasizing the importance of this relationship.

## Orders Are Orders: Direct Commands as an Antecedent of Aggression

Suppose that while walking along the street, you were stopped by a total stranger who handed you a loaded gun and demanded that you fire upon another person standing blindfolded against a wall. How would you react? In all probability, you would refuse; indeed, unless the stranger had some obvious way of enforcing his or her demands, you might well beat a hasty retreat and seek help in subduing this obvious madman. But now imagine a somewhat different set of circumstances. You are a soldier, and the person handing you the gun is a general with many decorations upon his uniform. How would you behave in this instance? Here the chances are quite high that you would obey and would quickly proceed to gun down in cold blood an individual you had never seen before.

Together, these hypothetical examples call attention to another important antecedent of aggression: direct orders from a source of authority. Although popular conceptions of aggression do not usually focus on the impact of this factor, even a moment's reflection suggests that it may be a crucial one. Many aggressive actions—especially those carried out by soldiers, sailors, and pilots—stem from the commands of superiors and *not* from any provocation or frustration suffered at the hands of the victims. In fact, it may well be the case that over the course of human history, more individuals have perished or been seriously injured as a result of commands initiating aggressive actions than as a result of any other single factor.

That authority figures can command such destructive, unquestioning obedience is far from surprising. Afer all, they usually have the full weight of their office—and society—behind their directives. More unexpected, however, is the suggestion that even persons lacking in such power and merely displaying the trappings of authority can frequently induce others to behave in harmful, destructive ways. The most systematic—and by far unsettling—evidence regarding such issues has been gathered by Stanley Milgram and his colleagues in a series of well-known and controversial experiments (Milgram, 1963; 1965a,b; 1974).

## Obedience in the Laboratory

In order to examine the ability of a relatively powerless source of authority to induce individuals to engage in antisocial, harmful actions, Milgram (1963) devised a simple but ingenious procedure. Briefly, subjects participating in his research were informed that they would be serving in an investigation concerned with the influence of punishment on learning. The task was then described as that of delivering electric shock to another subject (actually an accomplice of the experimenter) each time he made an error in a learning task. These shocks were to be delivered by means of 30 numbered switches located on the apparatus shown in Figure 18, and the subject was instructed to follow a simple rule: each time the learner made an error, the next higher switch was to be thrown. Since the first switch on the apparatus supposedly delivered a shock of 15 volts, the second a shock of 30, and so on throughout the series, it was clear that if the learner made any sizable number of mistakes, he would soon be receiving powerful and potentially dangerous jolts of electricity. Indeed, according to labels on the equipment, the final shock in the series would consist of fully 450 volts! In reality, of course, the accomplice never received any shocks during the experiment; the only real shock ever employed was a mild pulse of 45 volts delivered to subjects from the third button, simply to convince them that the apparatus was actually functional.

When all instructions were clear, the session began, and in accordance with a prearranged schedule, the accomplice quickly made a large number of errors. As a result, the subject soon found himself facing an extremely disturbing dilemma: he could continue "punishing" the learner with what appeared to be increasingly painful shocks, or he could refuse to continue and call a halt to the proceedings. To make matters worse, the experimenter did not stand idly by and allow him to reach this decision undisturbed. Rather, each time he indicated a desire to stop, the experimenter ordered him, in an increasingly authoritative manner, to continue. Thus, on the first occasion when the subject expressed unwillingness to continue, the experimenter said, "Please continue," or "Please go on." On the next occasion, he stated,

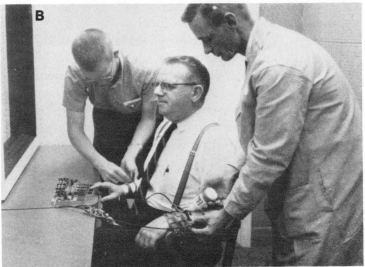

FIGURE 18. The apparatus employed by Milgram (1963) to investigate destructive obedience under controlled laboratory conditions (A). Subjects were informed that the switches on this equipment delivered increasingly strong electric shocks and were then ordered by the experimenter to move to higher and higher levels in "punishing" another person (B) for errors on a bogus learning task. (Photos courtesy of Dr. Stanley Milgram.)

"The experiment requires that you continue." If the subject still objected, the experimenter remarked, "It is absolutely essential that you continue," and if even this failed, he would sternly state, "You have no other choice, you *must* go on." As a result of these actions by the experimenter, the subject could terminate the session only by openly defying the commands of a stern and imposing individual.

As may already be apparent, these procedures are quite similar, in several respects, to the standard teacher–learner paradigm for the study of aggression devised by Arnold Buss (1961; refer to pp. 54–62). One important difference between them, however, should not be overlooked. In Milgram's procedures, subjects were first told—and later commanded—to punish each error with increasingly powerful shocks. In Buss's procedures, in contrast, they were given complete freedom concerning the strength of these jolts. As a result of this difference, studies employing Buss's methodology are generally viewed as yielding information concerning the occurrence of voluntary aggression, while those employing Milgram's technique are viewed as providing evidence concerning the occurrence of aggression carried out in response to direct commands from others.

Before describing the results of Milgram's study, we must note that the individuals participating in it were *not* college students seeking to earn extra credit or to fulfill a course requirement. Rather, they were a heterogeneous group of adult males ranging in age from 20 to 50 and in occupations from unskilled laborer to engineer, recruited through newspaper advertisements requesting paid volunteers. Since they had no direct connection with the university at which the research was conducted and were volunteers who had agreed to participate in the research of their own free will, it might be expected that they would be highly resistant to the experimenter's demands that they inflict seemingly dangerous electric shocks on another person. Yet, as shown in Figure 19, fully 65% demonstrated total obedience, proceeding during the session to the final 450-volt shock. Of course, as might be expected, many individuals protested and urged that the session be terminated. When confronted with the experimenter's stern demands that they continue, however, most yielded and shocked the victim time and time again. Moreover, they continued to obey despite the fact that at 300 volts, the learner pounded on the wall (as if in pain) and soon afterward stopped pro-

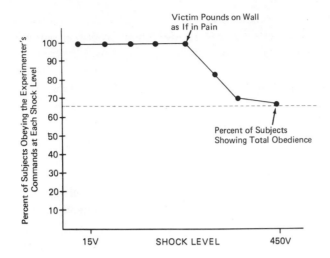

FIGURE 19. Direct commands from an authority as an antecedent of aggression. Fully 65% of the participants in Milgram's (1963) initial experiment were totally obedient to commands requiring that they deliver increasingly strong electric shocks to another person. (Based on data from Milgram, 1963.)

viding answers on the bogus learning task. In view of the fact that the experimenter actually had no means of enforcing his commands —subjects were totally free to leave any time they desired and had already received payment for their time—the tremendous capacity of even a relatively powerless authority figure to elicit aggression on the part of many persons was made abundantly clear.

In further experiments, Milgram (1965b, 1974) found that similar results could be obtained even under conditions that would be expected to reduce such obedience markedly. For example, when the study was moved from its original location on the campus of a highly prestigious university to a run-down office building in the business district of a nearby city, subjects showed only a slight and nonsignificant reduction in obedience. Similarly, a large proportion (62.5%) continued to obey even when the accomplice complained about the painfulness of the shocks and begged to be released from the study. Finally, and most surprising of all, many (fully 30%) continued to obey even when obedience required that they grasp the victim's hand and physically force it down upon the shock plate! Considered as a whole, these findings leave little doubt that orders from a source of authority can induce many individuals to physically harm victims who have neither frustrated nor provoked them in any manner.[2]

Before concluding this discussion of Milgram's research, we should note that although the influence of authority figures is often great, it *can* be counteracted. In particular, two factors seem quite effective in reducing the ability of such persons to command hostile actions on the part of their subordinates.

First, and perhaps of greatest importance, obedience is often sharply reduced under conditions in which individuals feel directly responsible for the consequences of their actions. In Milgram's studies, participants were informed by the experimenter that he would take personal responsibility for the safety and well-being of the victim. This was a reasonable procedure, for in many life situations, it is the persons in authority who, in the final analysis, must bear the blame for any untoward acts. (Recall that it was Lieutenant Calley and not the men under his command who was finally held accountable for the tragic Mylai massacre during the Vietnam war.) Given the presence of this condition in Milgram's research, it is not very surprising that many participants showed total obedience to the experimenter's commands; after all, it was *he* who would take the blame if the victim was harmed. But what if they themselves were to be held responsible for any negative outcomes? Would obedience be reduced? Evidence regarding this question has been obtained in several recent experiments. For example, in one investigation (Tilker, 1970), subjects were found to be far less willing to obey when they had been informed that the responsibility for the victim's health and welfare rested entirely with them. Further, individuals have been found to demonstrate far less obedience when they themselves must deliver the shocks to the victim, than when they must merely transmit the experimenter's orders for increasingly powerful jolts to another person, who then carries them out (Kilham & Mann, 1974). Increased responsibility for one's actions, then, seems to counteract strongly the tendency to obey in a blind and unthinking manner.

A second factor that also seems to be effective in this regard is suggested by careful observation of situations in which the orders of such persons are actually defied. In many such cases, the following pattern emerges: first, one brave and dedicated individual, or a few

[2] For a discussion of the complex ethical issues raised by Milgram's research, see Elms (1972) and Milgram (1974).

such persons, defy the source of authority, and then many others follow. This pattern of events suggests that one effective means for counteracting blind obedience to the directives of authority figures may be that of exposing their followers to *disobedient models*—others who refuse to obey. That such procedures may actually be highly effective in reducing obedience is suggested by the results of several interesting experiments (Milgram, 1965a; Powers & Geen, 1972). For example, in the earlier of these investigations (Milgram, 1965a), obedience was reduced from 65% to only 10% when subjects were exposed to two other persons (confederates) who defied the experimenter's commands at two different points during the session (see Figure 20).

Together, these findings concerning responsibility for one's own actions and exposure to disobedient models provide a ray of hope to counteract the generally gloomy picture painted by Milgram's investigations. Although the power of authority figures to command obedience even with respect to dangerous acts of aggression is great, it *can* be counteracted under appropriate conditions. The long and ever-growing list of atrocities carried out in the name of "orders," however, suggests that active steps must be taken if such conditions are to be attained.

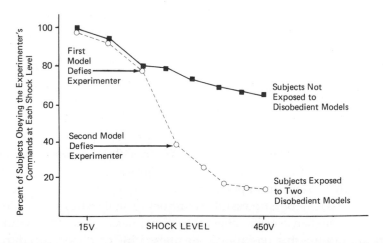

FIGURE 20. Counteracting destructive obedience. Subjects exposed to two disobedient models demonstrated a much lower tendency to obey the experimenter's commands than subjects not exposed to such models. (Based on data from Milgram, 1965b.)

## THE "INNOCENT BYSTANDER" STRIKES AGAIN: THIRD-PARTY INSTIGATION OF AGGRESSION

Many aggressive actions take place under conditions where only the aggressor and his or her victim are present on the scene (e.g., in dark alleys, on deserted city streets). In many other cases, however, acts of aggression occur in settings where several additional persons not directly involved in such behavior are also present. This fact leads to an interesting question: Can such individuals, by their mere presence or overt actions, influence the aggression that ensues? Informal observation suggests that this may well be the case. Crowds of onlookers often urge angry individuals on and in this manner facilitate the occurrence of dangerous altercations. Conversely, the presence of some individuals, at least, may strongly inhibit the performance of overt acts of aggression (e.g., consider the potential influence of heavily armed police). In short, there appear to be reasonable, informal grounds for assuming that uninvolved bystanders can strongly affect the frequency or probability of overt aggression in several different contexts. More formal evidence in support of this suggestion has also been obtained in a number of different experiments. Although all of this research has been concerned with the impact of bystanders upon aggression, it divides, logically, into two groups of studies, which have focused, respectively, upon the words and actions of such persons, on the one hand, and on their mere presence and apparent values, on the other. Thus, we will consider these two lines of investigation separately.

### Third-Party Instigation of Aggression: The Words or Actions of Bystanders

The earliest study concerned with third-party instigation of aggression was conducted by Stanley Milgram (1964). As an extension of his earlier research on obedience, Milgram sought to determine whether suggestions from peers, as well as commands from a source of authority, would be successful in inducing male subjects to deliver seemingly intense electric shocks to a helpless, innocent victim. In order to examine this possibility, he altered his original procedures so that three "teachers," rather than only one, took part in each session. Two of these individuals were confederates of the experimenter, who assisted the third person—the naïve subject—in instructing the learner in the experimental materials. Another major change from the original procedures was that in this study, there was no requirement that the subject increase the level of shock directed to the victim each time he made an error. Instead, the shock administered was to be decided by the teachers and would be set at the lowest level suggested by any of these three individuals. During the experiment, however, the two confederates continuously urged the subject to raise the shocks to the learner each time he made an incorrect response. In this manner, participants were exposed to steady social pressure in the direction of increasing assaults against this person.

Not surprisingly, the confederates' recommendations had a strong effect upon the subjects' behavior. As shown in Figure 21, they gradually raised the strength of the shocks they employed over the course of

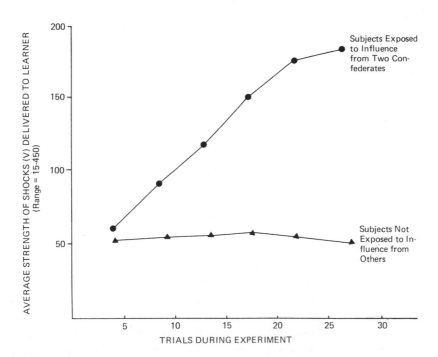

FIGURE 21. Third-party instigation of aggression. Subjects exposed to suggestions from two confederates that they increase the strength of their shocks to the learner delivered much stronger jolts to this person than subjects not exposed to such social influence. (Based on data from Milgram, 1964.)

the session. In contrast, participants in a control group, who performed in the absence of the confederates, chose to administer constant, mild punishment to the victim. In short, the repeated urgings of
the accomplices induced subjects to behave in a more aggressive manner than would have otherwise been the case.

That similar effects can be induced by passive spectators as well
as by active participants in the experimental setting is indicated by the
results of an additional study (Borden & Taylor, 1973). Here, subjects
competing with a fictitious opponent in the Taylor reaction-time task
(see pp. 66–68) were urged by an audience of three individuals to raise
the strength of their shock settings. Results indicated that the subjects
were strongly influenced by such suggestions and did increase the
strength of their jolts significantly over those used in a period when
they were alone in the experimental room. Moreover, in one condition, they maintained this heightened level of aggression even after
the spectators left. Fortunately, there is one ray of hope in other findings of this investigation: when urged to lower the level of their
shocks, participants also complied. (Disappointingly, however, they
did not retain this reduction in aggression after the spectators departed.)

Together, the findings of these experiments and those conducted
by other researchers (cf. Gaebelein, 1973) suggest that the verbal
statements of bystanders may often play an important role in instigating overt aggression. Apparently, peers as well as sources of authority
can facilitate aggressive behavior through calls or recommendations
for such actions.

### *Third-Party Instigation of Aggression: The Presence and Apparent Values of Bystanders*

That bystanders can influence the occurrence of aggression
through their overt actions is hardly surprising; many forms of behavior are affected by social pressure, and there is no obvious reason why
aggression should prove impervious to such effects. Somewhat less expected, however, is the finding that such individuals may strongly affect aggressive behavior when they take no direct action to produce
such results. In particular, it appears that bystanders can often influence the occurrence of aggression through their simple presence on
the scene. For example, in the first study concerned with this issue

(Baron, 1971a), male subjects were provided with an opportunity to aggress against a confederate within the usual teacher–learner paradigm either while alone in the experimental room or while in the presence of an audience of two persons described as a visiting professor and a graduate student. Results indicated that when the audience was present throughout the session, it inhibited aggression against the victim. Similarly, Scheier, Fenigstein, and Buss (1974) noted that the presence of an audience of two individuals (a male and a female) significantly reduced later aggression by male subjects, provided they maintained a high level of eye contact with the spectators. Together, these initial studies seemed to suggest that the presence of other persons often reduces the strength or likelihood of overt aggression. A more recent investigation by Borden (1975), however, indicates that whether the presence of an audience will facilitate or inhibit later aggression depends quite strongly upon the apparent values of these persons.

In this study, male subjects competed with a fictitious opponent on the Taylor reaction-time task. During the first half of the session, the subject performed in the presence of a male or a female observer. For half of the participants, the observer appeared to be a pacifist, opposed to aggression (he or she wore a coat with a prominent peace symbol and was introduced as a member of a pacifistic organization). For the remaining half, the observer appeared to be an individual who might well approve of aggression (he or she wore a coat with a large patch indicating membership in a karate club and was introduced as an instructor of this martial art). Halfway through the session, the observer left, and the subject continued to compete with the fictitious opponent while alone in the room. On the basis of previous research, it was predicted that the presence of the pacifistic observer would inhibit aggression, while the presence of the aggressive observer would facilitate such behavior. As can be seen in Figure 22, these predictions were generally confirmed. Subjects were considerably more aggressive in the presence of the aggressive observer than they were after this person departed and were slightly less aggressive in the presence of the pacifistic observer than they were once this person had left.

As noted by Borden (1975, p. 571), these results, when combined with the findings of previous studies, suggest that whether the presence of bystanders will facilitate or inhibit aggression depends quite strongly upon whether the aggressors anticipate approval or disap-

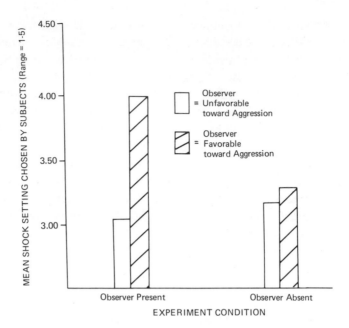

FIGURE 22. The effects of bystanders (observers) upon aggression. The presence of a by-stander who seemed to hold favorable attitudes toward aggression facilitated assaults by subjects against their opponent, while the presence of a bystander who seemed to be opposed to aggression inhibited such behavior. (Based on data from Borden, 1975.)

proval from these persons for engaging in such behavior. When they anticipate approval, aggression will be enhanced, while when they anticipate disapproval, it will often be reduced. Regardless of the direction of such effects, however, it is clear that bystanders can influence the likelihood and magnitude of aggression through their simple presence on the scene, as well as through overt, explicit actions.

## SUMMARY

Aggression does not occur in a "social vacuum." Rather, it often stems from aspects of the social environment that instigate its occurrence and influence both its form and its direction. The social antecedent of aggression that has perhaps received most attention in this regard is *frustration*—the blocking of ongoing, goal-directed behavior. Although this factor is widely assumed to enhance overt aggression, evidence regarding its influence has been quite mixed. While some experiments suggest that interpersonal thwarting enhances later aggression, others suggest that it exerts only weak effects in this regard or may totally fail to elicit such behavior. Although no final resolution regarding this controversy is yet at hand, existing evidence suggests that frustration is a relatively weak antecedent of aggression, and will facilitate its occurrence only when relatively intense or viewed as arbitrary and unexpected by the persons who endure it.

A second factor, and one that seems to exert somewat stronger and more consistent effects upon aggression, is that of direct provocation from others. With respect to physical provocation, a large number of studies suggest that individuals respond to such treatment in a highly reciprocal fashion, returning blow for blow and assault for assault. Further, many persons seem to respond aggressively to the mere suggestion that others harbor hostile intentions toward them, regardless of whether these are translated into overt actions or not. Turning to verbal provocation, existing evidence suggests that insults, taunts, and related provocations often elicit physical replies. As a result, incidents that begin with verbal exchanges frequently escalate into overtly violent ones.

Exposure to the actions of aggressive models—other persons acting in a highly aggressive manner—is another powerful elicitor of overt aggression. Eye-witness accounts of the events occurring during riots and similar events suggest that live aggressive models may play an important initiating role in collective violence—an observation that is supported by many laboratory studies. Most research concerned with the impact of aggressive models, however, has focused on the influence of portrayals of violence in the mass media. Such research has gone through three distinct phases, characterized by growing sophistication and methodological refinement. The major findings, however, have remained constant in suggesting that exposure to a steady diet of media violence may indeed increase the tendencies of observers to engage in similar actions themselves.

During time of war, many aggressive actions—including frightening atrocities—are performed in response to the directives of authorities. Intriguing research conducted by Stanley Milgram and others suggests that such effects may be quite widespread. Indeed, when ordered to deliver strong and potentially dangerous electric shocks to another person, many individuals readily yield and follow the commands of even a relatively powerless source of authority. Fortunately, it appears that such tendencies to engage in blind, destructive obedience can be counteracted by assigning responsibility for any harm produced directly to the individuals involved and by exposing such persons to disobedient models who refuse to obey.

Many instances of aggression take place in the presence of other persons not directly involved in their occurrence. Growing evidence suggests that such bystanders can exert important effects upon aggression in two distinct ways. First, they can either enhance or inhibit its magnitude through direct actions (e.g., verbal recommendations that it be increased or reduced). Second, they can produce similar effects simply through their presence on the scene. Specifically, it appears that the presence of bystanders may enhance overt aggression when aggressors anticipate approval from spectators for engaging in such behavior but will inhibit such behavior when aggressors anticipate disapproval or censure for such actions.

# 4

# *Environmental and Situational Determinants of Aggression*

It's a hot and steamy day, with temperatures in the high 80s, so you utter a sigh of resignation as you enter your office and find that the air-conditioning is out of order for the third time within a week. As the morning passes, you find yourself growing more and more uncomfortable. Your clothes become soaked with perspiration, and soon, even the simplest tasks begin to seem quite burdensome and difficult. Just when you feel you are approaching your limit, one of your co-workers, a pleasant fellow named Tim, approaches your desk. He is relatively new on the job and often asks your help and advice. As luck would have it, on this occasion, he has even more questions than usual. As you leaf through the large pile of papers he has brought for you to examine, you find yourself becoming increasingly irritated. Why, you reason, should you have to do his work as well as your own? Oblivious to your growing annoyance, however, he continues to pose one question after another. Finally, unable to control your temper any longer, you sweep the papers onto the floor and shout at him in a threatening and hostile manner. Tim beats a hasty retreat and avoids you for the rest of the day. Later, when the air-conditioning is functioning once again, you find yourself feeling guilty for your outburst. Tim had done nothing, after all, to deserve such harsh treatment, and you regret having upset and embarrassed him. Was it the heat, you wonder, that caused you to behave in such an obnoxious manner?

For the past two weeks, your friend Beth has been away on a vacation with her fiancé Steve. Much has happened in her absence, so you have a great deal to discuss and are looking forward to a very pleasant lunch. As you sit thinking about all the things you want to tell her, she appears at the table and takes a seat at your side. She is in a very good mood and looks both rested and tanned. Yet, there is one thing quite puzzling about her appearance: despite the fact that it is a very pleasant spring day, she is wearing a long-sleeved sweater with a high turtleneck collar. After a few minutes of animated and friendly conversation, you casually call this fact to her attention. Beth's first reaction is to blush and

125

refuse to answer. When you press her on the matter, however, she glances around and, once sure no one is looking, rolls up a sleeve. You are surprised to see a number of bruises upon her arm. And when she pulls down her turtleneck collar so you can see inside, you notice several distinct sets of teeth marks upon her neck. "It's Steve," she whispers. "He gets pretty aggressive when he gets romantic. But I like it!" At this, she giggles, and you both laugh a good deal about this unexpected turn in your friend's love life. When she leaves, though, you find yourself wondering about this seeming link between sex and aggression. Do flames of passion really ignite violent actions? Or is there some other explanation for the surprising behavior of your friend and her lover?

You are enjoying a quiet drink at an elegant cocktail party. Everyone around you is dressed in the height of fashion, and you recognize many of the other guests as being among the most successful and prominent people in town. On your right is a noted surgeon, on your left a wealthy banker, while behind you, surrounded by a crowd of admirers, stands a young attorney widely acknowledged to have a bright future in the realm of politics. As you lounge against the bar, considering your good fortune at finding yourself in such company, your thoughts are suddenly interrupted by a harsh and surly voice: "What in blazes are you staring at? Would you like a punch in the nose?" Startled, you look up and notice that wholly without intention, you have been staring in the direction of a burly, middle-aged fellow. Quickly, you stammer an excuse, but your words are to no avail. In fact, they only seem to irritate your adversary further. The exchange continues, with added apologies on your part, but no matter what you say, he takes it the wrong way and grows increasingly angry. Soon, in fact, he is shouting at you at the top of his lungs. When he removes his coat and squares off for a fight, however, several other guests rush to restrain him, and he is quickly dragged—still shouting—from the room. At this point, the host approaches and quietly remarks, "Don't pay any attention to Frank. He always gets a little raucous when he's had too much to drink." The disturbance passes quickly, and soon the party continues as before. Things are not quite the same for you, however. Still shaken by your experience, you contemplate the glass in your own hand. Was it really a simple overdose of alcohol that accounted for this unpleasant outburst? Or was some other factor responsible for its occurrence? Still pondering these thoughts, you walk to the bar and pour yourself another drink.

At first glance, these incidents seem totally unrelated. In reality, however, all illustrate an important yet frequently overlooked fact: contrary to popular belief, aggression does not always stem from the words or deeds of other persons. Rather, in many cases, it is elicited and encouraged by a wide range of factors not closely related to the ongoing process of social interaction. Thus, in the first example presented above, aggression was enhanced by unpleasantly warm temperatures. In the second, it seemed to spring from heightened sexual arousal, while in the third, it stemmed, largely unprovoked, from the influence of a popular drug. Of course, in these and all other instances, aggression remains a form of social behavior and is directed toward other persons. Further, it generally seems to follow some specific action on the part of the victim. Careful examination of such incidents, however, suggests that their major antecedents often lie outside the statements or actions of the targets of violence and are *not* primarily social in nature.

As suggested by even the few examples presented on pp. 125–126, many different factors not directly related to social interaction seem capable of influencing the occurrence of overt aggression. Among the most important of these, however, are several relating to the physical environment and several involving various situational conditions. It is upon such variables that the present chapter will focus. In particular, we will examine the impact upon aggression of such environmental factors as *noise, crowding,* and *heat,* as well as that of situational factors such as *heightened arousal,* the presence of *aggressive cues,* and the influence of various *drugs.* As will soon become apparent, these and related variables often seem to play as crucial a role in the elicitation of human violence as the more widely studied social conditions we examined in Chapter 3.


## ENVIRONMENTAL DETERMINANTS OF AGGRESSION: NOISE, CROWDING, AND HEAT

Anyone who has ridden regularly on crowded subways or buses, worked next door to a noisy construction project, or lived through intense heat waves without the benefit of air conditioning knows from his or her own experience that behavior can often be strongly affected by the physical environment. Our physiological state, the way we feel, and even our performance on many tasks is often strongly influenced by various aspects of the physical world around us (cf. Glass & Krantz, 1975; Proshansky, Rivlin, & Ittelson, 1976). Moreover, such effects often seem to spill over into our relations with others, affecting our judgments about them, our liking for them, and even our willingness to offer them aid (see Altman, 1975; Glass & Singer, 1972; Freedman, 1975). Given the existence of such effects, it seems only reasonable that aggression, too, might be affected by the physical environment. Not surprisingly, this suspicion has been confirmed by a growing body of empirical evidence (see O'Neal & McDonald, 1976). A number of different factors, ranging from darkness on the one hand (Page & Moss, 1976), through phases of the moon on the other (Lieber & Sherin, 1972), have been investigated in this research. By far the greatest amount of attention, however, has been focused on the impact of three variables: *noise, crowding,* and *heat.*

## Noise and Aggression: The Sound of Violence?

As an unpleasant side effect of increasing industrialization, widespread arrival of the two- or even three-car family, and rapidly growing air traffic, noise levels in many major cities have risen sharply in recent years. Health authorities have reacted to this increase with stern warnings regarding the potential hazards it may pose (Dey, 1970; Kryter, 1970). Indeed, it now appears that the levels of noise commonly encountered in many locations within urban areas may, over a period of time, cause permanent hearing losses and even deafness. Certainly, this result is serious enough in and of itself. Unfortunately, though, it may not be the only type of harmful effect produced. The findings of several recent investigations suggest that under some conditions, loud and unpleasant noise may also facilitate the occurrence of interpersonal aggression (e.g., Donnerstein & Wilson, 1976; Geen & O'Neal, 1969; Konečni, 1975b). This is far from an obvious finding and requires careful consideration. Before turning to the psychological mechanisms that seem to underlie it, however, we will examine the empirical evidence itself.

The first investigation concerned with the possible impact of noise upon aggression was conducted by Geen and O'Neal (1969). Basically, their study consisted of two major parts. In the first, participants (male college students) viewed short excerpts taken from either a highly aggressive boxing film or a nonaggressive track-race film. In the second, they were asked to evaluate an essay supposedly written by a male confederate in a special manner. Briefly, subjects were to express their evaluations in terms of the number and strength of electric shocks they delivered to this person. Good essays were to receive a small number of (and perhaps relatively weak) shocks, while bad ones were to "earn" a larger number of (and presumably stronger) jolts. While delivering their evaluations to the confederate, the subjects wore earphones, and half were exposed to white noise, presented at 60-db (decibel) intensity; the remaining individuals heard nothing over the earphones. The results of the study are summarized in Figure 23. As can be readily seen, exposure to the noise did affect the level of aggression directed toward the confederate, but only in the case of subjects who had previously witnessed the violent film. Among individuals in this experimental condition, the presence of the noise seemed to enhance assaults against the victim. Similar effects were not observed, however, among participants who had viewed only the nonviolent track film. Indeed, in this case, aggression was slightly higher when the noise was absent. In short, findings suggested that noise could in fact enhance ongoing aggression, but only under fairly specific circumstances.

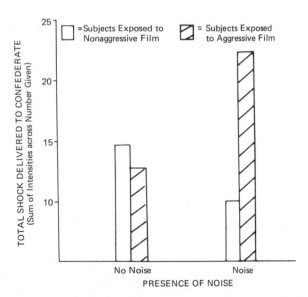

Figure 23. The effects of noise upon aggression. Among subjects exposed to an aggressive film, white noise facilitated attacks against a male confederate. (Based upon data from Geen & O'Neal, 1969.)

Results pointing to similar general conclusions have also been reported in two recent investigations conducted by Donnerstein and Wilson (1976). In the first of these studies, male subjects were first angered or not angered by a confederate (he evaluated an essay they wrote favorably or quite harshly) and were then provided with an opportunity to aggress against this person within the teacher–learner paradigm devised by Buss (1961). While serving as the teacher and delivering electric shocks to the confederate, subjects wore earphones and were exposed to one-second bursts of either low-intensity (65-db) or high-intensity (95-db) noise. Results were quite straightforward: in the case of participants who had previously been angered by the confederate, aggression was sharply enhanced by the high-intensity noise. In the case of those who had been treated in a less provocative manner by this person, however, similar effects failed to emerge (see Figure 24).

In a second and closely related study, Donnerstein and Wilson

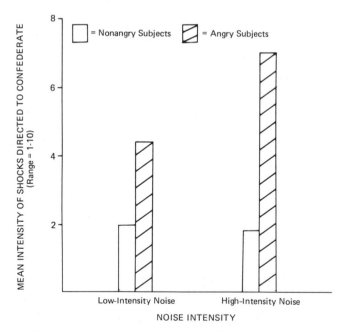

FIGURE 24. Effects of low-intensity (65-db) and high-intensity (95-db) noise upon aggression. Exposure to high-intensity noise facilitated aggression, but only by angry individuals. (Based on data from Donnerstein & Wilson, 1976.)

(1976) added a no-noise control group to the design of their research and also arranged conditions so that subjects were exposed to the presence or absence of noise prior to their opportunity to aggress against the confederate rather than during this period. Further, a condition in which subjects were led to believe that they could terminate the aversive noise simply by requesting its cessation was also included in the experiment. Despite these changes, the results were quite straightforward: when the subjects had previously had no control over the noise they heard (the same conditions as those prevailing in the first study), exposure to high-intensity stimulation of this type significantly facilitated assaults against the victim by angry but not by nonangry individuals. Under conditions in which participants had previously been told that they could control the noise they heard, however, similar effects failed to emerge. As noted by Donnerstein and Wilson, this may have been the case because under these latter conditions (i.e., when the subjects believed that they could terminate the noise at will), they found it to be less arousing or unpleasant than when it was not under their influence.

Together, the findings reported by Geen and O'Neal, Donnerstein and Wilson, Konečni, and others suggest that exposure to loud and presumably irritating noise may indeed sometimes facilitate aggression. In particular, the fact that such effects seem to occur only among angered individuals or those who have witnessed filmed violence points to the following conclusion: noise may facilitate ongoing or later aggression, but only when such behavior represents a relatively strong or prepotent tendency among potential aggressors. That is, if such individuals have been angered, annoyed, or otherwise instigated to aggress, the presence of loud noise in the environment may facilitate such actions. In the absence of these and similar predisposing conditions, however, noise will probably fail to enhance direct assaults against others.[1]

This is an interesting suggestion, and one quite consistent with existing empirical evidence. Yet, in and of itself, it is only part of the picture. Why, it may reasonably be asked, should this be the case?

[1] One puzzling aspect of the research conducted to date that should be mentioned in passing is that while Geen and O'Neal obtained increased aggression in response to noise of only 60 db, higher intensities of such stimulation have been required to produce such effects in later research. This discrepancy suggests that the precise manner in which noise is delivered to subjects and the context within which it is presented may have important effects that should be subjected to systematic study.

What psychological mechanisms underlie the seemingly restricted impact of noise upon aggression? One possible answer is suggested by the fact that exposure to loud noise induces heightened physiological arousal (see Glass & Krantz, 1975). It is a well-established fact within psychology that increased arousal, in turn, tends to facilitate the performance of dominant responses. Thus, as argued by Bandura (1973), the heightened arousal stemming from noise, or any other environmental condition, would be expected to facilitate overt aggression only under conditions in which such behavior represents a strong or dominant response among the persons involved. Given the frequency with which we are all exposed to annoyance or provocation from others, these proposals have unsettling implications. In particular, they suggest that the high levels of noise present in many urban areas may often play an important role in enhancing, if not actually in initiating, harmful instances of interpersonal aggression. While further evidence is clearly needed before any definitive conclusions regarding this issue can be reached, the mere possibility that such effects exist adds a telling argument to recent appeals for the control of our growing "noise pollution" (cf. Baron, 1970).

## The Effects of Crowding

Despite all efforts to the contrary, world population continues to increase at an alarming rate. At the same time, of course, the amount of physical space available for human habitation remains essentially unchanged. The result is all too obvious at many locations around the globe: in the closing decades of the 20th century, crowding has become a very common state of affairs (see Figure 25).

The presence of very large numbers of human beings within a limited geographic area poses many problems. Natural resources are strained to the limit, and irreversible damage may be inflicted on the physical environment. But what of the impact of such conditions upon social behavior? Does crowding exert adverse effects in this respect as well? And, more directly related to the context of the present discussion, do such conditions influence the occurrence of overt aggression?

Informal observation seems to suggest positive replies in both cases. For example, the incidence of serious crime, juvenile delinquency, out-of-wedlock births, and other signs of social disintegration does seem to be much higher in the "sinful" cities than in peaceful

FIGURE 25. Crowding is an all-too-common condition in the late 20th century.

rural or suburban areas (although the magnitude of this difference has decreased sharply in recent years). And common sense suggests that the greater the number of persons present in a given area, the greater the likelihood that two or more will become involved in aggressive encounters. Unfortunately, in sharp contrast to the simplicity of such suggestions, systematic research on these issues has painted a much more complicated picture.

First, with respect to the possibility of a relationship between crowding and social disorder, recent, sophisticated investigations have yielded largely negative findings. For example, in one well-known study, Freedman, Heshka, and Levy (1975) obtained two measures of crowding—the number of persons per residential acre and the average number of individuals per room—for 338 different neighborhoods within New York City. They then related these two indices of crowding to such signs of social disintegration as the incidence of juvenile delinquency, the prevalence of venereal disease, infant mortality, and the frequency of illegitimate births. Results at first suggested a strong link between crowding and such negative outcomes. That is, the greater the degree of crowding, the higher the social pathology. When the impact of such factors as income, educational level, and ethnic background of the persons involved was statistically controlled, however, no important relationship remained. Indeed, crowding and social pathology appeared to be totally unrelated.

Turning to the possibility of a relationship between crowding and aggression, correlational studies have again yielded generally negative findings (see Altman, 1975; Freedman, 1975). In particular, such investigations have failed to uncover any significant relationship between urban density and crime. Further, no indication of a link between crowding and the incidence of crimes of violence—such as murder, rape, or aggravated assault—has come to light. Such findings suggest that aggression—at least in its most dangerous forms—may not be strongly affected by the density with which human beings are packed into a given geographic area.

In contrast to the uniformly negative findings of such field investigations, however, the results of laboratory experiments have been quite mixed. For example, in one interesting study, Freedman and his colleagues (Freedman, Levy, Buchanan, & Price, 1972) had groups of from 6 to 10 persons (all men, all women, or both sexes) listen to tape recordings of what were purported to be five actual trials. After hearing each case, subjects were asked to decide whether the defendant was guilty or innocent and, if guilty, to recommend an appropriate sentence. In one experimental condition, all of these procedures took place in a very small room, in which each participant had only 12 square feet of space at his or her disposal. In a second, the same procedures were conducted in a larger room, in which each subject had 25 square feet available. The results indicated that the effects of this manipulation depended upon the sexual composition of the groups. In the case of groups consisting entirely of males, crowding increased the severity of the sentences assigned to the defendant. In the case of groups consisting entirely of females, it produced the opposite effect. And in the mixed-sex groups, crowding had no appreciable influence upon the subjects' recommendation whatever. If the severity of the sentences handed down by the participants is accepted as representing an indirect measure of aggression, these findings may be interpreted as suggesting that crowding may indeed enhance aggression, but only on the part of males.

Such conclusions are called into question, however, by other studies, which have reported that crowding may *reduce* rather than enhance overt aggression. For example, in one such experiment, Loo (1972) allowed 4 to 5-year-old children to play together in groups of six in either a large area (265.1 square feet) or a much smaller one (90 square feet). Their behavior during a 48-minute session was carefully observed, and the incidence of aggressive responses was recorded. As can be seen in Figure 26, the results were quite different from those reported by Freedman *et al.* (1972): in the case of males, aggression was sharply reduced by crowded conditions. While females failed to show similar effects, this latter negative finding may be largely artifactual in nature; the girls demonstrated such a low level of aggression even in the uncrowded condition that further reductions in such behavior may not have been possible. In any case, it is clear that in this investigation, crowding *inhibited* rather than facilitated overt acts of aggression.

Together with the results of other investigations (e.g., Hutt &

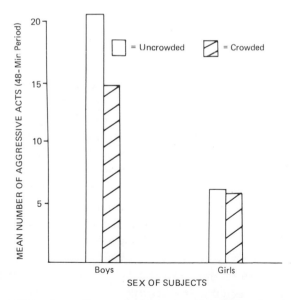

FIGURE 26. The effects of crowding upon aggression. Crowding reduced overt aggression among 4 to 5-year-old boys, but failed to produce similar effects among girls of the same age. (The latter finding may be artifactual, however; see text for further discussion.) (Based on data from Loo, 1972.)

Vaizey, 1966), the findings reported by Freedman and his colleagues and those reported by Loo present a confusing picture. Can crowding both facilitate *and* inhibit aggression by persons subjected to it? A theoretical framework presented recently by Freedman (1975) suggests that this may actually be the case. Basically, Freedman suggests that crowding acts primarily as an *intensifier* of behavior. More specifically, he proposes that it intensifies or enhances an individual's typical reactions to any situation. If these are positive, then crowding will make them even more favorable, while if they are negative, crowding will magnify their unfavorable nature. In Freedman's own words:

> I propose that crowding by itself has neither good effects nor bad effects on people but rather *serves to intensify the individual's typical reactions to the situation.* If he ordinarily would find the circumstances pleasant, would enjoy having people around him, would think of other people as friends, would in a word have a positive reaction to the other people, he will have a more positive reaction under conditions of high density. On the other hand, if ordinarily he would dislike the other people, find it unpleasant having them around, feel aggressive toward them, and in general have a negative reaction to the presence of the other people, he will have a more negative reaction under conditions of high density. (pp. 89–90)

The type of intensification to which Freedman refers is a phenomenon with which most of us are quite familiar. For example, consider a basically pleasant situation: eating a good meal in a fine restaurant. Freedman's theory suggests that we will find this experience more enjoyable under crowded than under noncrowded conditions, and informal observation indicates that this is clearly the case. Indeed, the pleasure derived from such a meal might well be entirely dissipated if we found ourselves to be the only diners in the entire establishment. Similarly, consider a somewhat unpleasant situation: waiting in a dentist's reception room. Here, Freedman's theory predicts that we will find the experience more unpleasant under crowded than under uncrowded conditions, and again, informal observation indicates that this would be true. More formal support for the intensification hypothesis has been obtained in several preliminary studies (see Freedman, 1975). However, discussion of this research would take us far afield from our main interest: the effects of crowding upon aggression.

Returning to this topic, it is readily apparent that Freedman's proposals lead to relatively straightforward predictions: under conditions in which our initial reactions to a situation or to other persons are unfavorable in nature, crowding may increase the likelihood of overt aggression, while under conditions in which such reactions are basically favorable, the opposite may be true. Interestingly, these suggestions seem to fit quite well with the results of previous research on crowding and aggression. For example, in the study conducted by Loo (1972), subjects were all drawn from the same class in school. Since they already knew each other quite well, it is reasonable to expect that their initial reactions to one another would be quite favorable and that crowding would thus reduce aggression—the results actually obtained. Correspondingly, it is also possible to explain the findings reported by Freedman, Levy, Buchanan, and Price (1972) within this framework if it is assumed that in American society, men often react to the presence of male strangers with suspicion or mild hostility, while women do not demonstrate such reactions. Granting this assumption, it would be predicted that men would be more aggressive under crowded than under uncrowded conditions, while women would not—again, the results actually obtained.

In short, Freedman's intensification hypothesis seems capable of accounting quite adequately for the findings of previous research concerned with the impact of crowding upon aggression. Unfortunately, though, it has not as yet been subjected to direct, independent test in this regard. At present, then, it is best viewed as a promising—but as yet unverified—possibility. Regardless of whether Freedman's proposals are confirmed or disproved by further studies, it seems reasonable, on the basis of existing evidence, to offer the following conclusions: crowding does not appear to exert any simple, global effects upon aggression. However, it seems capable of both facilitating and inhibiting such behavior under appropriate—but as yet only partially understood—conditions.

### Aggression and Heat: The "Long, Hot Summer" Revisited

During the late 1960s and early 1970s, a wave of dangerous riots swept through the United States and several other nations. Not surprisingly, many different factors—ranging from continued social injustice on the one hand, through provocative actions by police and other civil authorities on the other—were suggested as possible causes of these events (U.S. Riot Commission, 1968). One variable that often received considerable "play" in this respect in the mass media, however, was ambient temperature. That is, newspaper, radio, and television accounts of these frightening events often suggested that uncomfortable heat played a crucial role in their initiation. More specifically, such descriptions suggested that prolonged exposure to temperatures in the high 80s or 90s (Fahrenheit) had shortened tempers, increased irritability, and so set the stage for the outbreak of collective violence.

In general, these suggestions rested largely on "common sense" and informal observation. Two indirect types of empirical evidence, however, were often marshaled in their support. First, the results of several laboratory studies conducted by William Griffitt and his colleagues (Griffitt, 1970; Griffitt & Veitch, 1971) pointed to the conclusion that consistent with "common knowledge," many individuals did indeed become more irritable, more prone to outbursts of temper, and more negative in their reactions to others under uncomfortably hot than under comfortably cool environmental conditions. Second, systematic observation revealed that a large proportion of the serious instances of collective violence occurring in major cities during the late 1960s did in fact take place during the hot summer months, when heat-wave or near-heat-wave conditions prevailed (Goranson & King, 1970; U.S. Riot Commission, 1968).

Together, these observations and findings seemed to provide convincing support for the existence of an important and relatively straightforward link between high ambient temperatures and the occurrence of overt aggression. But is this actually the case? Does exposure to uncomfortable heat always—or even usually—facilitate the later development of assaults against others? More than five years of research on this topic by the present author and his associates suggests a qualified "no" to such questions. While there does indeed seem to be a link between ambient temperature and aggression, it has turned out to be far more complex and intricate in nature than that suggested by such phrases as "hot under the collar," "the heat of anger," or "the long, hot summer." In fact, the findings of recent research on this relationhip suggest that under appropriate conditions, uncomfortable heat can actually inhibit—as well as facilitate—overt acts of aggression.

Given the unexpected nature of these results and their potentially important implications regarding the occurrence of aggression in naturalistic settings, investigations concerned with the impact of ambient temperature upon aggression seem worthy of careful attention. While such research has proceeded in several different directions and has involved more than the usual share of false starts and empirical blind alleys, it can be divided into three distinct phases: (1) naïve empiricism; (2) preliminary theory construction; and (3) later theory construction and validation. Accordingly, the present discussion will parallel this order of development.

## Naïve Empiricism: Is the "Long, Hot Summer" Really Hot?

The first investigation undertaken to examine the impact of high ambient temperatures upon aggression (Baron, 1972a) was, in an important sense, purely empirical in nature. Basically, it was designed to examine the "common-sense" suggestion that hot and uncomfortable environmental conditions would cause individuals to become tense and irritable and would thus increase the likelihood that they would aggress against others.

In order to investigate this suggestion, male subjects were first either angered or not angered by a male confederate of the experimenter (he evaluated essays they had written either favorably or unfavorably) and were then provided with an opportunity to aggress against this person within the standard teacher–learner pardigm. For half of the participants, these procedures were carried out under comfortably cool ambient temperatures (72–75°F), while for the remainder, they were conducted under extremely hot conditions (91–95°F). On the basis of previous research (e.g., Griffitt, 1970) and repeated references to the irritating impact of the "long, hot summer" in the mass media, it was tentatively predicted that among angered subjects, at least, high ambient temperatures would facilitate assaults against the victim.

As shown in Figure 27, these seemingly straightforward predictions were definitely *not* confirmed. While angered subjects did in fact demonstrate higher levels of aggression than those who had not been provoked by the confederate, exposure to uncomfortable heat failed to produce the expected effects. In fact, such environmental conditions actually seemed to *reduce* rather than to enhance aggression by both angered and nonangered participants.

At first glance, such findings were both unexpected and puzzling. Fortunately, however, one possible explanation for their occurrence was suggested by comments made by subjects during postexperimental debriefing sessions. In many cases, individuals in the high-ambient-temperature condition volunteered the information that they

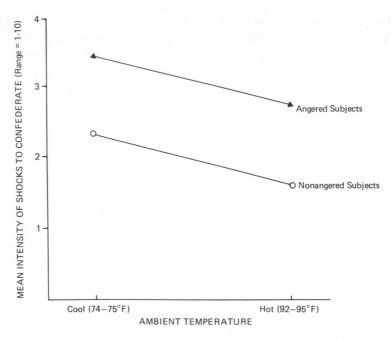

FIGURE 27. The effects of ambient temperature upon aggression. Surprisingly, uncomfortably high temperatures (92–95°F) were found to *reduce* aggression by both angered and nonangered subjects relative to comfortably cool temperatures (74–75°F). (Adapted from Baron, 1972a.)

had found conditions in the experimental rooms so unpleasant that they sought to complete the study as quickly as possible. In particular, many noted that they had employed shocks of short duration and relatively low intensity in order to avoid doing anything "controversial" that might prolong the session—and their agony! In short, it appeared that for some participants, at least, escape from the stifling laboratory had been a stronger behavioral tendency than aggression against the confederate. This reaction was hardly surprising; after all, even subjects in the angry condition had experienced only relatively mild instigation to aggression. However, it raised an interesting—and theoretically important—question: what would happen if aggression were a somewhat stronger and more dominant response in the subjects' behavior hierarchies? Would high ambient temperatures then produce the expected increments in aggression? These questions, in turn, suggested a possible link between the puzzling findings obtained in this initial study and a theoretical framework for understanding the nature of aggression proposed by Bandura (1973). Attempts to adapt this theory to the relationship between ambient temperature and aggression then led, quite logically, to a second phase in such research.

## Early Theory Construction: Heat as a Source of Arousal

While Bandura's theory is both sophisticated and complex, the portion most directly relevant to the impact of heat upon aggression is quite straightforward. Basically, it holds that virtually any type of aversive treatment serves to induce heightened emotional arousal among the individuals subjected to such conditions. This heightened arousal, in turn, will enhance the frequency or strength of later aggression under conditions in which these persons are "prone to behave aggressively" (Bandura, 1973, p. 56)—that is, when such responses are strong or dominant in their behavior hierarchies. In short, Bandura's theory proposes that almost any type of aversive, unpleasant treatment or experience—anything from severe frustration through actual physical discomfort—may facilitate later aggression when such behavior represents a strong or prepotent response among potential aggressors. When other responses—and especially those incompatible with aggression—are dominant, however, aversive treatment may actually inhibit rather than enhance assaults against other persons.

Given the fact that most individuals find exposure to high ambient temperatures quite unpleasant (Baron, 1972a; Griffitt, 1970) and the added finding that such conditions do indeed induce increments in arousal (Provins & Bell, 1970), Bandura's theory seems readily applicable to an understanding of the impact of ambient temperature upon aggression. Even more important, it seems capable of specifying those conditions under which uncomfortably high temperatures will either facilitate or actually inhibit subsequent aggression. Specifically, it seems to suggest that uncomfortable heat will encourage assaults against others when aggression is a dominant behavior tendency among subjects but will actually inhibit such actions when aggression represents only a weak, subordinate response.

Several different experiments have now been undertaken to test the accuracy of these predictions (Baron & Bell, 1975; Baron & Lawton, 1972). Perhaps the most informative of these, however, is the study conducted by Baron and Bell (1975). In this investigation, it was reasoned that two factors that might strongly influence the dominance of subjects' tendencies to aggress would be (1) the degree of provocation they experienced at the hands of the victim and (2) exposure to the actions of an aggressive model. Previous research concerning the effects of both of these variables suggested that if subjects were strongly provoked and then witnessed the behavior of an aggressive model before attacking their tormenter, aggression would represent a prepotent or dominant response in their behavior hierarchies (see, e.g., Zillmann, 1978, for a summary of this work).[2] In contrast, under conditions in which they were neither provoked nor exposed to the actions of the model, aggression would be a far less dominant reaction. On the basis of such considerations, it was predicted that high ambient temperatures would be most likely to facilitate overt aggression under the former circumstances and least likely to produce such effects under the latter conditions.

In order to examine these seemingly straightforward predictions, male subjects were first strongly provoked or treated in a totally nonprovocative manner by a male confederate. (In this case, provocation consisted of a highly derogatory personal evaluation from the confederate, while the absence of provocation involved favorable and flattering feedback.) Following these procedures, subjects were provided with an opportunity to aggress against this person by means of electric shock. The context within which this opportunity to aggress was presented, however, was somewhat different from that in the standard teacher–learner paradigm. Since it has been employed in several other studies that we shall consider in both the present and later chapters, it seems worthy of some comment.

Briefly, in these modified procedures, subjects were informed that they would be participating in a study concerned with the impact of unpleasant stimuli (in this case electric shock) upon physiological reactions. The rationale for delivering shocks to the learner, then, was simply that the experimenter wished to examine this person's physiological responses to such treatment. In order to lend credibility to these statements, the experimenter wired the confederate to an impressive-looking polygraph in full view of subjects, and the experi-

---

[2] While either strong provocation or exposure to an aggressive model alone would be expected to render aggression dominant in subjects' response hierarchies, it was assumed that in combination, these conditions would tend to raise its prepotency to relatively high levels.

menter pretended to make records of his physiological reactions throughout the shock portion of the study. These procedures were adopted in place of the basic Buss paradigm in the light of findings (Baron & Eggleston, 1972) suggesting that they yield a measure of aggression less contaminated by any altruistic motives (e.g., a desire to help the victim "learn" faster and so avoid future shocks). It should be noted, however, that results obtained with this modified approach have generally been quite consistent with those yielded by the more common teacher–learner strategy.

Returning to the design of the Baron and Bell (1975) study, a second factor, in addition to prior provocation, involved exposure to the actions of an aggressive model. In one experimental condition (the *model* group), the subjects were exposed to the behavior of a highly aggressive model prior to their own opportunity to shock the confederate. This individual was a second confederate of the experimenter, whose task in the study was also that of delivering electric shocks to the victim. He was arbitrarily selected by the experimenter to perform these activities first and pushed *only* buttons 8, 9, and 10 for from two to three seconds on each shock trial. In a second experimental condition (the *no-model* group), the subjects were chosen to shock the victim first, and so aggressed prior to witnessing the model's behavior.

Finally, of course, half of the subjects within each of these other conditions took part in the study under comfortably cool environmental conditions (temperatures of 72–75°F), while the remainder participated under uncomfortably hot conditions (temperatures of 92–95°F). In sum, the design of the study involved three factors: prior provocation from the confederate, exposure to an aggressive model, and ambient temperature. To reiterate our earlier statements, it was predicted that high ambient temperatures would be most likely to facilitate aggression under conditions in which subjects had previously been provoked and had witnessed the behavior of the model but would be least likely to induce such effects when they had not been provoked and had not witnessed the actions of the model. As can be seen in Figure 28, these expectations were *not* confirmed. Instead, it appeared that regardless of exposure or lack of exposure to the model, high ambient temperatures increased later aggression by nonangered subjects, while actually inhibiting such behavior by those who had previously been provoked!

Needless to say, these findings were quite unexpected. Moreover,

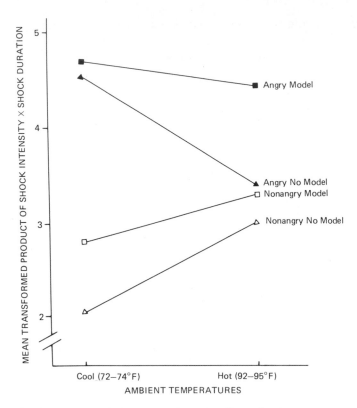

FIGURE 28. Further puzzling findings regarding the effects of ambient temperature upon aggression. Contrary to predictions, uncomfortably high temperatures reduced aggression by angry individuals, and increased aggression by nonangry individuals. Moreover, such effects occurred regardless of exposure to the actions of an aggressive model. (Adapted from Baron & Bell, 1975.)

together with other, confirming studies (Baron & Bell, 1976), they cast doubt upon the usefulness of applying Bandura's (1973) theory to explaining the impact of uncomfortable heat upon aggression. But how, then, were the effects of such environmental conditions to be explained? If arousal was not the crucial mediating variable in this complex relationship, what was? Fortunately, tentative answers to these questions were suggested by the replies of subjects in these studies to items on postexperimental questionnaires and in their comments during lengthy debriefing sessions. Together, these sources of information led to a third—and more definitive—line of research, which we will now consider.

*Later Theory Construction and Validation: Heat and Negative Affect*

In all of the studies described so far, subjects were asked to rate their feelings along several different affective (feeling) dimensions (e.g., comfortable—uncomfortable; pleasant—unpleasant). Careful analyses of these data indicated that without exception, participants experienced considerably more negative reactions under hot environmental conditions than under comfortably cool ones. Moreover, in several cases (Baron & Lawton, 1972; Baron & Bell, 1975), the most negative feelings of all were reported by individuals who had been exposed to prior provocation and had taken part in the study in the presence of uncomfortable heat. Such findings, of course, are neither surprising nor highly informative in and of themselves. When combined with other data, however, they take on a much more suggestive meaning.

Specifically, in several of the studies conducted (Baron & Bell, 1975, 1976), subjects were also asked to indicate the strength of their desire for the experiment to end. In all instances, those exposed to the combination of high ambient temperature and prior provocation reported by far the strongest desires to gain release from the study. Moreover, these findings were supported by comments volunteered by many participants during debriefing sessions (e.g., "The only thing I thought about was getting the hell out of here!").

Together, these data regarding subjects' current affective states and their expressed desire to escape from the experimental session pointed to an interesting possibility: perhaps the crucial psychological process underlying the impact of ambient temperature upon aggression was not heightened arousal in response to aversive conditions but rather the degree of induced negative affect—the level of unpleasant feelings experienced by subjects. In particular, it seemed possible that in the context of a negative evaluation from another person, high ambient temperatures served as the proverbial "last straw," causing participants who endured such conditions to feel so uncomfortable that minimization of discomfort rather than aggression became the dominant response in their behavior hierarchies. The result, of course, was that aggression was reduced. In the context of a positive evaluation from the confederate, however, the negative affect induced by high temperatures may have served only to annoy or irritate subjects to the point where aggression became more dominant than would otherwise have been the case; thus, such behavior was enhanced.

In short, the possibility of a curvilinear relationship between the level of negative affect experienced by subjects and the strength or dominance of aggression in their behavior hierarchies was suggested. This hypothetical relationship is illustrated in Figure 29; verbally, it may be stated as follows. Up to some determinable point, aggression becomes increasingly dominant as negative affect—induced by high temperatures, unpleasant odors, negative evaluation from others, or any other factor—rises. Beyond this point, however, the tendency to engage in such behavior may decrease as other responses incompatible with aggression (e.g., escaping from the extremely aversive situation) become increasingly prepotent.

Several investigations have recently been undertaken to examine this possibility (Baron & Bell, 1976; Bell & Baron, 1976, Rotton et al., 1977), and in general, results have been consistent with these suggestions. For example, in the study conducted by Bell and Baron (1976), male subjects in eight different groups were exposed to experimental conditions designed to vary their degree of negative affect from very

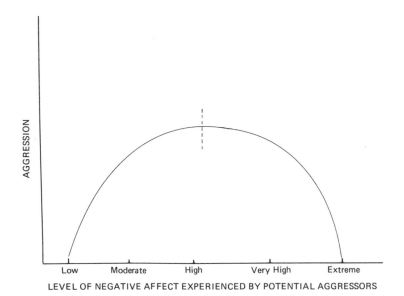

FIGURE 29. Hypothetical relationship between negative affect (unpleasant feelings) and aggression. At first, aggression increases as negative affect rises. Beyond some determinable point, however, further increments in negative affect lead to decreasing aggression. (Adapted from Baron & Bell, 1976.)

low to very high levels. Three independent variables (shown in previous research to exert strong effects upon subjects' affective state) were employed for this purpose: type of evaluation from another person (positive or negative), degree of attitude similarity to this same individual (low or high), and ambient temperature (cool or hot). A preliminary pilot investigation demonstrated that varying combinations of these factors produced the intended effects. That is, the subjects' level of negative affect ranged from very low (under conditions in which they received a positive evaluation from a confederate, learned that this person shared their attitudes, and participated in the study under comfortably cool conditions) to quite high levels (under conditions in which they received a negative evaluation, learned that the confederate did not share their attitudes, and participated in the experiment under uncomfortably high temperatures).

In accordance with the hypothesis of a curvilinear relationship between negative affect and aggression outlined above, it was predicted that the subjects' level of aggression would first increase as their level of negative affect rose but then actually decrease as the experimental conditions became even more unpleasant. As can be seen in Figure 30, these predictions were strongly confirmed: aggression and negative affect were indeed curvilinearly related. These findings suggest that the impact of ambient temperature upon aggression may well be mediated by negative affect rather than by general arousal and further, that this mediation, in turn, is underlain by the type of curvilinear relationship shown in Figure 29. In short, they suggest that whether high ambient temperatures will facilitate or actually inhibit subsequent aggression depends, quite strongly, upon the level of discomfort experienced by the subjects. If their levels of discomfort are initially quite low, high ambient temperatures may indeed facilitate overt aggression. If their levels of negative affect are already quite high, however, the introduction of uncomfortable heat may have the paradoxical effect of *lowering* later aggression. Under these latter conditions, individuals may simply feel so miserable that assaults against others become the furthest thing from their mind! (Anyone who has experienced total debilitation as a result of prolonged exposure to heat-wave conditions has had firsthand experience with such effects.)

Needless to say, further evidence is needed before the present theoretical framework can be accepted with any confidence. Two additional, confirming pieces of information might, however, be men-

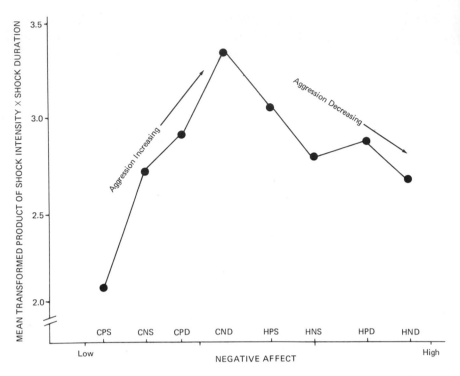

FIGURE 30. Empirical evidence for a curvilinear relationship between negative affect and aggression. Letters along the ordinate correspond to various groups in the experiment (e.g., CPS = cool, positive evaluation, similar attitudes; HND = hot, negative evaluation, dissimilar attitudes). See text for further explanation. (Adapted from Bell & Baron, 1976.)

tioned in passing. First, unpleasant cold seems to induce effects quite similar to those of uncomfortable heat, as the curvilinear hypothesis would predict (Bell & Baron, 1977; Calvert-Boyanowsky et al., 1976). And second, effects consistent with this model have also been observed in field as well as laboratory settings (Baron, 1976). Regardless of whether these suggestions are confirmed by further research, however, it seems reasonable, on the basis of existing evidence, to suggest the following general conclusions. First, the relationship between ambient temperature and aggression is far more complex than was once suggested. As a result, it does not seem appropriate to accept any broad or sweeping generalizations regarding the impact of such conditions upon collective violence. And second, the complexity of the relationship between heat and aggression indicates that the frequent occurrence of riots, looting, and similar events during the hot summer months does not stem directly or exclusively from the presence of uncomfortable heat during such periods. Rather, other factors—such as the greater number of people out on the streets, the longer hours of daylight, and the presence of teen-agers home from school—may also play an important role. In sum, the "long, hot summer" may well be hot, but only under highly specific conditions and not for the very simple reasons once proposed.

## Situational Determinants of Aggression

Together, the environmental factors we have just considered, and the varied social determinants of aggression examined in Chapter 3 constitute a very imposing list. In sharp contrast to simplistic assumptions regarding the origins of aggression (e.g., the suggestion that it always stems from frustration), it is now apparent that such behavior may be initiated or enhanced by a large number of different variables. Yet, not even the factors we have considered so far represent the entire picture. A number of additional antecedents remain to be considered. Specifically, it is often the case that aggression stems from various aspects of the situation or general context within which it occurs, and is not strongly determined either by the words and deeds of others or by various aspects of the physical environment. Such *situational determinants* of aggression, as they are often termed, are very diverse in nature. Thus, we could not hope to consider all of them here. Instead, we will focus upon three that have often been viewed as being among the most important, and that have been singled out for considerable empirical research: (1) situationally induced heightened arousal; (2) the presence of aggressive cues; and (3) the impact of various drugs (e.g., alcohol and marijuana).

### Heightened Arousal and Aggression

Suppose that you are an early-morning jogger and that on one of your trots through the neighborhood, you stop to chat with an acquaintance. During the course of this conversation, he insults you in a highly obnoxious manner. Would you be more likely to aggress against this individual under these conditions, when you are in a state of heightened physiological arousal as a result of your run, than would be the case under other conditions? In short, would your heightened arousal increase the likelihood that you would respond to his provocation in an aggressive manner? Interestingly, the results of a number of recent experiments suggest that this might well be the case (see Rule & Nesdale, 1976a, for a review of this work). Indeed, such research indicates that heightened arousal stemming from sources as diverse as participation in competitive activities (Christy, Gelfand, & Hartmann, 1971), vigorous exercise (Zillmann, Katcher, & Milavsky, 1972), and injections of stimulating drugs (O'Neal & Kaufman, 1972) can facilitate aggression, at least under some conditions. The phrase "under some conditions" should be strongly emphasized, however, for it is now also clear that increased arousal stemming from situational factors will exert such effects only under relatively specific circumstances.

We have already considered the first of these restrictions in our earlier discussion of the effects of noise upon aggression. As may be recalled, we noted at that time that exposure to loud noise—and the increased arousal so produced—seems to facilitate later aggression only when such behavior represents a strong or dominant response tendency among potential aggressors (e.g., Donnerstein & Wilson, 1976; Konečni, 1975b). Extending these suggestions to the present context, it seems reasonable to expect that heightened arousal stemming from other sources, too, will operate in a similar fashion. Evidence that this is indeed the case has been obtained in several studies (e.g., Konečni, 1975b; Zillmann, Katcher, & Milavsky, 1972). For example in the experiment conducted by Zillmann and his colleagues, subjects were first provoked or not provoked by a male confederate, next engaged in either two and a half minutes of strenuous physical exercise or performed a nonarousing task, and finally obtained an opportunity to deliver electric shocks to the accomplice. Consistent with the view that heightened arousal facilitates aggression only when such behavior is a strong or dominant response, physical exercise was found to enhance later assaults only by participants who had previously been strongly angered by the victim.

A second factor that seems to exert strong effects on whether heightened physiological arousal will lead to increased aggression is the manner in which individuals label or interpret such feelings. A series of complex but ingenious studies conducted by Zillmann and his associates (Zillmann & Bryant, 1974; Zillmann, Johnson, & Day, 1974) suggests that heightened arousal will facilitate later aggression in cases in which subjects misinterpret or mislabel such feelings as anger, but will fail to bring about such effects when subjects correctly attribute such reactions to their original source. As an example of this research, let us consider the experiment conducted by Zillmann, Johnson, and Day (1974).

In this study, male subjects previously found to be high, moderate, or low in physical fitness were given two opportunities to aggress against a male confederate. The first took place in the total absence of provocation from this person, while the second occurred after the participants had experienced harsh treatment at his hands. This latter opportunity to retaliate against the accomplice, however, did not take place immediately after provocation. In one experimental condition, the subjects were first asked to sit quietly for six minutes, then engaged in physical exercise on a bicycle-pedaling device for one and a half minutes, and only then obtained a chance to retaliate against the confederate. It was reasoned that in this condition, the fact that retaliation followed physical exercise immediately would lead subjects to label any increased arousal they experienced—whether stemming from the confederate's prior harsh actions or from the physical exercise—as due to this latter factor. As a result, they would not be expected to increase the strength of their assaults against the victim relative to the first session. In a second experimental condition, in contrast, the order was reversed: subjects first exercised, then sat quietly, and only then obtained their opportunity for retaliation. Here, it was reasoned that since a six-minute period intervened between exercise and retaliation, subjects would be less likely to attribute any increased arousal remaining at the time of retaliation to such activity. Instead, they might well label it as anger and attribute it to the confederate's prior actions. As a result, aggression would be enhanced.

As shown in Figure 31, this was precisely the pattern of findings obtained: for all participants except those who were most physically fit, aggression was indeed enhanced only in the group for whom exercise preceded retaliation by several minutes. (The absence of similar effects among the most physically fit group appeared to stem from the fact that these persons recovered from the exercise so quickly that they had virtually no heightened arousal remaining to misinterpret as anger.)

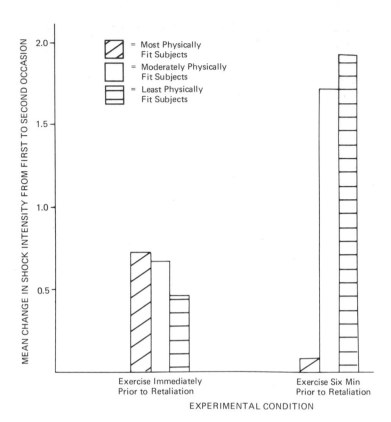

FIGURE 31. Heightened arousal and aggression. Increased arousal stemming from physical exercise facilitated aggression only under conditions where subjects could misattribute such reactions to provocation from the confederate (i.e., only when the opportunity to retaliate was delayed for six minutes following exercise). (Based on data from Zillmann, Johnson, & Day, 1974.)

Together with the findings of other research (cf. Rule & Nesdale, 1976a; Tannenbaum & Zillmann, 1975), these results suggest that a crucial factor determining whether heightened arousal facilitates later aggression is the ease with which individuals can become confused about the source of such feelings. If it is clear that their reactions stem from exercise, competitive activities, unpleasant noise, or similar sources unrelated to aggression, increased arousal will be labeled correctly and fail to enhance assaults against others. However, if the source of such feelings is no longer easily identified—perhaps because some time has elapsed since the arousing event or because several possible sources of arousal are present—individuals may become "confused" and label their feelings as anger, annoyance, or irritation. In such cases, heightened aggression may well result. In sum, existing evidence suggests that increased physiological arousal will not always or automatically facilitate attacks against others. Under specific conditions, though, it may well exert such effects.

### Sexual Arousal and Aggression: Facilitation or Inhibition?

Our discussion up to this point suggests that heightened arousal, whatever its situational source, will influence aggression in the manner already described. One particular type of arousal that has been of special interest to researchers for several years, however, is the sexual excitement stemming from exposure to erotic stimuli. Interest in this topic may be traced to repeated suggestions in the psychological literature regarding a "special" link between sexual and aggressive motives. For example, Freud (1933) proposed that desires to hurt or to be hurt by one's lover form a normal part of heterosexual relations and should be viewed as pathological only when they become extreme. Similarly, in a popular volume that attained near best-seller status, Berne (1964) suggested that the arousal of aggressive motives or feelings often serves to heighten sexual pleasure for both men and women. These and related proposals seem to imply that sexual arousal will often, if not always, encourage the occurrence of overt aggressive actions. Surprisingly, though, investigations undertaken to examine the accuracy of this suggestion have yielded inconsistent results.

On the one hand, several experiments have reported that heightened sexual arousal may indeed facilitate overt attacks against others by angry individuals—and perhaps even by those who have not been provoked as well (e.g., Jaffe et al., 1974; Meyer, 1972; Zillmann, 1971). For example, in the well-known study by Zillmann (1971), male subjects exposed to an explicit erotic film directed stronger shocks against a male confederate who had previously annoyed them than did subjects who were also angered by this person but who viewed only a neutral travel movie. Indeed, those in the erotic-movie condition actually demonstrated higher levels of aggression than participants exposed to a violent prizefight film. In contrast to such findings, however, several additional studies (Baron, 1974b, c; Baron & Bell, 1973; Frodi, 1977) have indicated that heightened sexual arousal induced through exposure to erotic materials may actually *reduce* later aggression.

At first glance, the contradictory nature of these results seems quite puzzling. How, after all, can sexual arousal both enhance and inhibit physical aggression? Fortunately, a resolution to this puzzle has been provided by further research. The first hint in this regard was suggested by a careful comparison of the procedures employed in the two sets of studies. This comparison revealed that those reporting an increase in aggression following exposure to erotic stimuli made use of relatively explicit materials of a highly arousing nature (e.g., films of young couples engaged in actual lovemaking, highly explicit and arousing erotic passages). In contrast, studies reporting a reduction in later aggression generally employed much milder and less explicit stimuli (e.g., *Playboy* and *Penthouse* nudes; pictures of attractive young women in bathing suits or revealing negligees). In short, there was some indication that mildly erotic stimuli might inhibit aggression, while more arousing materials of this type might facilitate such behavior. Direct evidence in support of this proposal has recently been obtained in an experiment conducted by the author (Baron & Bell, 1977).

In this study, male subjects were first angered or not angered by a male confederate who either praised or insulted them and were then provided with an opportunity to aggress against this person by means of electric shock. The study was described to subjects as one concerned with the effects of unpleasant stimuli upon physiological reactions, and participants were further told, at one point, that it would be necessary to wait for several minutes in order to allow the supposed victim's physiological responses to return to base level. During this interval, they were asked to examine and rate one of five different types of stimuli that the experimenter planned to use in further studies: neutral pictures of scenery and furniture; "cheesecake" pictures of young women in bathing suits and negligees; nudes taken from *Playboy* magazine; explicit pictures of sexual activities; or explicit erotic passages. In accordance with previous research, it was predicted that subjects' level of aggression against the confederate would be sharply reduced by exposure to the mildly erotic stimuli (e.g., the cheesecake and the nudes) but would be enhanced by exposure to more explicit materials (e.g., the erotic passages). As can be seen in Figure 32, results were generally in agreement with the suggestions. While aggres-

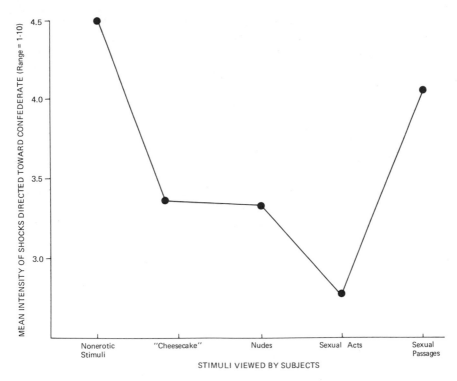

FIGURE 32. The effects of heightened sexual arousal upon aggression. Mild arousal inhibits such behavior, while stronger arousal returns aggression to initial levels. Additional findings (not illustrated here) suggest that very high levels of sexual arousal may
actually facilitate later aggression. (Adapted from Baron & Bell, 1977.)

sion was reduced by the pictures of cheesecake, the nudes, and sexual
acts, it was returned to initial levels by the erotic passages. Further,
there was some indication that even more arousing erotic materials
would have produced the expected increase in aggression. When combined with the findings of other research (Baron, 1974b,c; Frodi,
1977), these results lend support to the general suggestion of a curvilinear relationship between sexual arousal and aggression.

The apparent existence of a curvilinear relationship between sexual arousal and aggression accounts for the seemingly contradictory
findings reported in studies concerned with this topic. Specifically, it
suggests that the inconsistent results reported in these experiments
stemmed from the fact that different investigators, by employing contrasting types of erotic materials, sampled different portions of the

function relating sexual arousal to aggression. Knowing the general shape of this function, then, helps us to resolve an intriguing empirical puzzle. Unfortunately, though, such information does not in itself clarify the psychological mechanisms accounting for such curvilinearity. While this issue is still under investigation, one interesting explanation has recently been proposed by Donnerstein, Donnerstein, and Evans (1975).

Basically, these investigators have proposed that erotic stimuli actually produce two distinct effects upon the individuals who view them. First, they increase the level of arousal experienced by these persons, and second, they distract their attention away from any provocation they have previously experienced. Whether such stimuli will enhance or inhibit later aggression, then, may depend primarily on which of these two effects predominates. Since mildly erotic stimuli would be expected to have only minimal effects upon arousal, their major impact might be that of distraction. Thus, they would be expected to reduce later aggression. In contrast, more explicit stimuli would be quite arousing and, as a result, might well facilitate later aggression, especially under conditions in which such behavior is a strong or dominant response among potential aggressors (e.g., following strong provocation).

In order to examine the accuracy of these suggestions, Donnerstein, Donnerstein, and Evans (1975) conducted an experiment in which male subjects viewed neutral stimuli (various advertisements), mildly erotic stimuli (*Playboy* nudes), or more highly erotic stimuli (explicit pictures of sexual activity) before gaining an opportunity to aggress against a male confederate. In one experimental condition, they were insulted by the accomplice prior to examining these stimuli. Under these circumstances, it was reasoned, mildly erotic stimuli would distract the subjects' attention away from the provocation they had experienced and so inhibit later aggression. Because of their strong arousing effects, however, the highly erotic stimuli would fail to inhibit aggression and might well facilitate such behavior. As shown in Figure 33, both of these predictions were confirmed.

In a second experimental condition, subjects were also insulted by the confederate, but in this case, only *after* examining the appropriate stimuli. Since any distracting effects of the mildly erotic stimuli would be inoperative at this time, it was expected that such materials would fail to exert an inhibiting influence. Indeed, it seemed possible that like the highly erotic stimuli, they might actually enhance later aggression. Once again, as shown in Figure 33, these predictions were confirmed. (Subjects in a third, control group were not insulted at any time, and as anticipated, their behavior was little affected by the three types of stimuli.)

Considered as a whole, the findings of the Donnerstein *et al.* (1975) experiment lend support to the suggestion that the curvilinear relationship between sexual arousal and aggression is underlain by the joint arousing and distracting effects of erotic stimuli. When distracting effects predominate, aggression is inhibited, and when

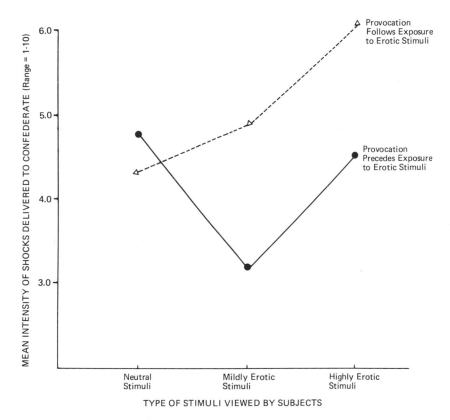

FIGURE 33. Further evidence concerning the influence of sexual arousal upon aggression. When provocation preceded exposure to erotic stimuli, mild sexual arousal inhibited aggression, while stronger arousal returned such behavior to initial levels. When provocation followed exposure to erotic stimuli, however, both mild and stronger sexual arousal facilitated aggression. (Adapted from Donnerstein, Donnerstein, & Evans, 1975.)

arousal effects take precedence, aggression is enhanced. We should note in passing, however, that other interpretations of this relationship have also been offered and have received some support. One of these—a view that emphasizes the impact of incompatible responses—will be considered at a later point (see Chapter 6).

Before we conclude, attention should be directed to one important fact that may already have become quite obvious: virtually all research concerning the relationship between sexual arousal and aggression conducted to date has involved only male participants. In view of this fact, it is obvious that additional investigations are needed to determine whether females are influenced in a similar manner by exposure to erotic stimuli. Given the high degree of similarity shown by the two sexes in other reactions to erotic materials (Byrne & Byrne, 1977), there appears to be little basis for anticipating marked differences between them in this instance. And in fact, the results of one recent experiment concerned with this topic (Baron, 1977a) suggests that heightened sexual arousal may well exert similar effects upon subsequent aggression by both genders.

In this study, female undergraduates were first angered or not angered by a female confederate, and then provided with an opportunity to aggress against this person by means of electric shock. Prior to aggressing, however, they were exposed to one of four different types of stimuli, chosen to be equivalent to those employed in previous studies conducted with males: nonerotic pictures of furniture, scenery, and abstract art; photos of seminude young males; pictures of nude young males; or pictures of couples engaged in various acts of lovemaking. Consistent with previous findings, results indicated that among angry participants, aggression was reduced by exposure to mild erotic stimuli (i.e., the "beefcake" pictures of seminude males), but significantly enhanced by exposure to more arousing materials (i.e., the pictures of sexual acts). Thus, heightened sexual arousal appeared to influence the behavior of females in a manner similar to that of males. Additional results, however, also pointed to the existence of subtle differences between the genders (for example, aggression by the female participants was *not* reduced by exposure to nudes—a type of erotic stimuli previously found to produce such effects among males). In view of these latter findings, the following, tentative conclusions seem most reasonable: heightened sexual arousal exerts generally comparable effects upon the behavior of males and females. However, subtle differences between the sexes may exist in this respect and should be examined in detail in future research.

## Conditioning and Aggression: The Role of Aggressive Cues

Contrary to the impression formed by many individuals during their first course in psychology, the process of classical conditioning is both an important and a pervasive one. Misunderstandings on this score often arise because such conditioning is frequently introduced, in beginning psychology, within the context of ringing bells and salivating dogs. Such examples, while certainly valid, seem to suggest that classical conditioning is a restricted process with little impact upon human behavior. As we shall soon see, nothing could be farther from the truth. In reality, it represents a central process with diverse and far-reaching effects.

Basically, the term *classical conditioning* refers to learning through association—instances in which one stimulus not initially capable of eliciting a particular form of reaction (the conditioned stimulus) gradually acquires this ability through repeated pairing (association) with another stimulus that *is* capable of producing such reactions (the unconditioned stimulus). Because this association between stimuli is a very common occurrence, classical conditioning plays an important role in a very wide range of behavior and emotional reactions. For example, consider the development of a strong sexual fetish. Here, specific articles of clothing not initially capable of eliciting strong sexual arousal (e.g., high-heeled shoes, black nylon stockings) are repeatedly paired with other stimuli capable of producing such reactions (e.g., the nude body of one's lover). As a result of this association, they gradually acquire the ability to elicit sexual arousal themselves (see Figure 34). Similarly, classical conditioning may play an important role in the acquisition of strong, irrational fears. This may occur in situations in which children who initially show little reaction to objects feared by their parents (e.g., snakes, insects), but who do become upset when they observe their mothers and fathers demonstrating fear, gradually come to react emotionally to the same objects. In short, classical conditioning may play an important role in many contexts where its impact might not at first be suspected.

Impressed by the pervasive influence of classical conditioning upon behavior, one noted researcher—Leonard Berkowitz (1964, 1969,

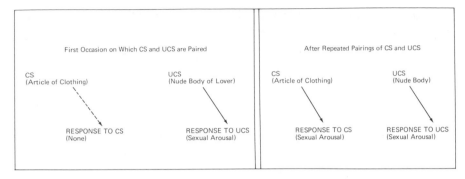

FIGURE 34. The role of classical conditioning in the acquisition of a strong sexual fetish. At first, some article of clothing (the conditioned stimulus) is incapable of eliciting sexual arousal. Through repeated pairing with an unconditioned stimulus, however, it gradually acquires this ability.

1974)—has proposed that aggression, too, may be strongly influenced by this process. In particular, he has suggested that people (and even objects) can acquire what he terms *aggressive cue value* through repeated association with anger arousal, witnessed violence, or aggression generally. And once they have acquired such cue value, Berkowitz reasons, their presence on the scene can serve to elicit or "pull" aggressive responses from persons who have been angered or otherwise made ready to aggress. In short, they will exert effects upon behavior analogous to those of any other conditioned stimuli.

Before proceeding further, we should pause for a moment to note that these proposals have recently been the subject of intense criticism. While this commentary upon Berkowitz's framework has been quite far-ranging in nature, much has focused upon the fact that it fails to specify the precise conditions required for the acquisition of aggressive cue value. Indeed, as noted recently by Zillmann (1978), it does not even seem to identify clearly the unconditioned stimulus initially capable of eliciting aggression, upon which such conditioning is based. While such criticism seems justified, at least to a degree, it is also true that Berkowitz's theoretical framework has generated a great deal of interesting empirical research and has called attention to several important facts about aggression. For these reasons alone, it seems worthy of careful consideration.

*Human Beings as Aggressive Cues: What's in a Name?*

In order to investigate the possible impact of an individual's aggressive cue value upon the strength of the attacks directed toward him, Berkowitz and his colleagues have conducted a number of related investigations (Berkowitz, 1965b; Berkowitz & Geen, 1966; Berkowitz & Knurek, 1969; Berkowitz & Turner, 1974). Basically, the procedures in this research have been as follows.

When subjects report for their appointments, they are informed that they will be participating with another individual (actually a confederate) in a study concerned with the effects of stress upon problem-solving ability. In order to study this topic, the experimenter notes, they will be asked to offer a written solution to a problem. Stress will be introduced into the situation by virtue of the fact that their solution will later be evaluated by the "other subject" (i.e., the accomplice), who will deliver from 1 to 10 shocks to them as an indication of his judgment of the work. After completing their solutions, half of the participants then receive only one shock from this individual (a very good evaluation), while the others receive fully seven shocks (a very poor evaluation). As a result, half are provoked by the accomplice, while the others are treated in a more neutral fashion.

Following this phase of the study, subjects view either an aggressive film, depicting a brutal prizefight, or a nonaggressive film containing scenes from an exciting track race. After observing these brief movies, they are presented with a problem solution ostensibly prepared by the confederate and asked to indicate their evaluation of it by shocking this person from 1 to 10 times. Measures of aggression are then obtained in terms of the number and duration of the shocks delivered by subjects to the victim.

In order to vary the confederate's aggressive cue value, attempts have been made, in such studies, to alter his degree of association with the witnessed film violence. For example, in an initial experiment (Berkowitz, 1965b), the confederate was described to half the subjects as a "college boxer" but to the remaining individuals as a "speech major." It was assumed that describing him as a boxer would link or associate him with the prizefight scene and thus increase his aggressive cue value (but only, of course, for the subjects who had witnessed this violent film). It was predicted, then, that the confederate would elicit the strongest attacks when he was introduced as a boxer and had angered subjects during the first phase of the study and when they had previously witnessed the prizefight film. Results offered support for these predictions: both the number and duration of shocks delivered to the confederate were greater under these conditions than under any others.

In several additional studies (e.g., Berkowitz & Geen, 1966; Geen & Berkowitz, 1966), attempts were made to link the confederate to the witnessed violence and thereby increase his aggressive cue value by means of his name rather than his college major. For example, in the study by Berkowitz and Geen (1966), which we mentioned briefly in Chapter 1, he was introduced to half the subjects as *Bob* Anderson and to the remaining participants as *Kirk* Anderson. Since one of the major characters in the boxing film was the actor Kirk Douglas, the confederate's name linked him to the witnessed aggression in the "Kirk" condition but not in the "Bob" condition. As expected, the subjects delivered the largest number of shocks to the accomplice when they were angry, had witnessed the violent film, and had heard him introduced as Kirk Anderson (see Table 8).

Considered together with more recent findings (e.g., Berkowitz, 1974; Berkowitz & Knurek, 1969), the results of these studies seem to provide consistent support for the view that the frequency or magnitude of the attacks directed against a particular person may be strongly influenced by his or her degree of association with previous or present anger instigators or with aggression generally. Indeed, these findings

TABLE 8
*Results of the Berkowitz and Geen (1966) Study*[a]

| Confederate's name[b] | Aggressive film | | Track film | |
|---|---|---|---|---|
| | Not angry | Angry | Not angry | Angry |
| Bob | 1.45[c] | 4.55 | 1.64 | 4.00 |
| Kirk | 1.73 | 6.09 | 1.54 | 4.18 |

[a] Based on data from Berkowitz & Geen, 1966.
[b] Subjects delivered the largest number of shocks to the confederate when they had witnessed an aggressive film, had been provoked by this individual, and his name associated him with the witnessed violence (i.e., when he was introduced as *Kirk* Anderson).
[c] Numbers shown represent the mean number of shocks delivered to the confederate by subjects.

suggest that even extremely subtle cues linking an individual with these events or persons may be sufficient to greatly alter his ability to elicit aggressive acts from others who have been "made ready" to behave in such a manner by previous provocation. It should be noted, however, that the procedures employed in such studies have been quite different from those that would normally be employed to establish classical conditioning. First, the confederate's name was linked with the witnessed violence on only one, or at most two, separate occasions. In general, such pairings must be repeated on numerous occasions to produce appreciable amounts of conditioning. Second, the interval between the presentation of the confederate's name and the viewing of aggressive film was considerably longer than that usually found to be effective in producing classical conditioning. And finally, as noted above, it is difficult, if not impossible, to identify the unconditioned stimulus in such cases. Was it the aggressor, the victim, the victim's reactions of pain in response to the beating he endured, or some other aspect of the situation? On the basis of Berkowitz's research, it is impossible to say.

In view of such considerations, it is far from clear that the findings of these studies stem from a process of classical conditioning through which the experimenter's accomplice acquired heightened aggressive cue value. Indeed, the precise mechanisms at work remain undetermined. What these experiments do seem to demonstrate, however, is that *some* form of association with witnessed aggression can sharply increase the capacity of specific individuals to elicit attacks from others. And this finding would appear to be of considerable importance in itself, regardless of the specific factors underlying its occurrence.

*Objects as Elicitors of Aggression: Does the Trigger Pull the Finger?*

Suppose that during the course of a meeting with a business associate, you were subjected to strong provocation. Further, imagine that these events took place in a room containing this person's large and varied collection of guns, swords, and daggers. Would you be more likely to aggress physically against him in these surroundings than in others? (Assume, before answering, that all of the weapons are securely bolted down and cannot be removed from their mountings.) By extension, Berkowitz's theoretical framework suggests that this might well be the case: your tendency to aggress against your acquaintance might in fact be enhanced by the mere presence of many weapons, even if you did not actually use them in your assault. This would be the case because as is true with people, *objects* that are repeatedly paired with aggression, anger arousal, or witnessed violence will acquire aggressive cue value. And, of course, weapons would frequently be encountered by most individuals under just such conditions.

Support for the existence of such effects has been reported in a well-known—but somewhat controversial—experiment conducted by Berkowitz and LePage (1967). In this study, male college students were first angered or not angered by a confederate and then were provided with an opportunity to aggress against this individual by means of electric shock. In one condition ( the *no-objects* control group), the apparatus employed by the subjects to shock the confederate was the only object present on the table as they directed their attacks against him. In two other groups, however, a .38-caliber revolver and a 12-gauge shotgun were lying on the table near the shock button. In one of these groups (the *unassociated-weapons* condition), it was explained that the weapons were being used in another experiment and had no connection with the present study, while in the second (the *associated-weapons* group), the experimenter indicated that they were being used by the victim in another study that he was conducting himself. Finally, in a fourth group, several *nonaggressive objects* (badminton racquets and shuttlecocks) were present on the table near the shock button.

In accordance with Berkowitz's views regarding the influence of aggressive cues, it was anticipated that the mere physical presence of weapons would facilitate aggression on the part of the angry subjects but would fail to exert similar effects upon the behavior of the nonangry subjects, who were not "ready" to aggress. As can be seen in Figure 35, these predictions were confirmed: among angry participants, the presence of weapons seemed to facilitate assaults against the accomplice.

Needless to say, such findings have important implications. In particular, they seem to suggest that the mere physical presence of weapons, even when they are not themselves employed in the performance of aggressive actions, may enhance the occurrence of such behavior. In Berkowitz's (1968) own words, "Guns not only permit violence, they can stimulate it as well. The finger pulls the trigger, but the

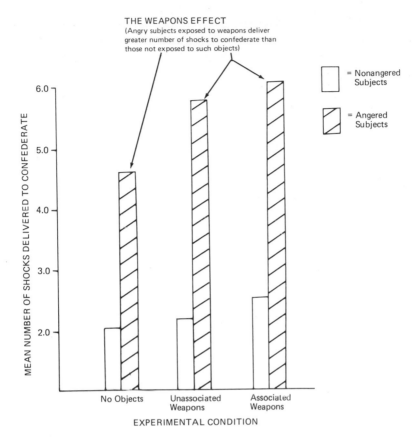

THE WEAPONS EFFECT
(Angry subjects exposed to weapons deliver
greater number of shocks to confederate than
those not exposed to such objects)

= Nonangered
Subjects

= Angered
Subjects

MEAN NUMBER OF SHOCKS DELIVERED TO CONFEDERATE

6.0

5.0

4.0

3.0

2.0

No Objects        Unassociated        Associated
                  Weapons             Weapons

EXPERIMENTAL CONDITION

Figure 35. The controversial "weapons effect." The physical presence of weapons facilitated aggression by angry individuals. Unfortunately, as explained in the text, it has not always been possible to replicate such findings. (Based on data from Berkowitz & LePage, 1967.)

trigger may also be pulling the finger" (p. 22). The existence of such effects would, of course, provide a strong argument in favor of strict government regulation of the sale of dangerous firearms. Before such conclusions can be accepted with confidence, however, and perhaps urged upon legislators, it is important to establish that they rest upon a firm empirical foundation. Unfortunately, this is not the case. While several experiments undertaken to replicate the original findings reported by Berkowitz and LePage (1967) have succeeded in demonstrating a similar "weapons effect" (e.g., Frodi, 1975; Leyens & Parke,

1975), several others employing virtually identical procedures have failed in this respect (Buss, Booker, & Buss, 1972; Page & Scheidt, 1971). For example, consider the investigation conducted by Buss and his colleagues.

In this research, a total of five separate experiments, employing almost 200 male subjects, were conducted. The first and second studies demonstrated that firing a weapon had no effect upon subsequent aggression. The third and fourth sought to determine whether individuals who had previously had experience with guns and those who had not might differ in this respect; however, no reliable findings emerged. Finally, in the fifth study, a very close replication of the initial study by Berkowitz and LePage was conducted. Surprisingly, the results indicated that the presence of weapons significantly *reduced* aggression against the experimenters' accomplice.

In the face of such findings—and other results suggesting that the aggression-enhancing impact of weapons may be observed only among subjects who are totally naïve with respect to the hypothesis under study (Turner & Simons, 1974)—it seems best to interpret the "weapons effect" with a degree of caution. The presence of guns, knives, and similar objects may indeed facilitate aggressive actions, but the precise conditions under which such effects occur remain to be determined.

### Aggressive Cues: A Concluding Comment

As we have already noted, Berkowitz's theoretical framework has been the subject of increasing criticism. Moreover, much of the research conducted to examine the accuracy of his proposals is currently quite controversial in nature. Indeed, it is now viewed by some investigators as heavily contaminated by the influence of demand characteristics (e.g., Didn't many subjects guess, when they saw the revolver and the shotgun in the Berkowitz and LePage study, that the experimenter had placed these objects there in order to make them more "aggressive"?). Regardless of such criticisms, though, it is clear that Berkowitz's more general proposal that aggression is "pulled" or elicited from without by external stimuli rather than merely "pushed" from within has attained widespread acceptance. In fact, it seems safe to conclude that his views in this regard have been highly influential in causing social psychologists to shift their search for the determinants of aggression largely from internal conflict and motives to external environmental factors. In this respect, certainly, there can be little doubt that his suggestions have had an important and beneficial effect upon the field.

### The Impact of Drugs: Alcohol, Marijuana, and Aggression

Anyone who has ever imbibed several cocktails before dinner, taken a powerful tranquilizer or pain killer under a doctor's prescription, or used "pep pills" to remain awake and alert on the night of a big exam knows from firsthand experience that drugs exert important effects upon behavior. Indeed, by swallowing appropriate substances, individuals are often able to change the way they feel, raise or lower their level of activation, and even alter their perceptions of the world around them. Given the wide-ranging impact of drugs upon behavior (see, e.g., Leavitt, 1974), it seems only reasonable to expect that they will also influence the occurrence of aggression, and in fact, recent research suggests that this is indeed the case. While a number of different substances have been found to exert such effects, two—alcohol and marijuana—have been the subject of special attention. In view of their widespread use at the present time, it seems only reasonable to make these substances the focus of the present discussion.

The first, alcohol, has long been viewed as a releaser or stimulator of aggressive actions. Drink too much, common sense suggests, and the chances of becoming involved in hostile interaction with others are increased (see Figure 36). In contrast, marijuana has often been held to be an inhibitor of overt aggression, presumably because it places its users in such a relaxed and pleasant state that aggression is the farthest thing from their minds.

While existing evidence is not entirely consistent in this respect (cf. Bennett, Buss, & Carpenter, 1969), a series of studies conducted by Stuart Taylor and his associates points to the conclusion that both of these suggestions are generally accurate (Taylor & Gammon, 1975; Taylor, Vardaris, Rawitch, Gammon, Cranston, & Lubetkin, 1976b). In these studies, male subjects in control groups were provided with special "cocktails" consisting of ginger ale and peppermint oil, while those in experimental conditions received the same drinks, to which small or large doses of two drugs—alcohol or THC (the active substance in marijuana)—had been added. After receiving these special

*"Oh, that wasn't me talking. It was the alcohol talking."*

FIGURE 36. Informal observation suggests that alcohol often increases the likelihood of aggression, and recent laboratory research lends support to this suggestion. Drawing by Dana Fradon; © 1975 The New Yorker Magazine, Inc.

drinks, the subjects participated in the type of competitive reaction-time task described earlier, in which the loser on each trial receives a shock from the winner. The measure of aggression obtained, of course, was the strength of the shocks set by the participants for their fictitious opponent. The results obtained in these investigations have been both clear and informative.

First, with respect to alcohol, findings indicate that small doses (0.5 ounces of vodka or bourbon per 40 pounds of body weight) tend to inhibit aggression, while larger doses (1.5 ounces of these beverages per 40 pounds of body weight) tend to facilitate such behavior. These findings lend support to the informal observation that one cocktail or a couple of beers may put people in a happy frame of mind and so reduce the likelihood of aggression, while a larger number of drinks

Table 9

*The Effects of Alcohol and Marijuana Upon Aggression*[a]

| Drug | Dose[b] | |  |
| --- | --- | --- | --- |
|  | Small | Large |  |
| Alcohol | 2.1[c] | 5.4 | (No-drug control= 3.9) |
| Marijuana | 3.1 | 1.9 |  |

[a] Based on data from Taylor *et al.*, 1976b.
[b] Small doses of alcohol seem to inhibit aggression, while larger doses facilitate such behavior. In contrast, small doses of marijuana have little effect upon aggression, while larger doses reduce it.
[c] Numbers shown represent the average strength of shocks set by subjects for their opponent in the Taylor reaction–time paradigm.

may serve to weaken their inhibitions and so increase the probability of dangerous altercations (see Table 9).[3] It is important to note, however, that even relatively high doses of alcohol do not necessarily facilitate aggression. Rather, such effects seem to occur only when the persons involved are provoked or threatened in some manner (Taylor, Gammon, & Capasso, 1976a).

Turning to marijuana, the results suggest that small doses of this drug have little impact upon aggression, while larger ones tend to inhibit such behavior (refer to Table 9). Further, there is some indication that even bigger doses (larger than those that could ethically be employed in the research conducted) might be even more effective in producing such reductions. Given the relatively small amount of evidence available at the present time, we will refrain from suggesting any implications of these results or from comparing the effects of alcohol and marijuana upon aggression. Readers, however, may wish to draw their own tentative conclusions in these respects.

## Summary

While aggression often springs directly from social interaction between individuals, it is also frequently initiated by factors not directly related to this ongoing process. First, it may be strongly affected by

[3] An interesting sidelight to these results is that vodka seems to exert a stronger influence upon aggression than bourbon, perhaps because it enters the bloodstream somewhat more quickly (Taylor & Gammon, 1975).

various aspects of the physical environment. Loud and irritating *noise* seems capable of facilitating overt aggression, but only when such behavior is a dominant response tendency among potential aggressors. *Crowding*, too, appears to influence aggression. Evidence regarding the direction of such effects, however, has been quite mixed. In some cases, crowding has been found to facilitate aggression, while in others, it has been found to inhibit its occurrence. One possible explanation for these puzzling findings lies in the suggestion that crowding is an intensifier of social behavior and reactions. Thus, in situations in which individuals' reactions to others are favorable, crowding may inhibit aggression. In situations in which their initial reactions are unfavorable, however, it may enhance the occurrence of aggressive actions.

A third aspect of the physical environment that seems capable of influencing aggression is *ambient temperature.* Informal observation suggests that individuals are often more irritable, prone to outbursts of temper, and negative in their reactions to others under uncomfortably hot than under comfortably cool temperatures, and these suggestions are supported by actual research. The effects of heat upon overt aggression, however, are somewhat more complex. Uncomfortable heat seems to facilitate overt aggression under conditions in which the level of negative affect experienced by potential aggressors is relatively low. However, it may actually inhibit aggression under conditions in which the level of negative affect experienced by such persons is already quite high. Apparently, in such cases, heat causes potential aggressors to feel so uncomfortable that escape or minimization of discomfort rather than assaults against others become their dominant responses.

In addition to the physical environment, aggression is also often influenced by various situational factors. One of these is externally induced *heightened arousal.* For many years, it was widely assumed that increased arousal, whatever its source, would facilitate overt aggression. Recent studies suggest, however, that arousal will produce such effects only under specific conditions. First, aggression must represent a strong or dominant response among potential aggressors. And second, such persons must mislabel their heightened arousal as anger or irritation. Only when such conditions are met will increased arousal facilitate overt aggression.

One particular form of arousal that has received considerable attention in recent years is the sexual excitement stemming from exposure to erotic stimuli. Initial findings suggested that such arousal facilitates aggression, but more recent evidence indicates that the relationship between sexual arousal and aggression is actually curvilinear in nature. Mild sexual arousal, induced through exposure to mildly erotic stimuli, inhibits aggression, while stronger arousal, induced through exposure to more explicit stimuli, facilitates its occurrence. Apparently, this curvilinear relationship is underlain by the fact that erotic stimuli exert two distinct influences upon aggressors: they distract their attention away from previous provocations and increase their level of arousal. When the distracting effects predominate (as in the case of mild erotic stimuli) aggression is inhibited, while when arousal predominates (as in the case of more explicit stimuli) aggression is enhanced.

A theoretical framework outlined by Leonard Berkowitz suggests that persons and objects that are repeatedly associated with anger arousal, witnessed violence, or aggression generally acquire gradually *aggressive cue value*—the capacity to elicit aggression from angry individuals. Research supporting this view has indicated that individuals whose first names or college majors associate them with witnessed violence are the targets of stronger aggression than individuals lacking such associations. Further, there is some indication that weapons—a class of objects frequently associated with aggression—can facilitate the occurrence of such behavior even when not used in its performance. Attempts to replicate this latter finding have not always been successful, however. Thus, it must be viewed as somewhat controversial in nature.

Recent investigations concerning the impact of drugs upon aggression have focused on the impact of *alcohol* and *marijuana*. Small doses of alcohol have been found to inhibit later aggression, while larger doses seem to facilitate its occurrence. In contrast, small doses of marijuana appear to have little impact upon aggression, while larger doses inhibit such behavior.

# 5

# Individual Determinants of Aggression: Personality, Attitudes, and Genes

It is a truism in social psychology that behavior is a joint function of the person and the environment. In short, an individual's actions in any given context are assumed to stem both from various aspects of the situation and from the numerous states, dispositions, or characteristics that he or she brings to it. This is an eminently reasonable generalization and one that has been supported by several decades of social research (cf. Shaw & Costanzo, 1970). Thus, it is not at all surprising to learn that it has also been widely accepted in the study of aggression. Indeed, most recent theorizing concerned with such behavior has assumed that it stems from both external variables involving the situation or environment and internal factors centering on individual aggressors (e.g., Bandura, 1973; Goldstein, 1975; Zillmann, 1978).

Given this fact, readers may well find themselves pondering the question of what has happened, in our discussions up to this point, to the "person" portion of this proposal. In preceding chapters, after all, we have focused primarily upon the social, situational, and environmental antecedents of aggression, while directing scant attention to the possibly crucial role of various dispositions and characteristics of potential aggressors. At first glance, this may well seem to be an unintentional oversight on the part of the present author. In reality, however, the decision to begin with the external antecedents of aggression and only then to turn to individual or internal factors was a deliberate one, based upon two important considerations.

First, as we noted in Chapter 1, widely known perspectives on aggression, such as the ones proposed by Freud and Lorenz, have generally tended to stress the individual or internal determinants of such behavior. In particular, they have frequently focused their search for the roots of violence within the personality dynamics, psychopathology, and even biology of individuals, while devoting far less attention to external influences on such behavior. As a result, "common knowledge" regarding aggression currently tends to overemphasize the importance of such internal factors, while at the same time understating the role of the many social, environmental, and situational variables considered in Chapters 3 and 4. It was partly to counteract this widespread misconception, then, that we chose to begin with and emphasize external antecedents of aggressive behavior.

A second reason for adopting this particular order of development may already be apparent from our previous discussions. Briefly, existing evidence suggests that external factors are indeed often the crucial ones with respect to both the elicitation and the maintenance of aggressive actions. Thus, they seem well deserving of careful and detailed attention.

For these reasons, then, we chose to begin with a careful consideration of several social, environmental, and situational influences upon aggression. Now that such external factors have been examined in detail, however, it seems both reasonable and appropriate to turn our attention "inward" and to focus upon what have often been termed *individual determinants* of aggression. Basically, these encompass antecedents of aggression centering primarily in the lasting characteristics or dispositions of potential aggressors. The term *lasting* is crucial in this definition, for in contrast to the types of relatively temporary emotional and affective reactions we have already considered, individual determinants of aggression are assumed to be quite stable over time. Thus, they are, in a sense, carried by individuals from situation to situation and influence their behavior in a wide range of settings.

Over the years, many different factors have been suggested as potentially important individual determinants of aggression. Fortunately, however, most seem to fall into three major categories, each of which will be considered in the present chapter. First, we will examine the influence of various *personality traits* or *characteristics* upon aggression. Informal observation suggests that certain individuals possess various traits that predispose them toward the performance of aggressive acts, and a substantial body of empirical research lends support to this proposal. A portion of this evidence, therefore, will be summarized in the present discussion.

Second, we will consider the impact of individuals' *attitudes, values,* and *internal standards* upon aggression. A rapidly growing literature suggests that such stable reactions or views often determine whether a given individual will aggress, how strongly he or she will assault others, and what specific targets will be chosen for attack.

Third, we will consider evidence relating to the possibility that aggression is strongly affected by specific *genetic factors*. Research on this topic is relatively recent and, at present, far from extensive. Yet, it has already stirred at least one heated controversy—that concerning the question of whether the possession of an extra "Y" chromosome predisposes individuals toward violence. Given the important implications of this controversy, it, too, seems deserving of careful attention.

Finally, in addition to these topics, we will briefly consider the question of *sex differences* in aggressive behavior. Do men and women differ in the tendency to aggress against others? And is one sex more likely than the other to become the target of such actions? Evidence concerning these and related questions will be both summarized and reviewed.

## Personality and Aggression: In Search of Violence-Prone Persons

Are there specific characteristics that predispose individuals toward or away from acts of violence? Informal observation suggests that this is certainly the case. With a little effort, you can probably bring to mind persons you have known who—because of unusually high or low "boiling points," offensive or inoffensive interpersonal styles, and other factors—tended to become involved in either far more or far less than their fair share of aggressive interactions. Personality, in short, seems to play an important role in determining the likelihood that specific persons will engage in assaults against others.

But what, precisely, are the crucial characteristics in this respect? What traits or tendencies predispose individuals toward the performance of overt aggressive actions? Information regarding such questions seems important in at least two respects. First, knowledge regarding the traits or dispositions associated with high and low levels of aggression may add to our understanding of such behavior generally and so prove useful from a theoretical perspective. Second, information on this issue may yield considerable practical benefit; after all, the ability to identify violence-prone persons may prove useful in future attempts to prevent or control such behavior. For these and other reasons, interest in the relationship between personality and aggression has seemingly increased in recent years (see Dengerink, 1976).

Basically, research concerned with this general issue has taken three major forms. First, many attempts have been made to identify those characteristics that predispose "normal" individuals—those who are free from gross pathology and who aggress only under appropriate conditions—toward such behavior. Second, considerable attention has been directed to the task of identifying the characteristics of "violent men and women"—persons who engage in aggression on a regular basis and for whom violence is a standard part of social interaction. And finally, a number of studies have been conducted to determine the characteristics of individuals who engage in extreme acts of violence—the type of savage and brutal incidents that so frequently make headlines in our local papers. The major findings of each of these lines of investigation will now be summarized.

### Loading the Dice in Favor of Violence: The Personality Traits of "Normal" Aggressors

Folklore and "common sense" suggest that a large number of different traits and dispositions might well be related to overt aggression. Indeed, with a little ingenuity, it is possible to make a fairly convincing case for the existence of direct links between aggression, on the one hand, and characteristics as varied in nature as self-esteem, the need for achievement, and the need for affiliation, on the other. Despite the seemingly reasonable nature of such suggestions, however, they have often proved difficult to verify in actual research. Investigations undertaken to explore the possibility of relationships between various traits and aggression have frequently yielded negative findings (see Dengerink, 1976; Larsen *et al.*, 1972). And even the positive findings obtained in such studies have often proved difficult to confirm. Several factors have probably contributed to this somewhat discouraging pattern.

First and foremost, lack of positive evidence in such investigations may simply reflect the fact that in many cases, situational factors of the type discussed in Chapters 3 and 4 exert a more powerful influence upon aggression than various personality traits. In short, the former simply overwhelm the latter and mask their effects upon behavior. This is an important point and one to which we will return below. For the present, suffice it to say that such dominance of situational over individual factors is a very real possibility and is currently accepted by many researchers, at least with respect to the actions of "normal" aggressors.

Second, negative findings in research on personality and aggression may often stem from a lack of reliability or validity in the measures of personality employed. A standard strategy in such research is that of comparing the behavior of individuals scoring "high" and "low" on various tests or other devices. As a result, any flaws in such instruments may prove fatal to the generation of positive findings. After all, one may end up comparing groups of individuals who do not actually differ with respect to the trait of interest.

And finally, the negative findings obtained in such research may reflect the fact that the link between personality and aggression is actually less close or less clear-cut than has often been assumed. Whatever the reasons behind the inconclusive results often obtained in this area, their existence suggests the need for extreme caution. As a result, attention will be restricted, in the present discussion, to variables for which evidence of a link to overt aggression is strong or consistent.

*Anxiety and Aggression: The Fear of Social Disapproval*

It has often been contended that fear—especially fear of punishment—may serve to inhibit aggression. For example, in their famous monograph, Dollard *et al.* (1939) stated, "The strength of inhibition of any act of aggression varies positively with the amount of punishment anticipated to be a consequence of that act" (p. 33).

Similarly, writing some years later, Berkowitz (1962) noted that "the strength of an individual's aggressive tendencies is directly associated with the extent that he anticipates punishment *or disapproval* for aggression" (p. 93; italics added).

If, as empirical research suggests (cf. Bandura, 1973), fear or anxiety does indeed inhibit aggression, it seems reasonable to suggest that individuals who are especially prone to such reactions—that is, those who are high in a general trait of anxiety—will often demonstrate lower levels of aggression than other persons. This would be the case because highly anxious or fearful individuals would be more likely to anticipate punishment, or at least social disapproval, for engaging in assaults against others. Evidence supporting this proposal has actually been obtained in several recent studies.

For example, in one of the first experiments concerned with this topic, Dengerink (1971) administered a personality questionnaire designed to measure anxiety (Lykken's Anxiety Scale; Lykken, 1957) to 500 male undergraduates. Then, 20 individuals scoring very high on this scale and 20 scoring very low were selected for further study. These persons then participated in the standard Taylor reaction-time task (refer to Chapter 2) under conditions in which they endured increasingly strong provocation from the fictitious partner. In accordance with the suggestions outlined above, it was predicted that individuals in the high-anxiety group would demonstrate lower levels of aggression in this setting than those in the low-anxiety group, and as shown in Figure 37, this prediction was partially confirmed: throughout most of the study, high-anxiety subjects did in fact set lower levels of shock for the opponent than low-anxiety subjects.

As can also be seen in Figure 37, however, this difference tended to decrease over the course of the session, so that by the final block of trials, it had entirely vanished. Thus, in the face of repeated and increasing provocation, even highly anxious individuals gradually came to respond in kind and met aggression with counteraggression.

This latter finding serves to underscore the important fact that we mentioned earlier and that we shall encounter again and again within the context of the present discussion: in many instances, situational factors seem capable of overcoming or counteracting even strong individual dispositions. As a result, even the meekest, most mild-mannered individuals may, like the proverbial worm, turn on their tormenters under appropriate external conditions.

While the results of Dengerink's (1971) study seem both clear-cut and convincing, they leave at least one important question unan-

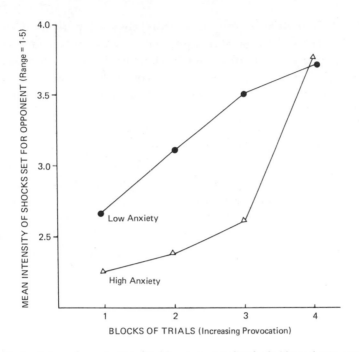

FIGURE 37. Anxiety and aggression. Highly anxious individuals (those fearing social disapproval) were initially less aggressive toward another person than subjects low in such anxiety. With continued provocation, however, this difference decreased and finally disappeared. (Adapted from Dengerink, 1971.)

swered: is aggression inhibited by a disposition toward general, "free-floating" anxiety or only by anxiety directed toward specific outcomes or events? More specifically, it seems possible that aggression may in fact be reduced by anxiety over punishment or social disapproval but not by more generalized anxiety or by anxiety directed toward unrelated issues (e.g., one's appearance, one's sexual adequacy). Questions of this type are also raised by the fact that in his research, Dengerink employed a personality scale often viewed as assessing primarily anxiety over social disapproval rather than more generalized fears. On this test, subjects are asked to choose between pairs of statements, one describing an unpleasant but nondangerous task (e.g., cleaning out a cesspool) and the other describing a task that entails the possibility of social disapproval (e.g., being seen naked by one's neighbor). High scorers on this scale, therefore, are individuals who consistently choose the nondangerous—but tedious—tasks over the potentially embarrassing ones. Thus, they are persons who prefer physical discomfort to social disapproval. In view of this fact, it seems possible that the results obtained in Dengerink's study are indicative of a relationship between anxiety over social disapproval and aggression, rather than of a relationship between more generalized anxiety and such behavior.

Evidence relating to this issue has been gathered in several studies. First, on the negative side, an experiment by Dorsky and Taylor (1972) reported no differences in the level of aggression demonstrated by males scoring high or low on a test of general anxiety (the Taylor Manifest Anxiety Scale). These findings suggest that a disposition toward generalized or free-floating anxiety is not closely related to aggression. On a more positive note, several additional studies have reported that individuals differing in the need for social approval (as assessed by the Marlowe–Crowne Scale of Social Desirability) do in-

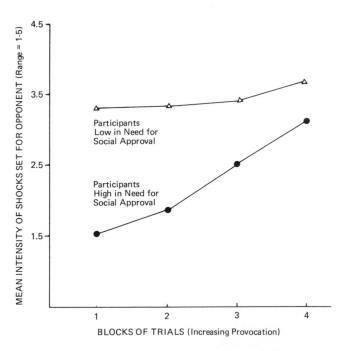

FIGURE 38. Need for social approval and aggression. Individuals low in the need for approval from others delivered uniformly strong shocks to their opponent, while those high in this characteristic started with mild shocks and raised the intensity of these jolts only with continued, increasing provocation. (Based on data from Taylor, 1970.)

deed differ in the strength of their assaults against others (Conn & Crowne, 1964; Fishman, 1965; Taylor, 1970). For example, in the most recent of these investigations (Taylor, 1970), individuals high in the need for social approval were found to direct lower levels of aggression against an opponent in the Taylor reaction-time task than individuals low in the need for approval. Since persons high in need for social approval are ones who express anxiety over censure or criticism from others, such findings point to the conclusion that it is indeed a disposition toward anxiety of this type, rather than a trait of generalized anxiety, that is closely related to aggression.

One additional feature of Taylor's findings should also be noted: while individuals high in need for social approval initially directed weaker shocks against their opponent than those low in need for such approval, this difference gradually disappeared over the course of the session, as participants in both groups were exposed to increasingly strong provocation (see Figure 38). This pattern of findings, is, of course, quite reminiscent of the one obtained by Dengerink and suggests once more that even strong individual dispositions can often be overcome or reversed by powerful situational forces.

Taken together, the findings reported by Dengerink, Dorsky, Taylor, Fishman, and others suggest that a trait or disposition toward anxiety over social disapproval is indeed related to aggression. Apparently, concern regarding censure from others may serve to inhibit overt assaults, at least in settings where strong situational factors do not serve to tip the balance in favor of such behavior.

## Aggression Guilt: Fear of One's Own Disapproval

In addition to fearing disapproval from others for engaging in aggression, individuals can—and seemingly do—often entertain anxieties regarding their *own* disapproval of such behavior. That is, they may anticipate experiencing strong feelings of guilt as a consequence of harming or even merely seeking to harm other persons. Given the fact that such reactions are usually quite unpleasant in nature, it seems reasonable to predict that individuals possessing a strong disposition toward experiencing guilt after aggressing will often be less likely to engage in such behavior than those not possessing such tendencies. Evidence relating to this possibility has been obtained in several different experiments (e.g., Gambaro & Rabin, 1969; Meyer, 1967). Per-

haps the most revealing study on this topic, however, is one reported
recently by Knott, Lasater, and Shuman (1974).

In this experiment, male undergraduates who had previously
been found to score either very high or very low on a measure of
aggression-associated guilt (the Mosher Incomplete Sentences Test;
Mosher, 1962), were placed in a situation in which they could, on a
number of occasions, deliver either a reward (an arbitrary point) or a
shock to an unseen partner. During an initial (base-line) portion of the
session, subjects received shocks and rewards from the confederate on
a purely random basis; nothing they did could influence his behavior.
It was predicted, of course, that during this phase, individuals high in
aggression guilt would deliver fewer shocks and more rewards (i.e.,
points) to the partner than those low in such reactions. As can be seen
in Figure 39, this expectation was confirmed: during the base-line
period, high-guilt subjects did in fact deliver fewer shocks to the confederate than low-guilt participants.

In contrast to conditions prevailing during the initial base-line
period, there was a direct contingency between subjects' responses
and the confederate's behavior during two subsequent phases of the
study. In one of these segments (*conditioning for aggression*), shocks by
subjects to the partner were followed, 90% of the time, by a reward
from this person, while rewards by subjects to the confederate were
followed, also 90% of the time, by a shock. Thus, during this phase of
the study, subjects were rewarded for behaving in a highly aggressive
manner (i.e., for shocking the confederate). In the remaining portion
of the study (*conditioning for nonaggression*), these contingencies were
reversed, so that shocks by subjects to the confederate elicited shocks
from this person, while rewards elicited reciprocal, friendly treatment.
(As might be expected, all participants were exposed to both of these
treatments, with the order of their presentation being carefully coun-
terbalanced.) It was predicted that individuals high in aggression guilt
would be affected to a lesser degree by conditioning for aggression,
and to a greater degree by conditioning nonaggression, than participants low in such guilt, and as can be seen in Figure 39, these predictions, too, were confirmed. During conditioning for aggression, the
high-guilt individuals increased their proportion of shocks to the confederate to a much smaller degree than the low-guilt subjects. During
conditioning for nonaggression, however, the high-guilt participants
decreased their proportion of shocks to this person to a much greater

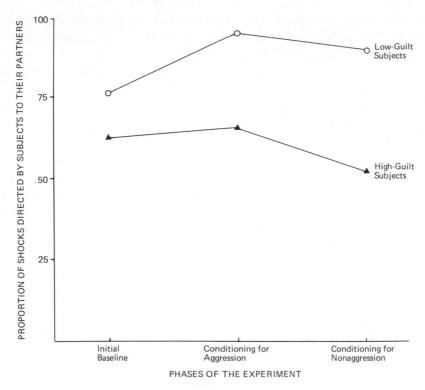

FIGURE 39. The effects of guilt upon aggression. During an initial base-line period, high-guilt subjects directed a smaller proportion of shocks against the partner than did low-guilt subjects. During a portion of the study when they were rewarded for aggressing, low-guilt participants sharply increased their proportion of shocks, while high-guilt subjects did not. Finally, in a portion of the study when the subjects were rewarded for behaving in a nonaggressive manner, high-guilt subjects reduced their proportion of shocks to a greater degree than low-guilt individuals. (Values for this phase of the study are adjusted to take account of an intervening base-line period.) (Based on data from Knott *et al.*, 1974.)

degree than the low-guilt subjects. These latter findings are of particular interest since they suggest that in this instance, individual dispositions could *not* readily be overridden by situational factors. In short, differences in subjects' levels of aggression guilt seemed to exert very powerful effects upon their behavior.

When combined with the findings of other investigations, those reported by Knott *et al.* (1974) suggest that to the extent that individuals anticipate pangs of remorse or stings of self-censure for engaging in assaults against others, they may refrain from participating in such actions. Moreover, this seems to be the case even in situations that appear to favor the development of aggression. These conclusions, in turn, point to intriguing speculations regarding the characteristics of highly aggressive persons. Are they, perhaps, individuals who have failed to acquire the ability to monitor—and censure—their own behavior (cf. Bandura, 1977)? In short, are such "violent men and women" persons lacking in the type of guilt that often accompanies or follows overt aggression against others? Such possibilities are beyond the scope of the present discussion, which, as may be recalled, is restricted to the behavior of "normal" aggressors. However, we will return to these and related issues in our later treatment of the characteristics of undercontrolled aggressors.

## Internals and Externals: Perceived Control and Aggression

There can be little doubt that most individuals wish to be the masters of their own fate. That is, most wish to exert control over the events and outcomes that befall them (Rotter, 1972). Largely because of this strong desire to exert control, individuals generally find situations in which they cannot influence their outcomes to be both unpleasant and unsettling. Moreover, recent evidence suggests that repeated exposure to such circumstances can exert lasting, detrimental effects upon the persons who endure them. Specifically, it appears that when human beings have been placed in settings where there is no contingency between their behavior and its results, they may learn to feel *helpless* and so suffer decrements both in motivation and performance. Even worse, such effects may then transfer to other settings, in which they *can* influence their outcomes, and interfere with performance in these as well (e.g., Maier & Seligman, 1976; Seligman, 1975).

Partly as a function of greatly varied life experiences with control or lack of control, individuals come to differ sharply with respect to beliefs concerning their ability to influence their destinies. Thus, at one extreme are a group often termed *internals*, who feel that they can readily influence events in a wide variety of contexts, while at the other are a group generally described as *externals*, who have largely "given up" and feel powerless to influence the course of the events around them. At first glance, such beliefs seem far removed from the realm of aggression. Yet, one line of reasoning, at least, suggests that these beliefs may well play a role in the occurrence of aggression. In particular, it seems possible that internals may view aggression as simply one additional technique for influencing the course of their lives. For example, they may perceive it as a means for attaining desired goals, for alleviating aversive, noxious treatment at the hands of others, or perhaps even as a rather drastic type of manipulative technique. In short, they may view it as one more form of instrumental behavior that they can employ to exert control over the shape of their lives. (Additionally, of course, they may aggress in a purely impulsive manner, in response to strong provocation; cf. Berkowitz, 1974.)

In contrast, externals—because of their largely fatalistic outlook on life—may perceive little instrumental value in aggression. Thus, they may be quite unlikely to adopt it, except in situations in which they are repeatedly and unendurably provoked. In sum, internals may engage in both instrumental and angry aggression, while externals participate, as a rule, only in the latter (see Buss, 1961; Feshbach, 1970). Evidence relating to the validity of these proposals has recently been reported by Dengerink and his colleagues (Dengerink, O'Leary, & Kasner, 1975).

In this experiment, a measure of belief in one's ability to control one's destiny—Rotter's Locus of Contol Scale (Rotter, 1966)—was administered to 210 male undergraduates. From these, 30 individuals scoring very high on this scale (externals) and 30 individuals scoring very low (internals) were selected for further study. Both groups then participated in the Taylor reaction-time paradigm under one of three different conditions. In one experimental treatment (the *increasing-attack* group), the partner began with low shock settings but then gradually increased the strength of these attacks over the course of the session. In a second (the *decreasing-attack* group), he began by setting strong shocks but gradually reduced the intensity of these assaults as the study progressed. Finally, in a third condition (the *constant-attack* group), he chose moderate shocks throughout the session.

On the basis of reasoning similar to that presented above, Dengerink and his colleagues predicted that internal subjects would respond quite readily to such differences in their partner's behavior. That is, those exposed to increasing attack would become increasingly aggressive themselves, those exposed to decreasing attack would reduce the strength of their shocks, and those exposed to a constant level of provocation would reciprocate with a constant level of aggression.

In contrast, it was predicted that external subjects would demonstrate much less responsiveness to the various experimental treatments. Presumably, this would be the case because they would believe that nothing they did would have any effect upon their partner's actions or the shocks they received. In particular, it was predicted that they would show less reaction to mounting provocation (the increasing-attack condition) than internal participants.

As can be seen in Figure 40, all of these predictions were confirmed: while the behavior of internal subjects varied significantly in the expected manner as a function of the partner's actions, that of externals showed somewhat less variation in this respect. Perhaps of

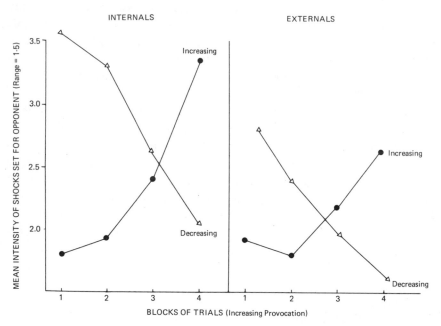

FIGURE 40. Belief in the ability to control one's outcomes or fate and aggression. Individuals who believed that they could control their own outcomes (Internals) varied their behavior in response to changes in their partner's actions (refer to left-hand panel). That is, they increased the strength of their shocks when he acted provocatively (in the Increasing condition) but decreased such assaults when he behaved in a friendly manner (in the Decreasing group). In contrast, subjects who did not believe that they could control their own outcomes (Externals) were far less responsive to changes in their partner's behavior (refer to right-hand panel). (Based on data from Dengerink, O'Leary, & Kasner, 1975.)

greatest interest, externals showed much smaller increments in aggression in the increasing-attack condition than internals. In short, they seemed largely to "turn the other cheek" in response to harsh treatment at the hands of the opponent.

While it is always somewhat risky to generalize findings obtained under carefully controlled laboratory conditions to events occurring in naturalistic settings, the findings obtained by Dengerink, O'Leary, and Kasner (1975), as well as those reported in related studies (e.g., Dengerink & Myers, 1977), seem to shed light on at least one puzzling question: why some persons, at least, seem willing to accept repeated, strong provocation from others without turning to aggression. The explanation suggested by the present research is that such persons are "external" in orientation and so feel quite powerless to do anything about their continued mistreatment. Further research is obviously needed to investigate this and related possibilities. Regardless of the outcome of such investigations, however, existing evidence seems to suggest quite strongly that beliefs concerning the ability to influence or control one's destiny often play an important role in the occurrence of overt aggression.

## The Coronary-Prone Behavior Pattern and Aggression: Another Reason Why Aggressors Die Young

One fascinating line of research conducted in recent years has been concerned with the possibility of a link between personality and coronary heart disease (see Glass, 1977). Briefly, investigations concerned with this topic have demonstrated that individuals showing a particular cluster of behavioral characteristics—*Type A*'s, as they are usually termed—are far more likely to experience serious heart attacks than individuals not demonstrating this cluster or *Type B*'s. More specifically, Type A persons seem to be characterized by three major behavioral tendencies.

First, they are hard-driving and competitive. Type A's, in short, are the kind of individuals who are greatly concerned with success and will push themselves to almost any limits in order to achieve it (see, e.g., Carver, Coleman, & Glass, 1976). Second, Type A's are generally characterized by a high degree of time urgency. They are always in a hurry and seem to be constantly working under pressure and against deadlines (e.g., Burnam, Pennebaker, & Glass, 1975). Finally, and most germane to the present discussion, they are assumed to be quite aggressive, particularly when others interfere with the hectic pace of their activities or with their achievement-oriented strivings (cf. Glass, 1977). Evidence relating to the last of these suggestions has recently been reported by Carver and Glass (1977).

In this experiment, a large group of male undergraduates first completed a questionnaire designed to distinguish between Type A and Type B individuals—the Jenkins Activity Survey (refer to Table 10). On the basis of their responses to this measure, 23 A's and 25 B's were then selected for further study.

During the experiment proper, half of the individuals in each of these categories were angered by a male confederate, who interfered with their performance on a complex puzzle and insulted their intelligence, while the remainder were not annoyed in this fashion. Following these procedures, all subjects were provided with an opportunity to aggress against the confederate by means of electric shock within the standard teacher–learner paradigm devised by Buss (1961).

TABLE 10

*Sample Items from the Jenkins Activity Survey*[a]

For each of the following items, please circle the number of the *one* best answer:[b]

1. Is your everyday life filled mostly by
   (1) Problems needing solution.
   2. Challenges needing to be met.
   3. A rather predictable routine of events.
   4. Not enough things to keep me interested or busy.

2. When you are under pressure or stress, do you usually:
   (1) Do something about it immediately.
   2. Plan carefully before taking any action.

3. How often are there deadlines on your job? (If job deadlines occur irregularly, please circle the closest answer below.)
   (1) Daily or more often.   2. Weekly.   3. Monthly.   4. Never.

4. How often do you bring your work home with you at night or study materials related to your job?
   1. Rarely or never.
   (2) Once a week or less often.
   (3) More than once a week.

[a] Adapted from Jenkins, Rosenman, & Zyzanski, 1972.
[b] This psychological test is designed to distinguish between individuals who demonstrate a hard-driving, competitive approach to life (Type A's) and those who do not (Type B's). Answers characterizing Type A's are circled.

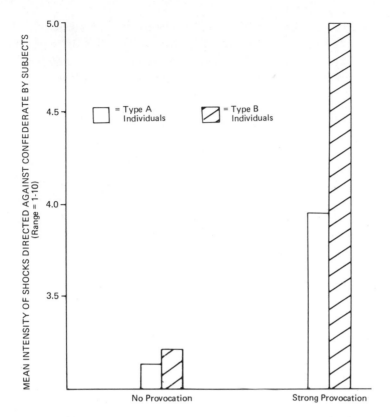

FIGURE 41. The Type A behavior pattern and aggression. Type A individuals directed higher levels of aggression against a male confederate than Type B's, but only when they had previously been provoked by this person. (Based on data from Carver & Glass, 1977.)

That is, they could deliver shocks of varying intensities to this person on a number of occasions when he appeared to make errors on a bogus learning task.

In accordance with the presumed characteristics of Type A and Type B individuals, it was predicted that in the case of subjects who had previously been provoked, A's would direct stronger aggression against the confederate than B's. In the case of nonangered participants, however, no differences of this type were anticipated. As can be seen in Figure 41, both predictions were verified: in the presence of prior provocation, Type A individuals made use of stronger shocks than Type B individuals. In the absence of such annoyance, however, both groups delivered similar, mild shocks to the accomplice. In short, important differences between Type A and Type B participants emerged, but only when these contrasting behavioral patterns were "engaged" or made relevant by appropriate situational forces.

*Personality and "Normal" Aggression: A Concluding Comment*

Our discussion up to this point has identified a number of different personality traits or dispositions that influence the occurrence of aggression. The list we have compiled, however, is by no means exhaustive, and it is important to note that many other factors, too, have been found to play such a role. For example, included in a sample of these would be *authoritarianism* (Elms & Milgram, 1966), *field dependence–independence* (Dengerink *et al.*, 1975), and *aggressivity* itself (Wilkins, Scharff, & Schlottmann, 1974). Rather than turning to a consideration of such additional characteristics, however, we will conclude the present discussion by addressing a question we raised—but considered only in passing—at several different points: the relative importance of personality and situational determinants of aggression. Specifically, we will conclude by inquiring how these two groups of variables "stack up" with respect to their influence upon such behavior.

In the opinion of most social psychologists, the answer is quite straightforward: personality variables come in a dim and distant second. That is, a majority believe that external factors, such as those examined in Chapters 3 and 4, are of much greater importance in influencing the occurrence, strength, and form of violent actions. This conclusion is based, in part, on the findings of studies such as the ones examined in the present section. As you may recall, many of these investigations seemed to suggest that situational forces often counteract the impact of individual traits or dispositions. Additional support for the view that situational factors dominate over personal ones also stems from direct comparisons between them.

For example, in one such study, Larsen and his colleagues (Larsen, Coleman, Forbes, & Johnson, 1972) related the scores obtained by a large group of undergraduate students on five different personality scales to their level of aggression in five different settings. Results indicated that *none* of the five scales employed (which presumably measured such traits as aggressivity, hostility, and Machiavellianism) was consistently related to subjects' behavior. In contrast, differences between the various experimental settings—that is, situational factors—exerted a powerful influence upon participants' actions. For example, subjects were much less aggressive toward a female than toward a male victim, aggressed significantly more strongly following exposure to an aggressive model than in the model's absence, and delivered significantly stronger shocks to the victim when urged to do so by two confederates than when alone in the experimental room.

On the basis of such findings, Larsen *et al.* (1972) concluded that

> it seems clear that the situational structure is the all-important variable in predicting behavior, and that persons in fact often act opposite to their predisposition to act when faced with situational pressure. (p. 294)

While the present author generally agrees, he would not go quite so far in this regard. Situational factors do indeed often dominate where aggression by "normal" individuals is concerned. This does not necessarily imply, however, that personality factors are of little or no importance. On the contrary, such variables, too, often exert a significant effect upon aggression. Such influence, however, is generally of a mediating nature. For example, personality factors may determine how strongly a given individual reacts to provocation, how strongly he or she is influenced by the actions of an aggressive model, or how aroused he or she becomes following exposure to erotic stimuli. In these and many other cases, the basic impact of important situational forces is still apparent—provocation still induces an instigation toward aggression, aggressive models still tend to stimulate similar actions, and erotic stimuli induce sexual reactions. Such effects, however, are filtered or modified by individual dispositions. In sum, personality factors do indeed seem to influence aggression, even by "normal" persons. However, such effects are generally exerted against a backdrop of social, environmental, and situational variables, which often serve to mask or conceal their influence.

### "Violent Men and Women": The Characteristics of Undercontrolled Aggressors

Up to this point, we have focused our attention upon the personality characteristics of "normal" aggressors. That is, we have concentrated upon the traits and dispositions associated with aggression on the part of individuals who show no signs of major psychopathology and who engage in such behavior only on relatively rare—and reasonably appropriate—occasions (e.g., following strong provocation). Now, however, we will shift our attention to another group of persons who, though quite small in relative numbers, are responsible for a large proportion of all violent behavior (cf. Goldstein, 1975). Because such individuals generally seem totally lacking in internal restraints or inhibitions against aggression, they have frequently been described as *undercontrolled* aggressors (e.g., Megargee, 1971). Another and perhaps more apt label for them, however, is *violent men and women*. Such a description is appropriate, for such persons have seemingly made violence a normal part of their lives. Indeed, it often serves as a major theme of their social interactions with others and involves much of their energies and attention. Because of their central role in a vast number of violent incidents, such undercontrolled aggressors have long been the subject of intensive study. Perhaps the most revealing work in this respect, however, is that conducted in recent years by Hans Toch (1969, 1975).

In order to study the personality characteristics of violent individuals, Toch adopted an intriguing and novel approach. Briefly, he arranged for prisoners and recent parolees from state penal institutions to conduct extensive interviews with other prison inmates and parolees who had a history of previous violent encounters. Needless to say, these interviews focused on the aggressive encounters in which the 77 subjects had been involved, and the information gathered in these conversations constituted the major data of the investigation.

Toch decided to employ such peer-interview procedures for two important reasons. First, he wished to improve communication with subjects who, in an important sense, often spoke a "different language" than the highly trained professionals who usually questioned them. And second, he wished to reduce subjects' inhibitions against providing various types of information—a common problem in such work. In conducting their interviews, Toch's assistants followed a prescribed set of guidelines for obtaining information concerning previous violent episodes. However, being similar to the subjects in background and experience, they consistently used language and forms of speech familiar to these individuals.

Interviews were tape-recorded and, once completed, were subjected to intensive analysis by study groups consisting of both professionals and nonprofessionals. Through a process of discussion to consensus, these groups attempted to formulate a summary of each incident that emphasized (1) the origins of the violent encounter (e.g., events leading up to its occurrence); (2) the general goals and orientation of the subject; and (3) any similarities between these first two points and corresponding information obtained in other interviews. The overall goal, of course, was that of identifying underlying themes that might then point to basic personality characteristics of violence-prone persons. A final step in the process was then that of reviewing all interview summaries in an attempt to extract common themes and patterns (see Toch, 1969, pp. 133–135).

On the basis of these procedures, Toch reached the conclusion that violent individuals may be divided into several distinct "types" who turn to aggression for somewhat different reasons. The final typology he derived is presented in Table 11; several of the categories listed will now be described.

## Self-Image Compensators

Perhaps the largest single group of violent individuals are those whose aggression stems from pronounced feelings of insecurity and low self-esteem. Basically, these persons hold a very low opinion of

TABLE 11
*The Typology of "Violent Men"*
*Proposed by Toch[a]*

| Type | Percent[b] |
| --- | --- |
| Self-image promoting | 27.5 |
| Self-image defending | 13.0 |
| "Rep" defending | 14.5 |
| Pressure removing | 11.6 |
| Exploiting | 10.0 |
| Bullying | 5.8 |
| Self-defending | 5.8 |
| Self-indulging | 4.3 |
| Norm enforcing | 4.3 |
| Catharting | 2.9 |

[a]Based on data from Toch, 1969.
[b]The figures indicate the percent of the subjects in his investigation who fell into each category.

themselves and are extremely concerned that others will come to share this view. In order to prevent such outcomes, therefore, they respond aggressively to even the slightest insult or challenge. An excellent example of this pattern is provided by the following description (Toch, 1969):

> The man states himself that he has paranoid feelings. . . . He cites a series of incidents in which, without any provocation from the other party, he gets the impression that he is being laughed at or belittled in different ways, and he invariably responds with violence to *defend himself* aganst the belittlement. . . . what seems to dominate him . . . is a kind of need to save his self-image and a need to hurt anybody who in any way whatsoever could cast aspersions on it. (pp. 147–148; italics added)

## Self-Image Promoters

A second and closely related group of violent persons also shares the suspicion that they are, in fact, quite worthless and unimportant. In contrast to self-image compensators, who attempt to refute such feelings by responding to real or imagined slights, however, self-image promoters actively set out to convince others that they are formidable and fearless. That is, they actually *seek* violent encounters as a means of demonstrating their own importance and worth. Consider the following example (Toch, 1969):

> The man has been flooded all his life with strong feelings of not being able to be what he should be. . . . He proves himself wrong by going out of his way to provoke fights to show he isn't afraid. He tackles the first "bully" he meets in a juvenile institution; he calls another one "punk" shortly thereafter. . . . And in every instance in which his little demonstration succeeds he feels great. As he puts it in relation to one victim, he was tempted to stand on the man's chest and "yell like Tarzan." (pp. 138–139)

## Self-Indulgers

The use of violence by a third distinct group of aggressors stems from somewhat different sources. Basically, these individuals hold an amazingly infantile view of the world, assuming that others exist simply to satisfy their needs and wants and will readily agree to fulfill this function. As suggested by Toch (1969), "They toddle about their way expecting to find a crib or breast around every corner" (pp. 265–266). Of course, they eventually—and repeatedly—discover that other persons do not always wish to cater to their every whim, and when they do, they frequently react to this "sudden treachery" with strong, repeated assaults.

## "Rep" Defenders

A fourth group of highly violent individuals uncovered by Toch consists primarily of persons who aggress against others because, quite simply, it is their assigned social role to do so. That is, these individuals occupy special positions within gangs or other peer groups that literally require that they become involved in aggressive encounters. Only in this manner, it seems, can they maintain and defend their reputations as tough, formidable opponents. A clear example of this intriguing pattern follows (Toch, 1969):

> The man appears to be defending his status as a gang leader, which in turn is expressed in his defense through violence of the integrity of his gang. . . . He is undoubtedly seen as a source of strength and support and is willing to help create and keep this image as a tower of physical strength for the group. (p. 151)

## Bullies or Sadists

In sharp contrast to the "types" we have considered so far is a group of violent individuals who seem to take actual pleasure in inflicting pain and suffering on others—a group often known to psychologists and other professionals as *sadists* but to their peers simply as bullies. In general, such persons choose as their targets individuals who are uniquely susceptible to their attacks. However, if such a victim cannot be located, they will seek to arrange conditions so that they have an unfair advantage and are sure to win. In short, there appears to be little sense of honor among such persons. Moreover, once their victim is down, they often redouble their efforts to harm or injure him, as indicated by the following vivid description (Toch, 1969):

> when the other person gives some indication of weakness (begs for mercy or asks him to stop) he accelerates his violence. . . . And at this point he resorts to walking over the person's chest, or stomping his face, or doing any number of other things that are obviously extremely cruel. (p. 162)

## Self-Defenders

A final group we shall consider are described by Toch as *self-defenders*. These are persons whose violence appears to stem from an

intense fear of others. Basically, they are afraid that if they do not
strike first, they will soon become victims themselves. Given such
views, it is not at all surprising that they frequently resort to violence
as a defense against what they perceive to be imminent danger. A
clear illustration of this pattern is provided by the following brief
description (Toch, 1969):

> This man shows a pattern which is dominated by basic fear of doom and
> the conviction that others are trying to kill him. He sees . . . many of the
> personal exchanges that he has become involved in as threats upon his life.
> Once he perceives this threat, he panics. He becomes enmeshed in extreme
> violence in an effort to handle this panic. He seems to resort to violence as
> a way of being assured that the other party is not going to kill him—at
> least, that is the way he feels. (p. 164)

### Undercontrolled Aggressors: Some Implications

Before concluding the present discussion, we should pause briefly
to consider the possible implications suggested by research on the
characteristics of violent individuals. First, as we have already noted,
investigations of this topic suggest that the predisposition toward repeated aggression stems from several different sources. There is not
simply one trait or even a single cluster of traits that causes people to
behave in a highly aggressive manner. Rather, there appear to be a
large number of different characteristics related to such actions. As a
result, it will probably not prove possible to develop a single set of
procedures for modifying the behavior of all—or even most—violent
men and women. Instead, different techniques will probably be
required for dealing with each distinctive type.

Second, Toch's research suggests that it will not usually be possible to alter the actions of violence-prone persons through such widely
accepted techniques as increasing the legal penalties for aggression,
strengthening police forces, or restricting sales of dangerous weapons.
This is the case, he contends, because such persons find aggression
personally satisfying and participate in it as a means of attaining goals
deeply rooted in their personality structure (e.g., defending their self-
image, removing imagined threats from others). The key to altering
their behavior, then, lies in psychological treatment focused upon increasing their self-confidence and moving them toward a more mature
outlook on life and relations with others. According to Toch, most violent persons are basically "children" who have learned to use force as
a means of compensating for their immature and undeveloped social

skills. Provide them with these skills, he suggests, and many of the factors predisposing them toward dangerous assaults against others will be removed.

And finally, Toch's investigations suggest that in the case of violence-prone persons, individual traits, characteristics, and dispositions are indeed of crucial importance in the occurrence of overt aggression. In sharp contrast to "normal" aggressors, who assault others primarily when situational factors push them in this direction, under-controlled aggressors actively seek such encounters and engage in them as a result of strong, internal forces. This is not to say, of course, that violence-prone persons aggress in a social or situational vacuum—obviously this is not the case. However, among such individuals, the predominance of situational over individual determinants of aggression that we emphasized so strongly in the first portion of this chapter appears to be lacking or, at the least, is sharply reduced. In the case of repeatedly aggressive men and women, the roots of violence seem, in an important sense, to lie at least partially within the traits or characteristics of individual aggressors.

## The Case of Excessive Violence: When Too Much Restraint Is a Dangerous Thing

SNIPER SHOOTS MOTORISTS FROM BRIDGE
VICTIM TURNED INTO HUMAN TORCH
MOTHER CHARGED IN BRUTAL CHAIN-SAW MURDERS
YOUNGSTERS BEAT TOT TO DEATH
TEEN LOVERS SUSPECTED IN PARENTS' DEATH

Headlines such as these appear with alarming frequency on the front pages of our morning or evening newspapers. In general, our reaction to these tragic events is one of profound bewilderment. How, we ask, could anyone commit such brutal crimes? What type of crazed or deranged monsters are responsible for these violent and seemingly senseless acts? Until quite recently, the answer to these questions provided by most psychologists, psychiatrists, and other professionals emphasized a breakdown in the usual internal restraints against aggression. Specifically, it was contended that the perpetrators of such acts are persons dangerously lacking in the normal controls and inhibitions that prevent most persons from engaging in such behavior.

At first glance, such an interpretation seems quite reasonable. After all, who but extremely aggressive persons totally lacking in such restraint would be capable of mass murder, assaults against children, or attacks on their own families? Surprisingly, however, closer examination of the individuals involved in such forms of extreme violence often reveals a sharply different picture. In case after case, the perpetrators of these shocking crimes are not the type of violent, assertive persons one might expect; rather, they turn out to be passive, mild-mannered men and women, totally lacking in a past history of aggressive encounters. Indeed, far from being impulsive or easily provoked, they frequently appear to be patient, long-suffering souls, possessed of truly extraordinary levels of restraint and control. While many examples of this pattern have come to light, the following case history is among the most vivid (Schultz, 1960):

> Jim came home by surprise one day and discovered his wife in bed with a neighboring farmer. He said he did not know what to do and merely closed the door and returned to the fields and cried. He added that he could have done "something" as there was a loaded rifle in the room adjoining the bedroom. Jim never brought up his wife's infidelity, and she, seeing so little objection, became more bold in her affair. The paramour began staying for meals, and on several occasions stayed overnight. Jim voiced no objections and even lent the paramour money, seed, and farm equipment, as well as labor. Finally, after this arrangement had gone on for three years, the paramour took a truck to Jim's farm while the latter was away, loaded up his household goods and livestock, as well as Jim's wife and four children, and took them away. Jim, though surprised at his wife's and children's absence, *did nothing to find out where she was or attempt to bring her back, nor did he ever approach his wife's lover.* (p. 106; italics added)

Certainly, it is hard to imagine a more amazing example of restraint in the face of repeated—and prolonged—provocation. Despite the brazen actions of his wife and her lover, Jim did nothing, failing to offer any type of protest during three long years. Only later, when he remarried and discovered that his second wife, too, was unfaithful, did he finally explode into violence, murdering her and her lover in a particularly brutal fashion.

After carefully analyzing a number of such cases, Edwin Megargee (1966, 1971) has reached the conclusion that many of the perpetrators of extreme acts of violence are in fact individuals of this type. That is, they are *overcontrolled aggressors,* possessing powerful inhibitions against the performance of overt aggressive actions. Reasoning from this initial finding, Megargee has also proposed that because of their rigid internal controls, such men and women usually show little overt reaction to provocation, choosing instead to mask their anger or resentment behind a cloak of extreme passivity. Over the course of time, however, provocations mount until even *their* excessive inhibitions are overcome. And then, these seemingly docile individuals erupt into sudden violence that often catches their victims totally by surprise. Following the completion of their aggressive outbursts, they quickly revert to their former, passive state, appearing once again to be persons without a temper, totally incapable of mild, let alone extreme, acts of aggression. According to Megargee, then, the individuals most likely to commit extreme acts of violence are not the chronically undercontrolled persons we considered in the previous section—who go about with the proverbial "chip on their shoulder"—but rather, chronically overcontrolled individuals whose excessive restraints against aggression turn them into walking powder kegs with a fuse of indeterminate length.

In order to investigate the validity of these suggestions, Megargee (1966) conducted a large-scale field study involving two groups of male juvenile delinquents (ages 11–17). Individuals in the first of these groups (labeled as *extremely assaultive*) had been incarcerated for extreme acts of violence (e.g., the murder of their own parents, brutal beatings of others), while those in the second (labeled as *moderately assaultive*) had been detained for more moderate acts of aggression (e.g., fist fights, attacks with nondeadly weapons such as can openers or sticks). On the basis of the reasoning outlined above, Megargee predicted that many of the persons in the extremely assaultive group would turn out, upon close study, to be chronically overcontrolled aggressors. In contrast, none of the individuals in the moderately assaultive group should fall into this category. Instead, they should all be chronically undercontrolled persons, of the type discussed in the preceding section. To the extent that these two different types of aggressors were differentially represented in the two major experimental groups, a further—and seemingly paradoxical—prediction could then be made: subjects in the extremely assaultive sample would actually be found to evidence *lower* levels of aggression both prior to and following their incarceration than those in the moderately assaultive sample. This would be the case because aside from their single, extremely violent act, they would demonstrate a pattern of restrained, passive behavior. (Largely for purposes of comparison, two nonag-

gressive groups of subjects, who had been arrested for property offenses and general incorrigibility, respectively, were also included in
the study.)

As a means of assessing the accuracy of these intriguing predictions, Megargee gathered a large amount of data regarding the actions
of all four groups of subjects both prior to and following their arrest.
With respect to behavior prior to their detainment, he examined the
subjects' school-attendance and conduct records, as well as pertinent
police files, while with respect to their actions following incarceration,
he obtained behavioral ratings from counselors who were in close
daily contact with the subjects at their juvenile institution. In general,
the results provided strong support for the major hypothesis under
study. For example, as expected, a greater proportion of individuals in
the extremely assaultive than in the moderately assaultive group were
first offenders who had not previously been in trouble with the law
(78% versus only 29%). Similarly, as shown in Table 12, the subjects
in the extremely assaultive group were rated by their counselors as
being more cooperative, more submissive, and more amiable than
those in the moderately assaultive group. (Also as predicted, the individuals in the two nonaggressive samples fell in between these two
extremes.) Finally, it should also be noted that on a number of psychological tests, the subjects in the extremely assaultive group were

TABLE 12

*Counselor Ratings of the Behavior of Four Groups of Juvenile
Delinquents[a]*

| Experimental Sample[b] | | | |
|---|---|---|---|
| Extremely assaultive | Property offenses | General incorrigibility | Moderately assaultive |
| 16.11[c] | 15.36 | 14.96 | 14.80 |
| ↑————————————————Key comparison————————————————↑ | | | |

[a] Based on data from Megargee, 1966.
[b] Those who had committed extremely aggressive acts were rated as being more
cooperative, more submissive, and more friendly than those who had committed
only moderately aggressive acts. The individuals arrested for property offenses or
because of general incorrigibility fell in between these two extremes.
[c] Higher numbers indicate ratings of greater cooperativeness, etc.

TABLE 13

*Scores on the Overcontrolled Hostility (O–H) Scale Obtained by Various Groups of Prisoners*[a]

| Sample | Mean O–H scale score[b] |
|---|---|
| Extremely assaultive probation applicants | 18.43 |
| Overcontrolled assaultive prison inmates | 16.24 |
| Moderately assaultive probation applicants | 15.07 |
| Nonviolent probation applicants | 13.39 |

[a] Adapted from Megargee, 1971.
[b] Higher scores indicate increasing hostility as well as increasing controls over such reactions.

found to possess stronger internal restraints against aggression than those in the moderately assaultive group.

Taken as a whole, the findings obtained by Megargee (1966) and those reported in additional studies (e.g., Blackburn, 1969) suggest that contrary to popular belief, the perpetrators of extreme acts of violence are frequently *not* individuals lacking in internal controls or restraints over the expression of overt aggression. Rather, they often appear to be persons possessing extremely powerful inhibitions of this type, who turn to violence only after a series of long and unendurable provocations.

Needless to say, this surprising finding is of considerable interest in its own right. Unless some means for identifying such overcontrolled individuals exists, however, it is of little practical significance. Fortunately, a psychological test designed for just this purpose has recently been developed by Megargee and his colleagues (e.g., Megargee, 1971; Megargee, Cook, & Mendelsohn, 1967). Although this test—known, appropriately, as the Overcontrolled Hostility (O–H) Scale—is still in the developmental stage, it seems quite promising. For example, when it is administered to groups of prisoners incarcerated for different types of offenses, differences in the expected directions are generally obtained (refer to Table 13). Should the O–H Scale be fully validated in further research, it will provide a useful tool for identifying individuals whose excessive restraints against aggression render them extremely—and unexpectedly—dangerous both to themselves and to their victims.

## Attitudes, Values, and Aggression

Suppose, for the sake of argument, that on a particular day, you were strongly provoked by two different persons—one you liked and one you disliked. Do you think that your reactions toward these two individuals might differ? Although existing empirical evidence concerning this issue is quite mixed in nature (e.g., Hendrick & Taylor, 1971; Kelley & Byrne, 1977), it seems only reasonable to predict that this would indeed be the case. Specifically, you would be much more likely to behave in an aggressive manner toward the latter than toward the former. Further, it seems safe to predict that this would be the case across a number of different situations and in many different contexts. Regardless of the particular circumstances, you might well react with forebearance and restraint when irritated by your friend but with anger and perhaps open hostility when treated in a similar fashion by your enemy. In short, your attitudes toward these two persons might well influence your reactions to them in a wide range of settings.

Now, consider a second hypothetical situation—one in which *you* serve as the annoyer and anger two different strangers. Further, imagine that one of these persons is a pacifist, strongly opposed to violence on the basis of deep religious convictions, while the other is a professional soldier, quite hooked on the "macho" cult of male toughness. Do you think that these individuals might react differently to your provocations? Once again, an affirmative answer seems justified. While the pacifist might well "turn the other cheek" and ignore your actions, the soldier would be more likely to grow quite angry and attempt to reciprocate in kind. Moreover, such reactions on the part of these persons would probably be observed in a wide range of settings. Regardless of the specific situation, the pacifist would refrain from aggressing, while the soldier might turn quite quickly to such behavior.

Needless to say, both of these examples represent gross oversimplifications. Many factors other than the ones we have mentioned would, of course, influence the actions of the persons involved. Yet, both serve to underscore an important point about aggression: personality is far from the only individual determinant of such behavior; in many cases, the *attitudes* and the *values* of potential aggressors are also quite important in this regard.

As you probably know from your own experience, attitudes and values are often highly enduring in nature. Barring strong external intervention, the opinions we hold today are very likely to be the ones we will hold tomorrow. Similarly, values shift exceedingly slowly, if at all, with the passage of time. Given this state of affairs, it is clear that individuals carry these psychological "entities" with them from situation to situation. Thus, to the extent that they are relevant to aggression, they may strongly affect such behavior.

While social psychologists have long been aware of the possible influence of attitudes and values upon aggression, it is only within the past decade that this relationship has been subjected to systematic study. Despite this fact, however, a great deal of valuable information has already come to light. Because this evidence suggests that attitudes, values, and internal standards are actually even more crucial in influencing aggression than was previously assumed, we will now examine a portion of these findings in some detail.

### The Mediating Role of Attitudes: Prejudice and Interracial Aggression

While many different attitudes might be expected to influence the occurrence of aggression, most attention has been focused, in social psychology, upon the impact of *prejudice*—strong negative reactions toward the members of racial, ethnic, or religious groups other than one's own. A great deal of informal evidence, including the long and ghastly record of atrocities to which we alluded in Chapter 1, suggests that these powerful negative attitudes often set the stage for high levels of violence. In particular, it appears that strong racial, religious, or ethnic prejudice often leads the persons holding such views to perceive the objects of their wrath as somehow less than human. And once they are defined in this manner, even the most extreme forms of violence against them seem to become permissible (e.g., Leamer, 1972).

The observation that strong prejudicial feelings often facilitate the occurrence of intergroup aggression points, quite logically, to the conclusion that such reactions also play an important role in the behavior of specific individuals. That is, it seems reasonable to expect that persons high in prejudice will often behave in a more aggressive manner than those lower in such beliefs, at least with respect to members of the groups they dislike (cf. Buss, 1961; Kaufmann, 1970). Somewhat surprisingly, experiments undertaken to assess this suggestion in a direct manner have yielded mixed and complex results (e.g., Baxter, 1972; Genthner & Taylor, 1973). However, other research, concerned primarily with the broader issue of *interracial aggression*, has yielded strong—if somewhat indirect—support for this relationship.

In these intriguing studies, most of which have been conducted by Edward and Marcia Donnerstein and their colleagues (see Donnerstein & Donnerstein, 1976), the participants' level of prejudice has not generally been assessed. Despite this fact, however, a portion of the findings obtained may be interpreted as suggesting that negative attitudes toward the members of groups other than one's own may strongly affect aggression across racial lines.

For example, in the earliest of these investigations (Donnerstein *et al.*, 1972), white undergraduate males were provided with an opportunity to deliver electric shocks to either a white or a black confederate in the context of the teacher–learner paradigm devised by Buss (1961). Within each of these two major conditions, half of the participants were led to believe that their identity would be concealed from the victim (the *anonymous* condition), while the remainder were informed that he could both see and identify them over closed-circuit TV (the *nonanonymous* condition). Further, within each of *these* groups, half of the subjects were informed, prior to the start of the shock trials, that when they finished, the learner would have the opportunity of shocking them (the condition of *prior–role-switching instructions*); in contrast, the remaining individuals were not told about this supposed reversal of roles until after they had finished shocking the victim (the condition of *subsequent–role-switching instructions*).

As might be expected, subjects' level of aggression was strongly affected both by the anonymous–nonanonymous variable and by the factor of prior role-switching–subsequent role-switching. That is, they generally evidenced lower levels of aggression in the nonanonymous group, where they could be readily identified by the victim, than in the anonymous condition, where they could not. And they also demonstrated somewhat less aggression in the prior–role-switching condition, where they were led to fear retaliation from the victim before shocking this person, than in the subsequent–role-switching group, where they learned of such retaliation only after completing their attacks. Of greater importance within the context of the present discussion, however, was the added finding that victim's race interacted strongly with both of these factors in influencing subjects' behavior.

Specifically, under conditions in which the subjects anticipated retaliation from the victim (i.e., in the nonanonymous and prior–role-switching conditions), they directed stronger levels of aggression against the white than against the black victim. In contrast, however, precisely the opposite pattern of findings was obtained under conditions in which the subjects did *not* anticipate retaliation from the victim (i.e., in the anonymous and subsequent–role-switching conditions). Here, stronger levels of shock were directed against the black than against the white confederate (see Figure 42). In short, subjects were *less* aggressive toward a black than a white target when they believed that retaliation was probable but were actually *more* aggressive toward a black than a white victim when they believed that no re-

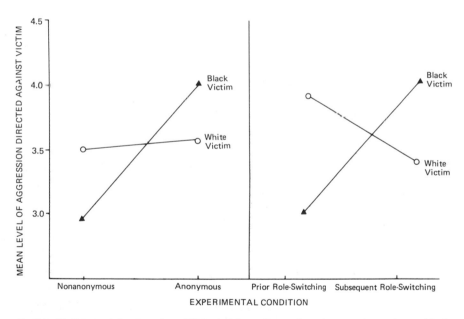

FIGURE 42. Interracial aggression. White subjects directed weaker attacks against a black than against a white victim when retaliation from this person was expected (i.e., in the nonanonymous and prior–role-switching conditions). However, they actually directed *stronger* attacks against a black than against a white victim when no retaliation seemed likely (i.e., in the anonymous and subsequent–role-switching conditions). (Adapted from Donnerstein *et al.*, 1972.)

taliation would be forthcoming and they could attack with total impunity.

While several different factors may have contributed to this pattern of findings, one reasonable interpretation is that even the relatively "enlightened" university students who took part in Donnerstein *et al.*'s research harbored negative attitudes toward blacks and that these reactions led them to direct heightened aggression against such persons when it seemed "safe" to engage in such actions. Further evidence that this may indeed be the case is provided by the fact that a similar pattern of findings has emerged in several follow-up studies (e.g., Donnerstein & Donnerstein, 1973, 1975). That is, in these experiments, too, white subjects inhibited assaults against blacks when retaliation seemed imminent but aggressed with considerable vigor when retaliation seemed unlikely.

That tendencies to direct stronger assaults against the members of a different race than against the members of one's own race are not restricted to whites is suggested by an additional study conducted by Wilson and Rogers (1975). In this experiment, the participants were black female students, who were provided with an opportunity to aggress against either a black or a white target. Half of the subjects within each of these groups were insulted by the confederate, while the remainder were not. Also, half were led to believe that they would be subject to retaliation from this person, while the remainder were assured that this would not be the case. The major findings of the experiment are summarized in Figure 43, where it can be seen that regardless of the presence of prior provocation or the threat of retaliation, the subjects directed stronger shocks against the white than against the black victim. Once again, several different factors may have contributed to these findings. However, the possibility that they stemmed from negative attitudes on the part of the participants toward individuals belonging to a different race than their own seems quite plausible.

Together, the findings reported by the Donnersteins and their colleagues, Wilson and Rogers, and others (e.g., Griffin & Rogers, 1977) may all be interpreted as supporting the view that negative attitudes—particularly in the form of strong racial, religious, or ethnic prejudice—can greatly enhance the occurrence of overt aggression. This possibility, in turn, takes on added importance when it is noted that such views are both long-lasting and resistant to change (cf. Jones,

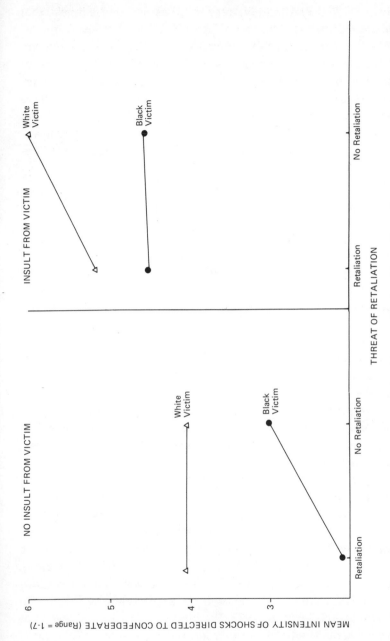

FIGURE 43. Further evidence regarding interracial aggression. Black subjects directed stronger aggression against a white than against a black victim regardless of the threat of retaliation from this person and regardless of whether she had previously provoked them. (Adapted from Wilson & Rogers, 1975.)

1972; Guthrie, 1976). Fortunately, recent investigations suggest that they can be altered through the technique of increased intergroup contact—provided that the conditions prevailing during such contacts are carefully arranged (Eaton & Clore, 1975; Taylor, 1974). Regardless of the specific actions taken to reduce or eliminate prejudice, however, one fact seems clear: the truly disastrous consequences that have stemmed from such reactions in the past suggest very strongly that *some* steps in this direction are essential. Only in this manner, it appears, can we succeed in avoiding what Wilson and Rogers aptly describe as "the fire *this* time."

## Internal Standards and Aggression: The Effects of Looking Inward

As we have already noted, individuals differ sharply in their views concerning aggression. Some find such behavior morally abhorrent and seek to avoid it at all costs; others perceive it as quite acceptable and turn to it readily in their social relations; and most fall somewhere in between these two extremes, avoiding or adopting aggression in accordance with their beliefs that it is or is not justified in a given situation (cf. Rule & Nesdale, 1976b). Needless to say, these differences stem from the fact that individuals possess internal standards and values regarding aggression that often strongly affect their tendencies to engage in such behavior. Further, since they carry such values and standards with them from situation to situation and setting to setting, these, too, seem to qualify as important individual determinants of aggression.

The impact of such values and standards upon overt violence, however, is far from automatic. In order for them to exert such effects, they must be made *salient* to the persons involved; that is, these individuals must notice and pay attention to them. In the absence of such salience, values will exert little, if any, impact upon aggression, which may, instead, be quite impulsive in nature (cf. Berkowitz, 1974). How, then, do such internal standards and values become salient? According to a theoretical framework proposed in recent years by Duval and Wicklund (Duval & Wicklund, 1972; Wicklund, 1975), one answer lies in the development of what has been termed a state of *objective self-awareness*. Specifically, Wicklund and his colleagues argue that because of a strong desire to know and understand themselves better, individuals often turn their attention inward in a self-examining manner. When they do, they enter a state of objective self-awareness in which their attitudes, values, and other characteristics are brought sharply into focus. This process, in turn, leads to attempts at self-evaluation, involving direct comparisons between such internal entities and overt behavior. To the extent that these are found to be consistent, positive reactions follow, and little, if any, pressure for change develops. After all, happy is the person who discovers that his or her behavior is consistent with strongly held ideals! To the extent that behavior and values are found to be discrepant, however, negative reactions develop, and strong pressures toward change may be generated. That is, the persons experiencing such reactions feel a strong pressure to bring their values and their actions into agreement. While alterations in either can eliminate such a discrepancy, internal standards and values are often quite resistant to change. Thus, it is often the case that overt behavior is the portion of the cognitive equation that "gives." In short, the ultimate result of looking inward may often be important changes in various forms of activity.

Extending these suggestions to the occurrence of aggression, it seems reasonable to predict that the impact of heightened self-awareness will depend, quite strongly, upon the values and standards regarding such behavior held by the persons in question. If aggression is viewed in a favorable light and is considered to be an acceptable form of activity, focusing attention inward will make such values salient and so increase the likelihood or intensity of overt violence. In contrast, if aggression is viewed in an unfavorable light and held to be an unacceptable form of activity, heightened self-awareness will make *these* values salient and so reduce the likelihood or strength of such behavior.

These predictions have recently been examined in a number of related studies (e.g., Carver, 1974, 1975; Scheier, Fenigstein, & Buss, 1974). The basic procedure for inducing heightened self-awareness employed in all of these experiments was simple yet ingenious: subjects in the high–self-awareness groups were exposed to their images in a mirror positioned over the experimental apparatus. (Previous research had demonstrated that this technique was highly effective in raising self-awareness; Wicklund, 1975.) The results obtained in these investigations have uniformly supported predictions derived from a self-awareness analysis. For example, in the first investigation on this topic (Scheier *et al.*, 1974), male subjects were provided with an opportunity to deliver electric shocks to a female victim either in the presence or in the absence of a mirror. Since most males view physical assaults against females as reprehensible and inappropriate, it was predicted that the presence of the mirror would serve to make this standard salient and thus inhibit subjects' aggression; this prediction was strongly confirmed. Similarly, in a follow-up investigation (Carver, 1974), male subjects were led to believe (through instructions) that strong shocks to a male confederate would help this person master materials on a bogus learning task. Under these conditions, it was reasoned, the subjects would consider aggression to be justified. Thus, the presence of the mirror would tend to make this standard salient and so enhance assaults against the confederate. As shown in Figure 44, this prediction, too was confirmed.

While these initial studies demonstrated that heightened self-awareness could in fact intensify the impact of widely held or situationally induced values and standards upon aggression, they did not focus primarily upon individual reactions in this respect. That is, in the first study, the impact of a value shared by almost all males in Western culture was examined, while in the second, the impact of a specific, situationally induced standard was investigated. Can self-awareness, then, also intensify the influence of idiosyncratic, individually held values regarding aggression? A recent investigation conducted by Carver (1975) was concerned with precisely this issue.

In this study, individuals previously found, on a brief questionnaire, to be either highly favorable toward the use of physical punishment (the *high-punitive* group) or strongly opposed to the use of such procedures (the *low-punitive* group) participated in the standard teacher–learner paradigm devised by Buss (1961). For half of the individuals within each of these groups, a mirror in which they could see their own reflection was present throughout the session, while for the remainder, the mirror was absent. On the basis of the suggestions outlined above, it was predicted that the presence of the mirror and the heightened self-awareness it induced would strongly facilitate aggression against the confederate by the subjects in the high-punitive group, while actually inhibiting such behavior by those in the low-punitive condition. This would be the case because the presence of the mirror would raise the salience of the pro- and antiaggression values

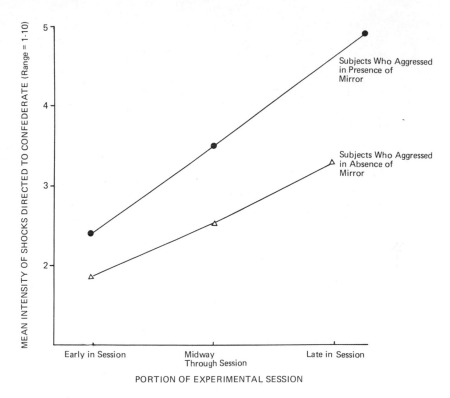

FIGURE 44. Self-awareness and aggression. The presence of a mirror facilitated aggression by individuals who had previously been led to believe that such behavior was beneficial to the victim. (Based on data from Carver, 1974.)

held, respectively, by these two groups of participants. As can be seen in Figure 45, both predictions were generally confirmed. The presence of the mirror significantly enhanced aggression by high-punitive subjects but tended to inhibit such behavior by those low in punitiveness.

It should also be mentioned, in passing, that the findings obtained by Carver can be interpreted in another, related manner. In particular, they can also be viewed as suggesting that while the behavior of the high- and low-punitive groups failed to differ in the absence of the mirror, the high-punitive individuals were much more aggressive in the presence of the mirror. In this respect, these findings support our suggestion on p. 208 that internal values and standards can

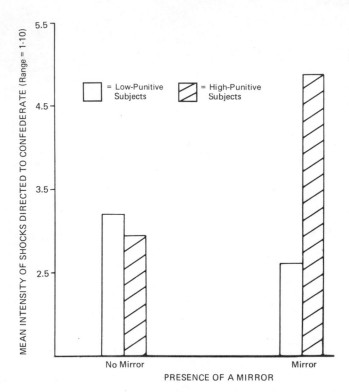

FIGURE 45. Personal values, self-awareness, and aggression. The presence of a mirror facilitated aggression by subjects holding positive views regarding the use of physical punishment (high-punitive individuals) but actually inhibited aggression by participants holding negative views toward such procedures (low-punitive individuals). (Based on data from Carver, 1975.)

indeed exert powerful effects upon aggression, but only—or at least primarily—when these are made salient to the individuals in question.

In conclusion, the studies we have considered and some additional, related experiments (e.g., Rule, Nesdale, & Dyck, 1976; Scheier, 1977) suggest that values and internal standards related to aggression can often exert important effects upon such behavior. Further, they suggest that such effects can be intensified by conditions that favor the development of heightened self-awareness. Apparently, focusing our attention inward not only yields the increased self-understanding or self-knowledge we seek; in many cases, it may also strongly affect the nature of our relations with other persons.

## Heredity and Aggression: The XYY "Syndrome"

Normally, the cells of the human body possess 46 chromosomes, two of which—the X and the Y chromosomes—play a crucial role in the determination of sex. More specifically, men possess one X and one Y and are designated XY, while women possess two Xs and are designated as being XX. On relatively rare occasions, however, men are encountered who possess an extra Y chromosome (XYY). Although the existence of this unusual pattern had been recognized for many years, it was viewed as merely an interesting but unimportant departure from normality until the mid-1960s. At that time, a team of researchers (Jacobs, Brunton, & Melville, 1965) reported that this unusual chromosomal pattern was much more common among individuals imprisoned for various crimes than among the population at large. Further, they described an XYY "syndrome," presumably shown by such persons, consisting of (1) excessive height; (2) mental retardation; and (3) occasional—and unpredictable—outbursts of extreme violence.

These early findings received a great deal of attention and were soon followed by a number of additional studies conducted in several countries around the world. Although the results of individual experiments were not always totally consistent, most tended to confirm the original findings reported by Jacobs, Brunton, and Melville (1965), indicating that the XYY chromosomal type does indeed occur more frequently among prisoners than among other groups of individuals. Indeed, while the rate of occurrence of this anomaly is approximately 1 in 1,000 among newborn male infants and normal adult males, it is more than 15 times higher in the case of prison inmates (Jarvik, Klodin, & Matsuyama, 1973; see Table 14).

On the basis of such evidence, some researchers concluded that possession of an extra Y chromosome predisposes individuals toward aggression. Indeed, a few went even further, suggesting that the high level of aggression often demonstrated by such persons implicates the single Y chromosome possessed by normal males in the occurrence of such behavior. As stated by one group of researchers (Jarvik, Klodin, & Matsuyama, 1973):

> The increased frequency of XYY individuals among perpetrators of such crimes suggests that an extra Y chromosome predisposes [individuals] to aggressive behavior. If any extra Y chromosome can lead to excessive ag-

gression or hostility, it is possible that *the single Y chromosome with which each normal man is endowed may itself be the genetic root of "normal" aggressiveness.* (p. 80; italics added)

While such conclusions are quite intriguing, they were greeted with skepticism by other scientists, who pointed to several important grounds for exercising caution in their acceptance. First, attention was called to a number of flaws in the research purporting to demonstrate a link between the XYY chromosomal type and heightened aggression. For example, it was noted that many such studies were based on only one or at most a few cases and that they often lacked appropriate control groups (cf. Witkin *et al.*, 1976). In view of such problems, existing evidence could hardly be accepted as convincing. Second, it was noted that most crimes of violence are committed by individuals possessing the normal XY chromosome combination. Thus, possession of an extra Y chromosome does not in itself seem to be a necessary condition for the performance of violent acts. Third, closer study of the XYY individuals found in prisons revealed that most were arrested not for attacks upon others but for less dramatic offenses, such as theft or burglary (Price & Whatmore, 1967). And finally, it was suggested that any tendency on the part of XYY individuals to become involved in violence more frequently than normal XY persons may stem primarily from social rather than genetic factors (Bandura, 1973). For example, being quite large for their age, such persons may often associate with friends several years older than themselves and so be exposed to violent, delinquent models at an early stage of development. Similarly,

TABLE 14

*The Incidence of XYY Individuals in Prison and Nonprison Populations*[a]

| Population | Number in sample | Number of XYY[b] in sample | Percent of XYY in sample |
|---|---|---|---|
| Prisoners | 5,066 | 98 | 1.93 |
| Newborn male infants | 9,904 | 13 | .13 |
| Normal adult males | 6,148 | 8 | .13 |

[a]Based on data from Jarvik, Klodin, & Matsuyama, 1973.
[b]Persons showing the XYY chromosomal pattern are more than 15 times as common among prisoners as among newborn infants or normal (nonprison) adult males.

being tall, they may often be rewarded for aggressing against others and thus quickly acquire such patterns of behavior.

In the face of such criticism, the suggestion that possession of an extra Y chromosome strongly predisposes individuals toward crimes of violence quickly became controversial in nature. On one side was a group of scientists who strongly supported its accuracy, while on the other was a somewhat larger group who expressed grave doubts in this respect. Such strong disagreement between the purported "experts" was quite discouraging in and of itself. Even worse, however, was the fact that this controversy often found its way into the popular press, where the complex and significant issues it involved were thoroughly clouded and confused.

In science, the existence of a heated controversy generally leads within a short period of time to the collection of additional, relevant data. In this respect, the controversy surrounding the possible existence of an XYY syndrome has been no exception. Indeed, a number of investigations quickly shed further light upon its nature and pointed the way to its resolution. While many of these studies have been quite informative, by far the most convincing—and definitive—appears to be one reported recently by Witkin and his colleagues (1976).

These investigators began by selecting as their experimental sample all males born within the city of Copenhagen between January 1, 1944, and December 31, 1947. The result, of course, was a very substantial initial sample, consisting of 28,884 individuals. Since previous research had indicated that XYY individuals are generally quite tall, however, Witkin *et al.* decided to focus their attention upon the tallest 16% of this group. Attempts were then made to visit all of these persons (a total sample of 4,591) in order to determine their chromosomal type. With perseverance, almost 91% of these individuals were successfully contacted. Within this group of 4,139 persons, 12 were found to be XYY, 4,111 to be XY, and 16 to be XXY (another relatively rare chromosomal anomaly). Information was then gathered from extensive public records regarding the (1) height; (2) intellectual functioning; (3) socioeconomic status; and (4) past criminal activities (if any) of all of these individuals. This information was then employed to assess the accuracy of several suggestions concerning the behavior and the characteristics of XYY individuals.

The first major finding of the study was a confirmation of the results reported in previous research. As expected, the XYY individuals showed an elevated rate of criminal offenses. While only 9.3% of the XY participants had previously been convicted of one or more crimes, fully 41.7% of the XYY participants fell into this category.[1] Thus, as reported by earlier investigators, XYY individuals seemed much more likely than their XY peers to become involved in criminal activities. But how was this seemingly elevated rate of antisocial behavior to be explained? What factors might account for the over-representation of XYY persons among criminal offenders? This, of course, was the major focus of the study.

In accordance with previous suggestions, Witkin and his colleagues concentrated their attention upon three alternative explanations for the elevated crime rate shown by the XYYs. The first—and by far most controversial—contends that XYY individuals are more aggressive than normal XYs and that, as a result, they more frequently turn to a life of crime. If this is indeed the case, it would be expected that XYY criminals would be found to have been involved in crimes of violence much more frequently than criminals showing the normal XY configuration. Yet, careful study of the offense records of both groups revealed no appreciable differences between them: XYYs were definitely *not* more likely to commit crimes of violence than XYs. Indeed, only one of the 12 XYY persons studied had ever been arrested for such behavior, and even this incident was of a relatively minor nature. Thus, there was definitely no indication that heightened tendencies toward aggression accounted for the overrepresentation of XYYs among the criminal elements of the population.

A second hypothesis investigated by Witkin and his colleagues contends that because they are often quite tall, XYY persons are more likely than others to be perceived as dangerous. As a result, they are also held in suspicion more frequently than shorter men and are more likely to be apprehended and convicted. Careful comparisons of the heights of the various groups of individuals participating in the study failed to yield any support for these contentions. While the XYY subjects were in fact slightly taller than XYs, there was no appreciable difference in the heights of criminal and noncriminal participants. In fact, if anything, criminals tended to be *shorter* than their more law-

[1] Both of these figures are somewhat inflated by virtue of the fact that they include convictions for relatively minor as well as more serious crimes.

abiding peers. Thus, height did not seem to provide an adequate explanation for the elevated crime rate evidenced by XYY persons.

In contrast to the negative findings we have outlined so far, results offered strong support for a third interpretation—one contending that XYYs are not as bright as normal individuals and, as a result, are much more likely to be apprehended and convicted than criminals showing the normal XY configuration. Two pieces of evidence supported this contention. First, as expected, XYYs were found to demonstrate lower levels of performance than XYs on standardized tests of intellectual functioning routinely administered to all Danish males. Second, among the XY control group, criminals evidenced significantly lower levels of intellectual functioning than noncriminals. Together, these two findings suggested to Witkin *et al.* that it is primarily intellectual dysfunction—not innate tendencies toward violence—that accounts for the overrepresentation of XYY individuals among prisoners and convicted criminals. Indeed, XYYs do not even engage in criminal behavior more frequently than XYs—they are simply punished for it more regularly! As noted by Witkin *et al.* (1976)

> People of lower intelligence may be less adept at escaping detection and so to be likely to have a higher representation in a classificatory system based on registered crime. The elevated crime rate found in our XYY group may therefore reflect a higher detection rather than imply a higher rate of commission of crimes. (p. 553)

In short, XYYs may not be any more likely than XYs to become involved in criminal activities. When they do, however, their lower level of intelligence may lead them to blunder in ways that sharply increase the chances of their being arrested and convicted.

Regardless of whether all of these suggestions are confirmed in further research, the findings reported by Witkin *et al.* leave us confronting a picture of XYY individuals far different from the one commonly reported by the mass media. In place of raving killers, lusting after violence, we find, instead, relatively dull and mild-mannered persons who are no more likely than others to engage in criminal behavior but who are more likely, when they do, to be apprehended. Admittedly, this pattern is far less exciting or intriguing than the earlier image of aggressive "supermales," genetically programmed for violence. Existing evidence, though, suggests that it is probably far closer to the truth.

## SEX DIFFERENCES IN AGGRESSION: GENDER AS A DETERMINANT OF VIOLENCE

Are there any important differences between the two sexes with respect to aggressive behavior? Both common sense and informal observation point to the possible existence of two major contrasts in this respect. First, it has often been held that men are more aggressive than women—more likely than their female counterparts to turn to physical or verbal assaults in the course of their interactions with others. And second, it is widely believed that other factors being equal, men are far more likely to serve as the target of aggression than women. These differences, in turn, have usually been attributed to both genetic and cultural factors. On the one hand, it has been argued that men, because of inherited characteristics, are more strongly predisposed toward aggression than women. And on the other, it has been noted that cultural stereotypes of masculinity and femininity teach individuals in many different societies that males are—and should be—"tougher" and more aggressive than females (cf. Deaux, 1976).

While such assertions regarding the existence of important differences between the sexes with respect to aggression seem quite reasonable in nature, we have already found at many points in this volume that common sense is often a faulty guide to an accurate comprehension of human aggression. Thus, before reaching any firm conclusions concerning such contrasts, we should turn to empirical evidence regarding their existence. A number of experiments provide information relevant to this issue, and as we shall soon see, they suggest that while there may in fact be some differences between the sexes with respect to aggressive actions, these are not nearly as simple or as clear-cut as has often been assumed (cf. Frodi, Macaulay, & Thome, 1977).

### Sex Differences in Aggression: Males and Females as Aggressors

Early investigations concerned with the influence of gender upon aggression generally reported findings consistent with expectations based upon informal observation: males usually *did* seem to be more aggressive than females (e.g., Bandura, Ross, & Ross, 1963a,b; Buss, 1963). More recent investigations, however, have generally failed to confirm such findings. For example, in several experiments conducted by the present author (Baron & Ball, 1974; Baron & Bell, 1976), male college students have *not* been found to direct stronger or longer-lasting shocks to a victim than females. Further, aggressive actions by both sexes have been found, in these studies, to be influenced in a highly similar fashion by variables as diverse in nature as direct insult, exposure to nonhostile humor, and the presence of unpleasant heat. Similar findings have also been reported by other researchers, in both laboratory (e.g., Gentry, 1970b; Taylor & Epstein, 1967) and field (Harris, 1974b) settings. Further, the absence of sharp or clear-cut sex differences in aggression has also been observed among young children (Liebert & Baron, 1972) and among subjects from racial, economic, and social backgrounds quite distinct from those of most college students (e.g., Shemberg, Leventhal, & Allman, 1968). Taking the results of all of these investigations into account, it seems reasonable to conclude that the strong and obvious sex differences reported in many early studies have all but totally vanished. While the reasons for this shift are by no means entirely clear, two tentative explanations for its occurrence may be readily suggested.

First, a careful comparison of the studies reporting large sex differences in aggression with those failing to observe such findings suggests that the two sets of investigations differ in one crucial respect: in most cases, those reporting large sex differences did not expose participants to strong provocation, while those failing to uncover such differences did employ such procedures. In short, significant differences between the sexes seem to emerge in the absence of strong provocation but vanish in its presence. This pattern of findings, in turn, suggests that there may well be a difference in the threshold for aggression on the part of men and women. Specifically, males may have a lower "boiling point" than females, so to speak, and turn to aggression much more readily or after milder provocation on many different occasions. Further, they may sometimes be strongly angered by forms of treatment (e.g., direct verbal insult) which seem to induce somewhat weaker emotional reactions of this type among women (see Frodi, 1977). Such conclusions seem consistent both with experimental findings and informal observation. It should be noted, though, that they are only tentative in nature, and must be subjected to further, direct experimental test before being accepted with any confidence.

Figure 46. Are men more aggressive than women? Recent evidence suggests that as shown in this cartoon, any differences between the two sexes in this respect may be sharply on the wane. (Source: King Features Syndicate, Inc.)

Second, the apparent disappearance of clear-cut sex differences in aggression may be related to more general changes in sexual roles and stereotypes that have occurred in recent years. As noted by several different observers (e.g., Deaux, 1976), these changes have involved a reduction in passivity on the part of women, as well as growing self-esteem and confidence. Together, such shifts may have served to render women less inhibited about responding aggressively to direct provocation. If this is indeed the case, then any remaining differences between males and females—including the proposed difference in threshold mentioned above—may continue to decrease with the passage of time and vanish entirely at some point in the future. In short, the two sexes may gradually become equal in their propensity for violence, as well as in their tendencies toward more desirable forms of behavior (see Figure 46).

### Sex Differences in Aggression: Males and Females as Targets of Violence

While the findings of investigations concerned with differences between the two sexes in their tendency to aggress have been both mixed and inconsistent, those relating to the likelihood that the members of each gender will serve as targets of such behavior have been much more uniform. Almost without exception, the results of studies in which the sex of the target has been varied have systematically confirmed the widespread belief that women are less likely to be the recipients of physical attacks than men and, further, that when they are, the magnitude of such assaults will be lower than for their male counterparts (cf. Frodi, Macaulay, & Thome, 1977). Such findings have been reported in a large number of studies employing sharply different procedures, measures of aggression, and subject populations (e.g., Buss, 1966a; Baron & Bell, 1973; Kaleta & Buss, 1973). For example, in an interesting study conducted by Taylor and Epstein (1967), male and female subjects competed in the Taylor reaction-time paradigm, described previously, with either a male or a female partner. Results indicated that as expected, both male and female participants set weaker shocks for their opponent when this person was a female than when he was a male. The fact that similar results have also been obtained in other experiments suggests that in general, women are less likely to serve as the target of aggression than men. Again, however, this situation may well change in the years ahead, as traditional conceptions of both masculinity and femininity continue to alter. At the present time, "chivalry"—at least with respect to aggression—is not quite dead; whether it will persist into future decades remains to be seen.

## SUMMARY

While aggression is strongly influenced by the type of situational, social, and environmental variables considered in earlier chapters, it is also often affected by the lasting characteristics of potential aggressors—those traits, values, or dispositions they carry with them from situation to situation. With respect to aggression by "normal" persons (i.e., those free from obvious psychopathology), several personality traits or dispositions have been found to affect the occurrence of aggression. Among these are fear of social disapproval, guilt concerning assaults against others, beliefs in one's ability to influence one's own fate, and a hard-driving, competitive approach to life.

In contrast to most individuals, who aggress only under appropriate conditions (e.g., following strong provocation), a relatively small group of persons, often described as "violent men and women," make such behavior a normal part of their social relations. Detailed study of such individuals indicates that they may actually be divided into several distinctive "types" and that the aggression of each stems from somewhat different factors or characteristics.

A third group of aggressors—the perpetrators of extreme acts of violence—demonstrate still a different pattern. Common sense suggests that such persons must be wild-eyed killers, totally lacking in the normal restraints that prevent most persons from performing violent acts. Yet, recent investigations suggest that in many cases, they actually turn out to be quiet, passive persons, possessing exceptionally powerful inhibitions against overt aggression. Apparently, these strong restraints prevent such individuals from expressing aggression until they have been provoked beyond endurance—at which time they literally explode into extreme and unexpected violence.

Aggression is also influenced by attitudes and internal standards or values. Among the most important attitudes affecting such behavior are various forms of prejudice. Such negative attitudes regarding racial, ethnic, or religious groups other than one's own seem to have been responsible for a long history of cruel atrocities. And, unfortunately, they still appear to be present and active today. For example, in the studies reported, white individuals directed stronger levels of aggression against blacks than against other whites when they feared no retaliation from these victims, and blacks aggressed more strongly against whites than against fellow blacks regardless of the threat of retaliation.

Individuals also differ greatly with respect to internal values or standards concerning aggression. While some find such behavior morally abhorrent and refrain from its performance, others view it as much more acceptable and quickly adopt it in the course of their social interactions with others. Several recent studies suggest that such values and standards exert a powerful effect upon aggression, providing they are made the subject of careful scrutiny by the persons involved.

The fact that individuals possessing an extra Y chromosome (XYYs, as they are often termed) are found with a higher-than-expected frequency among prison populations has led to speculation that this genetic abnormality predisposes such persons toward violence. However, growing evidence suggests that this is not the case. XYY criminals are not more likely than their XY counterparts to become involved in aggressive crimes; in fact, they only rarely participate in such episodes. Thus, their overrepresentation among prison populations seems to stem primarily from their low level of intelligence, which leads to their being apprehended far more frequently than other criminals for various property offenses (e.g., theft, burglary).

It has generally been assumed that men are more aggressive than women. Recent empirical evidence, however, suggests that this may be the case only in the absence of strong provocation. When subjected to strong annoyance, women as well as men may turn to aggression in their interactions with others. Despite increasing equality between the sexes with respect to willingness to aggress, however, other findings suggest that both men and women are still less likely to direct overt assaults against female than against male targets.

# 6

# The Prevention and Control of Human Aggression

Aggression is, by definition, a dangerous and harmful form of behavior. Further, as we have noted on several different occasions, its incidence in social interaction is alarmingly high. Given these facts, it seems only reasonable to expect that over the years, researchers concerned with the study of human violence would devote considerable attention to techniques for preventing or controlling such actions. Surprisingly, however, this has not been the case. A careful survey of existing psychological literature on aggression reveals that while a great many investigations have focused upon various social, situational, environmental, and individual antecedents of violence, a much smaller number have examined means for preventing or controlling its occurrence (cf. Kimble, Fitz, & Onorad, 1977; Pisano & Taylor, 1971). Further, many of the studies that *have* been concerned with these latter topics have been conducted primarily within an applied context. As a result, they have often sought means for controlling aggression under specific circumstances or among special populations and have *not* attempted to establish basic principles that might prove useful in lowering the incidence of aggression generally (cf. Bandura, 1973). While many different factors have contributed to this surprising and somewhat unsettling state of affairs, two seem to be of greatest importance.

First, there appears to have been a widespread—albeit largely implicit—assumption on the part of many researchers to the effect that aggression can be controlled in what might be termed a largely "negative" fashion, that is, through the removal of factors serving to elicit its occurrence. According to this view, investigations of the possible

225

antecedents of aggression might well provide a double "payoff." On the one hand, information concerning the conditions facilitating human violence would be obtained, while on the other, knowledge useful in attempts to reduce or control such behavior would be provided. At first glance, this seems to be an eminently reasonable suggestion: to eliminate aggression, simply eliminate the conditions enhancing its performance. Unfortunately, though, the persuasiveness of this argument is sharply diminished by the ever-growing list of social, environmental, and situational antecedents of such behavior. Short of the attainment of Utopia, it is difficult to visualize a situation in which all—or even most—of the aggression-enhancing conditions examined in earlier chapters of this volume could be removed from the environment. How, for example, can frustration, aggressive cues, crowding, and related factors be entirely eliminated? The fact that they cannot raises strong doubts concerning the ultimate effectiveness of control strategies based largely upon the removal of such factors.

Second, and perhaps of even greater importance in accounting for the past neglect of techniques for the prevention and control of aggression, is the fact that until quite recently, many psychologists believed that they already knew the best means for attaining such goals. Specifically, it was widely believed that two factors—*punishment* and *catharsis*—are the most effective deterrents to human violence. And since, presumably, these were already well understood, little further research on them was needed (cf. Berkowitz, 1962). In short, the "big picture" had already been established; all that remained was the task of filling in the minor, unresolved details. This was a comforting view but, unfortunately, one that has now been called into serious question. Recent investigations concerned with punishment and catharsis suggest that neither is quite as effective in controlling overt aggression as was once believed and, further, that both operate in a far more complex manner than was previously assumed. Thus, while both may be of some use in this regard, they do not, either singly or in combination, provide a panacea for all human violence.

As the restraining influence of the beliefs outlined above has waned in recent years, the volume of research directly concerned with means for preventing or controlling human violence has risen sharply. Not surprisingly, much of this work has represented extensions of earlier research concerned with punishment and catharsis and, in this respect, has both increased and refined our knowledge regarding the impact of these two factors. Many other studies, however, have examined additional techniques for reducing aggression, including such approaches as the introduction of *nonaggressive models,* the induction of *incompatible responses* among potential aggressors, and the role of various *cognitive factors* (e.g., the provision of reasonable explanations for past provocation). Evidence regarding the influence of all of these potential deterrents, as well as that of punishment and catharsis, will be described in the discussion that follows. In addition, whenever existing data seem to warrant such generalizations, attempts will be made to outline possible applications of research findings to the control of aggression in various natural settings.

## ACTUAL AND THREATENED PUNISHMENT: EFFECTIVE DETERRENTS TO HUMAN AGGRESSION?

Over the course of several decades, scientific opinion concerning the impact of punishment upon human behavior has swung from one extreme to the other. Initially, such procedures were accepted as representing a highly effective means for modifying behavior; indeed, in his original *law of effect,* Thorndike (1911) assumed that punishment is equal, in this respect, to positive reinforcement. Yet, in apparent contradiction of this view, early empirical evidence seemed to suggest that the impact of punishment is only temporary in nature (Estes, 1944; Skinner, 1938). Largely on the basis of such findings, the usefulness of punishment was called into serious question, and it soon fell into severe disfavor as a technique for altering human behavior (cf. Skinner, 1971). More recently, however, the pendulum has swung the other way, and it is now generally agreed that providing certain conditions are met, punishment may indeed produce relatively lasting changes in overt behavior (see Church, 1969; Fantino, 1973).

In sharp contrast to these wide swings in scientific opinion concerning the overall influence of punishment, the views of most psychologists regarding the impact of this factor upon aggression have remained surprisingly constant. In particular, punishment has generally—and consistently—been assumed to operate as an effective deterrent to such behavior. For example, in their famous monograph on frustration and aggression, Dollard *et al.* (1939) stated, "The strength of inhibition of any act of aggression varies positively with the amount of punishment anticipated to be a consequence of that act" (p. 33). And writing some 27 years later, Richard Walters (1966)—a noted developmental psychologist—remarked, "It is only the continual expectation of retaliation by the recipient or other members of society that prevents many individuals from more freely expressing aggression" (p. 69).

Clearly, punishment does sometimes serve as an inhibitor of human violence; to argue otherwise would be sheer folly. But does it *always* exert such effects? Given the sweeping nature of the statements listed above, one might assume that overwhelming empirical evidence points to this conclusion. Indeed, in commenting upon the proposal by Dollard *et al.*, Leonard Berkowitz (1962)—an established authority on aggression—has categorically stated, "This principle, as it stands, *cannot be disputed*" (p. 73; italics added).

Yet, in reality, this is far from the case. Recent investigations concerned with the influence of punishment upon aggression suggest that the relationship between these two variables is quite complex. Moreover, there has been a growing awareness, in recent years, of the possibility that punishment may itself involve several consequences or "side effects" that, together, largely counter its effectiveness as a deterrent to violent behavior. The appropriate question, then, appears to be "*When* does punishment inhibit aggression?" not "*Does* it produce such effects?" In order to facilitate our discussion of this important issue, we will consider, in separate discussions, evidence bearing upon (1) the impact of threatened punishment and (2) the actual delivery of such aversive treatment.

### Threatened Punishment as an Inhibitor of Overt Aggression

Over the centuries, virtually every human society has established specific punishments for murder, rape, assault, and similar aggressive actions. One major factor behind the development of such codes, of course, has been the almost universal belief that threats of strong punishment will serve to deter or inhibit many would-be aggressors from performing such behaviors. Threaten violent persons with enough pain and suffering, it has been contended, and their willingness to attack their fellow citizens will be held in check. Obviously, this is a deeply ingrained belief—one not easily surrendered. Yet, as we shall soon see, existing evidence suggests that it is only partially correct and must be accepted with some degree of caution. Threatened punishment may indeed serve to deter overt aggression, but only, it appears, under specific, restricted conditions.

Early attempts to investigate the aggression-inhibiting influence of threatened punishment followed a somewhat indirect route to this goal, based largely on methodology quite different from that in wide use today. Basically, participants in these studies were provided with opportunities (either actual or hypothetical) to aggress verbally against targets differing sharply in *status* or *social power* (e.g., Cohen, 1955; Graham *et al.*, 1951). It was then predicted that since victims high in status or power would be perceived as possessing greater ability to punish hostile actions, they would receive weaker levels of aggression than targets of low status or power. In general, the results tended to confirm these expectations. For example, in one well-known study (Worchel, 1957), college students were first strongly insulted and then were provided with an opportunity to aggress verbally against the experimenter, a faculty member, or a student assistant. As expected, stronger verbal hostility was directed against the assistant than against the relatively high-status professor. Similarly, in a related study, Thibaut and Riecken (1955) arranged conditions so that individuals belonging to the air-force reserve were strongly annoyed by another person who was then described as being higher or lower in military rank than themselves. It was expected that when later given a chance to communicate with this person, participants believing he was higher in rank than themselves would make fewer hostile comments than those believing he was lower in military rank, and in general, this prediction was confirmed. Together, studies employing these basic procedures seem to provide indirect support for the view that under some conditions, at least, threats of later punishment can inhibit verbal aggression.

Additional and more direct evidence concerning the possible aggression-inhibiting impact of threats of punishment has already been reviewed in our earlier discussion of interracial aggression (see Chapter 5, pp. 204–208). You may recall that in several of the studies considered at that point, various groups of subjects were provided with information suggesting either that the victim of their attacks would have no opportunity to retaliate against them at a later time or that he would, in fact, obtain such an opportunity. It may also be recalled that the results of these investigations have been quite consis-

tent in suggesting that aggression toward the target person is considerably lower when the opportunity for punishment (i.e., retaliation)
exists than when it is absent (e.g., Donnerstein *et al.*, 1972; Donnerstein & Donnerstein, 1975; Wilson & Rogers, 1975). Thus, there is
some indication that under certain conditions, at least, physical aggression, too, may be deterred by the threat of later punishment or retaliation for such actions.

Our comments up to this point, of course, seem mainly to confirm
the "common-sense" belief in the aggression-inhibiting influence of
threatened punishment. Unfortunately, though, this is only part of the
total picture. You may have noticed that throughout the present discussion, the phrase "under some conditions" has appeared and reap-
peared with notable frequency. Our use of these words has been far
from accidental. In fact, it has been included to direct attention to the
important fact that while threats of punishment are often effective in
inhibiting overt aggression, they are by no means always successful in
this regard. Indeed, taken as a whole, existing empirical evidence
points strongly to the conclusion that their effectiveness in deterring
various assaults is strongly mediated by at least four important factors.

First, it appears that the impact of threatened punishment in deterring aggression depends quite strongly upon the level of anger or
provocation experienced by potential aggressors: when such individuals have been exposed to mild annoyance or provocation, threats of
punishment may be quite effective in deterring such behavior. When
they have been subjected to more powerful annoyance, however,
threatened punishment may be far less useful in inhibiting later aggression. Perhaps it is useful to illustrate this important relationship
by means of a few examples. First, imagine the case of a child who is
continually taunted by a neighborhood bully. Eventually, he or she
may turn on the tormentor, despite the certainty that such actions will
result in a sound thrashing. Similarly, consider the case of a soldier
who, after witnessing the death or the mutilation of a close comrade-
at-arms, launches a desperate and seemingly senseless attack against
the hated enemy, regardless of the fact that such behavior will almost
certainly result in serious injury or death. An actual instance of such
behavior is reported in the following description of events occurring
during the bloody struggle for independence by the people of Bangladesh (Leamer, 1972):

> Some of the Bengalis were so fierce in their fury, so outraged, that they
> could not be held back, and they ran forward into the cantonment until
> they were cut down by machine-gun bursts, a few of them rising again to
> throw their spears arching up into the sky. (p. 88)

Here the degree of anger experienced by the persons involved was so great that they literally threw themselves headlong into the guns of their Pakistani foes, seemingly oblivious to the fact that they were in this manner courting certain death.

While such eye-witness accounts are quite dramatic and often informative, they cannot, of course, take the place of empirical data. Thus, we must ask whether this apparent relationship between the degree of provocation endured by potential aggressors and the effectiveness of threatened punishment in preventing such persons from assaulting others has been verified in actual research. In fact, it has. A recent experiment conducted by the present author has been directly concerned with this issue.

In this study (Baron, 1973), male college students were first either strongly provoked (the *angered* group) or treated in a more neutral fashion by a male confederate (the *nonangered* group). Following these procedures, both groups were provided with an opportunity to aggress against this person by means of electric shock under the guise of studying the effects of such stimuli upon physiological reactions. Threat of punishment (in the form of possible retaliation from the victim) was then varied in a systematic manner by informing one-third of the participants that the victim would never have an opportunity to shock them (the *low probability of retaliation* condition), a second third that he might have such an opportunity (the *moderate probability of retaliation* condition), and the final third that he would definitely obtain such an opportunity (the *high probability of retaliation* group). On the basis of the reasoning outlined above, it was predicted that threatened punishment would be highly effective in inhibiting subsequent aggression under conditions in which the subjects had not previously been angered by the victim but would be relatively ineffective in this regard under conditions in which they had previously endured strong provocation at the hands of this individual. As can be seen in Figure 47, both predictions were confirmed: as anticipated, the level of shocks employed by subjects in the nonangered group dropped sharply as the threat of punishment rose, while the behavior of the

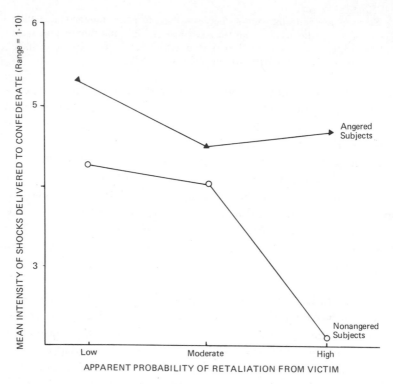

FIGURE 47. The effects of threatened punishment and prior anger arousal on physical aggression. Only subjects who had not previously been provoked were deterred from later aggression by the threat of retaliation from the victim. (Adapted from Baron, 1973.)

participants in the angered condition was largely unaffected by this factor. Together with the findings of other research (e.g., Knott & Drost, 1972a), these results point to the conclusion that threatened punishment may indeed be effective in inhibiting physicial aggression—but only when potential aggressors have not been strongly angered or provoked.

A second factor that also seems to exert an important mediating influence upon the aggression-inhibiting impact of threatened punishment is the apparent probability that such treatment will actually be delivered. Informal observation suggests that threats of punishment that are perceived as having little chance of being enacted often fail to deter later violence; indeed, such "empty" threats may sometimes backfire and yield quite the opposite result. Evidence indicating that this may indeed be the case has been gathered in several laboratory studies (e.g., Baron, 1971c, 1973, 1974b). Briefly, the findings of these experiments indicate that aggression decreases in a regular manner as the apparent probability of punishment for such behavior rises. Unfortunately, it is often the case in many natural settings that the probability of punishment for a given aggressive act is perceived as being quite low, or ambiguous at best. Thus, as we shall soon note in more detail, the effectiveness of potential punishment in deterring such actions may frequently be severely curtailed.

Third, the impact of threats of punishment upon overt aggression seems to be strongly mediated by the magnitude of aversive treatment expected by potential aggressors. In their famous text on aggression, Dollard and his colleagues (1939) suggested that the relationship between these two factors is linear in nature, with increments in the strength of anticipated punishment producing regular reductions in the magnitude of aggression. Certainly, this is a reasonable "first guess" and one that has attained widespread acceptance (see p. 228). Yet, it should be noted that there is some indication in existing data that the link between these variables may actually be curvilinear in nature, as shown in Figure 48. Specifically, it may be the case that large reductions in aggression are not attained until relatively high levels of threatened punishment are reached (cf. Shortell, Epstein, & Taylor, 1970). Further evidence is needed before any definite conclusions along these lines may be obtained. At present, though, there appear to be sufficient grounds for concluding that the success of threatened punishment in inhibiting subsequent violence is strongly mediated by the magnitude of the punishment anticipated.

Finally, additional evidence suggests that threatened punishment will be successful in deterring overt aggression only when potential aggressors have relatively little to gain through such behavior (Baron, 1974d). When, in contrast, aggression serves an important instrumental function, threats of punishment for engaging in such actions may fail to deter their occurrence. Unfortunately, as noted by Buss (1971), aggression often "pays" quite handsomely in precisely this manner: criminals, prizefighters, soldiers, athletes, and many others frequently gain important social or material rewards through successful assaults against others. In situations in which this is the case, the cards seem

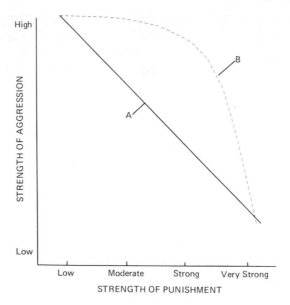

FIGURE 48. While Dollard *et al.* (1939) seemed to assume that aggression decreases in a linear manner with increasing strength of punishment as shown in (A), recent evidence suggests that the relationship between these two factors may actually be curvilinear as shown in (B).

to be severely stacked against the effectiveness of threatened punishment, and such procedures may totally fail to inhibit the performance of dangerous aggressive acts.

In sum, existing evidence suggests that the impact of threats of punishment for aggression is strongly mediated by several different factors. As a result, such procedures will usually succeed in inhibiting overt violence only when (1) the persons preparing to aggress are not very angry; (2) the magnitude of punishment they anticipate for such actions is great; (3) the probability that such unpleasant treatment will actually be delivered is high; and (4) the aggressors have relatively little to gain through assaults against others. Together, these apparent limitations on the influence of threatened punishment seem to offer unsettling implications for our present system of criminal justice. In particular, they suggest that existing conditions, under which the probability of being both apprehended and convicted of a single violent crime is exceedingly low, may be operating largely to nullify the potential influence of the penalties established for such crimes. In short, unless potential aggressors can be made to believe that their chances of being punished for assaults against others is high, the deterrent effect of even extreme and severe legal penalties will be slight. Such considerations, in turn, suggest that the current heated debates over the use of capital punishment may, in a sense, be irrelevant: since criminals fully realize that such penalties are exacted only in extremely rare cases, any inhibitory effects they might otherwise produce may be effectively neutralized.

We should hasten to add, of course, that such extensions and generalizations from laboratory research to pressing social issues are somewhat speculative in nature and should be viewed with a degree of caution. Empirical evidence pointing in the direction of such conclusions, however, seems both convincing enough and consistent enough in scope that they should, at the least, be given careful consideration.

## Actual Punishment as a Deterrent to Overt Aggression

While threats of punishment may indeed often fail to inhibit overt aggression, "common sense" suggests that the actual delivery of such unpleasant treatment might be somewhat more effective in this regard. At the very least, it might be argued, the delivery of punishment may serve to convince aggressors that society— or the particular persons they have attacked—"mean business" and will not tolerate aggressive outbursts. And if carried to relatively extreme levels, punishment may actually incapacitate aggressors or physically restrain them from engaging in further violent actions (cf. Buss, 1961). Formal evidence indicating that actual punishment can indeed frequently play a restraining role with respect to aggression has been obtained in several different studies.

For obvious ethical reasons, it has generally been impossible to investigate the effects of strong, physical punishment in such research. However, one investigation, conducted within a clinical framework, has, in fact, made use of such procedures (Ludwig, Marx, Hill, & Browning, 1969). In this study, attempts were made to alter the violent behavior of a female schizophrenic who frequently launched surprise, violent attacks against other patients and the professional staff at a mental institution. The pattern of behavior shown by this individual was quite ingenious in terms of achieving her aggressive ends. First, she would threaten other persons and then would appear to calm down. Once her intended victim had relaxed and lowered his or her guard, she would then strike quite suddenly and without warning, often inflicting considerable harm upon her unsuspecting target.

In order to modify this dangerous behavior, Ludwig and his colleagues administered strong electric shocks to the violent patient in a highly systematic manner. At first, the shocks were delivered only following physical attacks. Later, they were delivered simply for verbal threats and, finally, for verbal complaints or accusations. The effects attained through such treatment were quite dramatic: over a short period of time, she ceased these forms of behavior and actually became quite friendly in her relations with others. That the patient herself perceived the magnitude of these changes is indicated by her remark that "You're trying to make a human being out of me." In this instance, then, painful physical punishment was highly successful in inhibiting a dangerous and ingenious form of aggression.

With the exception of this single study, other investigations concerned with the impact of punishment upon aggression have employed much milder forms of treatment, based largely upon social disapproval or the removal of positive reinforcers (e.g., Brown & Tyler, 1968; Deur & Parke, 1970; Hollenberg & Sperry, 1951; Tyler & Brown, 1967). For example, in one well-known experiment conducted by Brown and Elliott (1965), relatively aggressive nursery-school boys were exposed to procedures in which they were ignored by their teachers each time they engaged in physical or verbal assaults against others. During the two-week period when such procedures were in effect, their level of aggression fell sharply (refer to Figure 49). However, in a subsequent three-week period when this treatment was discontinued, it increased. Importantly, though, it did not return to the level previously shown. Finally, when the "ignoring" procedures were reinstituted during another two-week period, both physical and verbal aggression were reduced once again, this time falling to extremely low levels. In short, even the very mild form of punishment employed in this study was sufficient to strongly inhibit such behavior.

Although the study conducted by Brown and Elliott (1965), as well as a number of related investigations, points to the conclusion that actual punishment may often be effective in deterring various forms of aggression, there appear to be several grounds for questioning the widespread assumption that such treatment will *always* be successful in this regard. First, it is clear that punishment may sometimes be per-

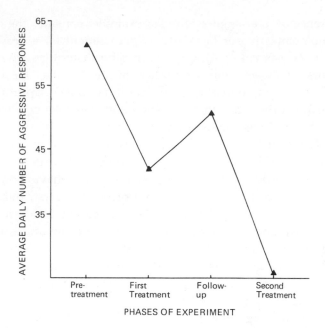

FIGURE 49. The effects of mild punishment upon aggression. Prior to the start of the experiment (pretreatment stage), the subjects showed a relatively high level of physical and verbal aggression. When they were ignored by their teachers following such actions (first treatment stage), however, the incidence of this behavior dropped sharply. It rose again when such treatment was discontinued (follow-up stage) but then dropped even more sharply during a second period in which teachers again ignored aggressive outbursts (second treatment). (Based on data from Brown & Elliott, 1965.)

ceived by its recipients as a form of physical or verbal attack and may thus serve to *elicit* rather than to inhibit overt aggression. As noted recently by Zillmann (1978), the crucial factor in this respect may be the degree to which the recipients identify the punishment they receive as legitimate. To the extent that they label it in this fashion and view it as consistent with accepted social norms, inhibitory effects may well be produced. To the degree that they label it as illegitimate or unwarranted, however, precisely opposite results may follow. Thus, in many cases, severe punishment may be far more likely to instill desires for revenge or reprisal than lasting restraints against interpersonal violence.

Second, the persons who administer punishment may sometimes serve as *aggressive models* for those on the receiving end of such discipline. In such cases, of course, punishment may serve to facilitate the occurrence of later aggression. For example, consider the case of a parent who spanks his or her child as punishment for a previous assault against a playmate and who, while administering such chastisement shouts, "I'll teach you to hit other children!" What the child may learn in such cases, of course, is that it is indeed appropriate to aggress against others but that one should always take care to select a victim smaller and weaker than oneself!

Finally, recent investigations concerned with the impact of punishment (cf. Church, 1969; Fantino, 1973) suggest that such procedures are effective in producing long-term changes in behavior only when administered in accordance with certain principles. First, punishment must be made directly contingent upon an individual's behavior, so that it regularly and predictably follows a particular undesirable action. And second, it must be administered as soon after the performance of such behavior as possible; if delayed, the strength of its inhibitory impact may be greatly reduced. Unfortunately, of course, punishment is rarely delivered in accordance with these principles in attempts to inhibit aggression. The perpetrators of violent crimes are only occasionally punished for such actions, and even when they are, punishment is usually delivered only after the completion of protracted legal battles, months—or even years—after the crucial aggressive act. In view of these facts, the failure of even long stays in uncomfortable prisons to deter convicted felons or their cohorts from engaging in antisocial behavior is hardly surprising.

For all these reasons, direct punishment may often backfire and totally fail to inhibit aggression—or may actually tend to increase its occurrence. This is not to say, however, that punishment is *never* successful in this respect. On the contrary, existing evidence suggests that it may be highly effective in deterring aggression under certain conditions. In particular, punishment would be expected to exert strong inhibitory effects when (1) it is administered in a sure and predictable manner; (2) it follows aggressive actions as swiftly as possible; (3) it is legitimized by the law and existing social norms, so as to avoid the possibility that it will be interpreted by recipients as an unwarranted attack; and (4) the persons charged with its administration are clearly differentiated from aggressive models. Under these circumstances, existing evidence suggests that punishment may well serve as an effective deterrent to human violence. Regrettably, however, these seemingly straightforward predictions remain, at the present time, only predictions. Largely because of the complex religious and moral issues they involve, no modern society has, as yet, been willing—or able—to put them to systematic test.

## CATHARSIS: DOES "GETTING IT OUT OF YOUR SYSTEM" HELP?

Suppose that on a particular occasion, one of your friends or acquaintances did something that made you very angry (e.g., insulted you in a highly obnoxious manner or caused you to "lose face" in front of other persons). Further, assume that your tormentor quickly left the scene, so that you had no opportunity to retaliate against him in a direct and immediate manner. If you then pounded your fist repeatedly on your desk, threw darts at a nearby dart board, or simply shouted at the top of your lungs, would you become less likely to aggress against this person the next time you met? Until quite recently, most psychologists believed that this would be true. In fact, it was widely assumed that providing angry individuals with an opportunity to "blow off steam" in some safe, noninjurious manner would (1) cause them to feel better (i.e., reduce their level of arousal) and (2) weaken their tendency to engage in overt—and potentially dangerous —acts of aggression.

These suggestions—which together are generally termed the *catharsis hypothesis*—can be traced to the writings of Aristotle, who held that exposure to moving stage drama could produce a vicarious "purging" of the emotions. While Aristotle himself did not refer directly to the purging of aggressive impulses or emotions, this seemingly logical extension of his views was propounded by Freud, who suggested that such reactions could be lessened through the expression of aggression-related emotions as well as through exposure to aggressive actions. In this respect, it is important to note that while Freud accepted the existence of such effects, he was relatively pessimistic regarding their usefulness in preventing or controlling overt aggression. Indeed, he seemed to regard them as both minimal in scope and short-lived in nature (see Chapter 1, pp. 16–18). The popular acceptance of the notion of catharsis within psychology, therefore, seems to stem instead primarily from certain statements made by Dollard and his colleagues in their frustration–aggression volume. According to these authors (1939), "The expression of *any act of aggression* is a catharsis that reduces the instigation to *all other acts of aggression*" (p. 33; italics added). In short, these scientists held that the performance of one aggressive act—whatever its nature—would serve to reduce an aggressor's tendency to engage in all other forms of aggression. Thus, for example, inducing an angry individual to engage in verbal or fantasy aggression against a hated enemy might well serve to lower substantially the probability that he or she will later engage in direct attacks against this person.

Largely on the basis of this and related suggestions, generations of parents urged their children to play with aggressive toys (e.g., Bobo dolls, punching bags), thousands of psychotherapists urged their patients to "release" their hostile feelings, and syndicated columnists advised frustrated persons to "vent" their aggressive urges through participation in vigorous sports or similar activities.

At first glance, the notion of catharsis seems to make good sense. Doing *something* when we are angry does indeed appear to be preferable to simply stifling our emotions and, in many cases, seems to lessen our annoyance. But is the catharsis hypothesis totally valid? Is it actually the case that the performance of one aggressive act—even a relatively noninjurious one—serves both to lower our level of emotional arousal and to reduce the probability that we will later engage in further aggressive actions? As we shall soon see, existing evidence seems to offer relatively strong support for the first of these suggestions, while leaving the second somewhat in doubt.

### Tension Reduction through Aggressive Actions: When It Feels Good to Hurt

Direct experimental evidence for the tension-reducing properties of aggression has been obtained in a series of ingenious studies conducted by Jack Hokanson and his colleagues (e.g., Hokanson & Burgess, 1962a,b; Hokanson, Burgess, & Cohen, 1963; Hokanson & Shetler, 1961). In these studies, subjects (typically, female college students) were first provoked by the experimenter and then were provided with an opportunity to aggress in one of several ways against this person or against other individuals. Participants' blood pressure was measured prior to the provocation, following these procedures, and again after aggressing, and in general, results provided evidence for catharsis: when permitted to aggress in a relatively direct fashion against the person who provoked them, subjects evidenced sharp reductions in arousal. Perhaps more detailed discussion of one of these experiments (Hokanson & Burgess, 1962b) will prove useful.

In this study, subjects were first asked to count backward from 100 to 0 by 3s, ostensibly as part of an experiment concerned with the relationship between performance on intellectual tasks and physiological responses. The experimenter then repeatedly interrupted and harrassed them, insisting that they start over on several separate occasions. Finally, he terminated this phase of the study in apparent disgust, remarking that the subject's "uncooperative attitude" had rendered her data useless. As might be expected, these highly provocative procedures induced marked increments in physiological arousal among subjects (i.e., both their blood pressure and heart rate increased sharply).

In order to determine whether this heightened arousal would then be reduced by an opportunity to aggress against the provocative experimenter, subjects were next divided into several groups and permitted to attack this individual (1) physically (by electric shock); (2) verbally (by ratings on a questionnaire); or (3) in their imaginations (by creating stories based on pictures they examined). Individuals in a fourth, no-aggression control group received no opportunity to retaliate for their harsh treatment at the hands of the experimenter. As shown in Table 15, results supported the notion of emotional cathar-

TABLE 15

*The Tension-Reducing Influence of Overt Aggression[a]*

| Measure of arousal | Type of aggression against the experimenter[b] | | | |
|---|---|---|---|---|
| | Physical[c] | Verbal | Fantasy | None |
| Heart rate (beats/minute) | 0.8[d] | −3.8 | 8.0 | 11.4 |
| Systolic blood pressure (millimeters) | 1.2 | 1.8 | 9.2 | 10.8 |

[a]Based on data from Hokanson & Burgess, 1962b.
[b]Preannoyance base level = 0.0.
[c]Both physical and verbal attacks against the person who had provoked them (the experimenter) were effective in reducing the subjects' degree of emotional arousal to preannoyance levels. However, fantasy assaults against this individual were not effective in this respect.
[d]Numbers shown represent elevations (positive values) or depressions (negative values) in heart rate and blood pressure relative to base levels during a preannoyance period.

sis: subjects provided with an opportunity to aggress against the experimenter either physically or verbally demonstrated marked reductions in arousal. However, as might be expected, fantasy attacks against this individual proved relatively ineffective in this respect. Only when subjects could aggress against the annoyer in a relatively direct fashion was physiological arousal reduced.

In later experiments, Hokanson and his associates observed that the occurrence of such cathartic effects is strongly influenced by certain characteristics of the victim. For example, Hokanson and Burgess (1962a) found that while assaults against a relatively low-status target (an individual described as an undergraduate student) produced reductions in subjects' level of arousal, aggression against a relatively high-status frustrater (an individual described as a faculty member) did not. And in related research, Hokanson, Burgess, and Cohen (1963) reported that aggression against an annoyer or against individuals closely associated with him produced reductions in physiological arousal, while assaults against "innocent victims" unrelated to prior provocation did not. Combined with the findings of other studies (e.g., Geen, Stonner, & Shope, 1975; Kahn, 1966), these results suggest that aggressors may indeed sometimes experience sharp reductions in emotional tension as a result of harming others. In this sense, at least, the informal observation that we often "feel better" after evening the score with someone who has strongly provoked us appears to have a basis in fact.

*Emotional Catharsis: Some Limiting Conditions*

Before we conclude the present discussion of what might reasonably be termed *emotional catharsis,* attention should be directed to two additional points. First, the fact that aggression against others often yields reductions in physiological arousal does not in any sense guarantee corresponding reductions in the likelihood of further assaults. Indeed, as noted by Hokanson (1970), such reductions in emotional tension are often quite pleasurable or rewarding and may, as a result, actually serve to strengthen aggressive tendencies. In brief, the sequence may proceed as follows: an individual is strongly provoked and aggresses against his or her tormentor. As a result of such actions, the unpleasant arousal he or she experiences is reduced. Such reductions, in turn, serve as positive reinforcement, thus strengthening this person's tendency to aggress on future occasions when annoyed by others. Thus, the occurrence of emotional catharsis in no way assures that successful attacks against others will lessen the future likelihood of such behavior; indeed, quite the opposite result may be produced.

A second point deserving of careful attention concerns the assumption that there is, in some sense, a unique link between aggressive actions and reductions in anger-induced emotional arousal. Until recently, it was widely believed that only assaults against the source of provocation—or closely related persons—could succeed in reducing the emotional arousal experienced by angry individuals. A number of ingenious experiments now point to the conclusion, however, that virtually *any* response that is successful in terminating aversive treatment from another person can acquire such "cathartic" properties (e.g., Hokanson & Edelman, 1966; Hokanson, Willers, & Koropsak, 1968; Stone & Hokanson, 1969). For example, in the study by Hokanson, Willers, and Koropsak (1968), the subjects were placed in a situation in which, on each of a number of occasions, they could push one of two different buttons either to reward another person (by giving him an arbitrary point) or to shock him. During an initial, base-line phase of the study, the subject's partner (a confederate of the experimenters) delivered shocks and rewards on a random basis, independent of the subject's behavior. As expected, it was found that during this period, the subjects demonstrated catharticlike reductions in emotional arousal when they responded aggressively to shocks from the partner—that is, when they responded with a countershock. In a second phase of the experiment, the conditions were changed so that the confederate's actions were now contingent upon those of the subject. Specifically, on 90% of the occasions when the male participants responded *non*aggressively to shocks from the opponent (i.e., by rewarding him), he, in turn, rewarded them on the next occasion. On 90% of the trials when they responded to shock from their opponent in an aggressive manner (i.e., by shocking *him*), however, he shocked them again on the next trial. It was predicted that under these conditions, the subjects would soon learn to respond to shocks from the confederate with rewards. Moreover, and of greater importance in the context of the present discussion, it was also expected that they would gradually come to demonstrate reductions in arousal after nonaggressive—but not after aggressive—responses. In short, it was predicted that they would evidence signs of emotional catharsis following nonaggressive behavior.

As shown in Figure 50, the results offered strong support for this prediction.

Additional and in some ways even more dramatic evidence for the view that reductions in anger-induced arousal are not linked in a unique manner to aggressive responding is provided by an experiment conducted by Stone and Hokanson (1969). Here, conditions were arranged so subjects could respond to shocks from their opponent in one of three ways: by shocking him, rewarding him, or by delivering a mild shock, weaker than the ones they received from their partner, to themselves. A contingency between subjects' behavior and that of their partner was then established, such that whenever they responded to shocks from this person with a self-shock, he rewarded them on the next occasion. Under these conditions, participants grad-

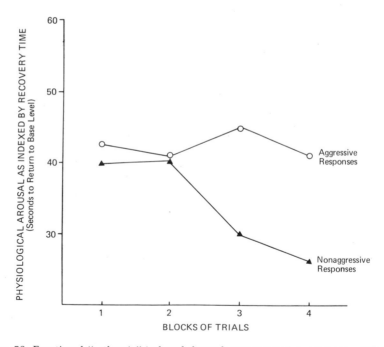

FIGURE 50. Emotional "catharsis" induced through nonaggressive responses. When the conditions were arranged so that male subjects received shocks for responding aggressively to shock from the partner but rewards for responding in a nonaggressive manner to such treatment, they gradually came to demonstrate reductions in arousal following nonaggressive responses. As shown above, however, aggressive responses failed to produce such "catharsis." (Based on data from Hokanson, Willers, & Koropsak, 1968.)

ually came to demonstrate catharsislike reductions in arousal following such responses. That is, they demonstrated rapid and sharp reductions in physiological arousal each time they engaged in what amounted to masochistic behavior! Combined with the findings of other research (e.g., Sosa, 1968), these results suggest quite strongly that there is no unique or special link between aggression and emotional catharsis. Under appropriate conditions, it seems, virtually any form of behavior can acquire such "cathartic" properties (see Quanty, 1976).

### Catharsis and Behavioral Aggression: Does Present Violence Lead to Later Mercy?

While the occurrence of emotional catharsis is certainly of considerable interest, a more important issue, from the point of view of controlling human violence, is the existence of *behavioral catharsis*—the second portion of the famous catharsis hypothesis. In particular, we must ask whether, as suggested by this hypothesis, the performance of relatively "safe" aggressive acts actually reduces the likelihood of more dangerous forms of aggression on later occasions. Unfortunately, as we noted earlier, existing evidence concerning this possibility is far from encouraging. In fact, it now seems safe to conclude that such effects occur only under highly specific circumstances and will not be observed in many situations in which they were previously assumed to exist. Perhaps it may prove useful to list some of these restrictions.

First, growing evidence suggests that the performance of aggressive acts will serve to reduce the likelihood of similar behavior only when the aggressors have previously been annoyed or provoked (e.g., Bramel, Taub, & Blum, 1968; Doob, 1970; Konečni, 1975a). Apparently, acts of violence committed in the "heat of anger" may sometimes tend to reduce or weaken the instigation to engage in such behavior, while those perpetrated in the absence of such arousal (i.e., in "cold blood") do not.

Second, it is now apparent that angry individuals cannot be restrained from aggressing through exposure to scenes of violence involving persons other than the ones who annoyed or provoked them (Berkowitz & Alioto, 1973; Goranson, 1970; Goldstein & Arms, 1971). Indeed, as we have already seen in Chapter 3 (cf. pp. 98–111), aggression is frequently *enhanced* by such procedures.

Third, common knowledge notwithstanding, allowing angry individuals to aggress against inanimate objects does not seem to be effective in reducing the strength of their tendencies to direct such behavior toward persons who have provoked them. In fact, there is some indication that subsequent aggression is actually *facilitated* by such activities (Mallick & McCandless, 1966). Although kicking furniture, punching a pillow, or throwing objects against a wall may cause many persons to "feel better" by reducing their emotional arousal, it is doubtful that such activities are effective in preventing them from engaging in aggression against the source of their annoyance.

And finally, it appears that verbal aggression against others will often fail to reduce the tendency to assault them physically on later occasions. Indeed, the results of several studies suggest that quite the opposite may be true (Ebbesen, Duncan, & Konečni, 1975; Mallick & McCandless, 1966). That is, the opportunity to "sound off" against others may actually enhance rather than reduce our willingness to aggress against them through other means on subsequent occasions.

In view of all these restrictions concerning the possible occurrence of behavioral catharsis, you may well be wondering by this point whether anything resembling this phenomenon *ever* occurs. In point of fact, a growing body of evidence leads to the conclusion that it does, but only, it seems, under conditions that severely limit its usefulness as a technique for preventing or controlling interpersonal aggression. Specifically, the results of a number of recent studies (Doob, 1970; Doob & Wood, 1972; Konečni, 1975a; Konečni & Ebbesen, 1976) suggest that behavioral catharsis may indeed occur under conditions in which angry individuals are permitted to aggress directly against the person responsible for their annoyance. As an example of this research, let us consider an experiment by Konečni (1975a).

In an initial phase of this study, male and female high-school students were either annoyed or not annoyed by a confederate, who either interfered with their performance on an anagrams task and insulted their intelligence or offered no interference and acted in a neutral manner. Following these procedures, the subjects in both conditions were exposed to one of three treatments: (1) they were simply asked to sit quietly in the experimental room and wait until the study could be resumed; (2) they were asked to work on a series of math problems for the same amount of time; or (3) they were provided with an opportunity to deliver electric shocks to the confederate within the context of a portion of the experiment concerned with the effects of punishment on recall.

Following the completion of these contrasting interpolated activities, all participants were provided with an opportunity to deliver a series of electric shocks to the confederate. The context for these shocks was a task supposedly concerned with "creative imagination," in which each subject read words to the confederate and then delivered as many shocks as he or she wished to this person for responses deemed to be low in "creativity." In accordance with the general notion of behavioral catharsis and the findings of previous research, it was predicted that angry individuals who had been provided with a previous opportunity to aggress against the confederate would deliver fewer shocks to him during this final task than those who had been asked simply to wait in the experimental room or to work on various math problems. As can be seen in Figure 51, this prediction was

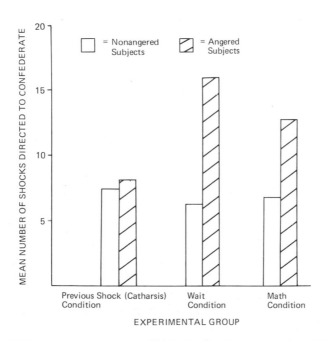

FIGURE 51. Evidence for the occurrence of behavioral catharsis. Angered individuals permitted to deliver shocks to the person who previously annoyed them on one occasion later directed fewer shocks to this person than subjects not provided with an initial opportunity to aggress (i.e., those in the "wait" and "math" conditions). (Based on data from Konečni, 1975a.)

strongly confirmed: angry subjects in the previous shock condition directed significantly fewer shocks to the confederate than those in the "wait" and "math-problems" groups.[1]

The findings reported by Konečni and those obtained in several other experiments (e.g., Doob, 1970; Doob & Wood, 1972; Konečni & Ebbesen, 1976) point strongly to the conclusion that catharsis may indeed occur under conditions in which angry persons are allowed to aggress directly against the individual who has provoked them. Further, additional findings (Doob & Wood, 1972) suggest that similar effects may occur when angry persons merely witness events in which their "enemies" are harmed by someone else. In view of such evidence, it seems reasonable to conclude that consistent with long-held beliefs, behavioral catharsis is indeed a real phenomenon.

We should hasten to add, however, that not all studies concerned with this topic have yielded confirming results. Indeed, at least one controversial study (Geen, Stonner, & Shope, 1975) has reported that an initial opportunity to aggress against an anger instigator may result in *stronger* rather than weaker tendencies to assault this person on later occasions. Given such conflicting evidence, the existence of catharsis may be accepted, but only with some degree of caution.

Even assuming that catharsis exists, however, it is important to note that it seems to take place only under conditions in which angry persons are permitted directly to harm—or to witness harm—to the objects of their wrath. In short, reductions in the likelihood or the intensity of future aggression may be obtained only at the expense of present acts of violence! Obviously, this is a far cry from past suggestions to the effect that reductions in aggression can readily be obtained through the performance of a wide variety of "safe" cathartic behaviors. Further, it should be noted that there is as yet little systematic evidence concerning the *duration* of any reductions in aggression produced by such procedures. Thus, the distinct possibility exists that these are of only a brief or a temporary nature. In view of such considerations, the following tentative conclusion seems justified: while participation in certain cathartic activities may sometimes succeed in re-

---

[1] It should be noted that these results were obtained under conditions in which the various interpolated activities occupied 7 minutes. When, instead, they lasted 13 minutes, there was some indication that working on the math problems, as well as a previous opportunity to aggress against the confederate, countered the effects of prior annoyance.

ducing later aggression, the potential benefits of such procedures have in the past been greatly overstated.

## The Effects of Nonaggressive Models: Can Restraint Be Contagious?

In an earlier discussion (see Chapter 3, pp. 99–100), we suggested that in one sense, at least, overt aggression may be quite "contagious." Specifically, we noted that an impressive body of empirical evidence points to the conclusion that exposure to the actions of aggressive models—individuals behaving in a highly aggressive manner—frequently serves to elicit similar actions on the part of observers. Further, we also called attention to the fact that such effects seem to be produced by both live and symbolic (e.g., filmed or televised) models.

One common explanation for the occurrence of this phenomenon centers on the presumed impact of aggressive models upon the restraints or inhibitions of observers. In particular, it has frequently been contended that witnessing the actions of such models induces sharp reductions in the strength of observers' restraints against overt aggression and, in this manner, facilitates the occurrence of this dangerous form of behavior. If, as existing evidence suggests (cf. Bandura, 1973), this is indeed the case, it seems only reasonable to expect that opposite effects, too, might be induced. That is, if restraints against aggression may be weakened through exposure to highly aggressive models, might they not also be strengthened as a result of exposure to *nonaggressive models*—individuals who behave in a restrained, nonbelligerent manner? Informal observation points strongly to the occurrence of such effects. Many tense and threatening situations seem to be "nipped in the bud," so to speak, by the presence and the actions of individuals who both demonstrate and urge restraint. And recently, informal procedures based on such an approach have been used—apparently with some success—to avert the occurrence of collective violence on several university campuses. More systematic evidence suggesting that nonaggressive models may often play a beneficial role in the prevention or the control of human violence has also been obtained in a number of laboratory studies (e.g., Baron, 1971e, 1972b; Baron & Kepner, 1970; Donnerstein & Donnerstein,

1977). Since we have already examined the investigation conducted by Baron & Kepner (1970) in Chapter 3, let us begin by returning to this research.

As may be recalled, the subjects in this study participated in the standard teacher–learner paradigm designed by Buss (1961) under conditions in which two teachers were present and took turns administering shocks to the learner on occasions when he made errors. One of these teachers was a confederate, and in two experimental groups, conditions were arranged so that each subject who played the role of the second teacher witnessed this person's actions before obtaining his or her own opportunity to aggress (i.e., the confederate served as the first teacher). In one of these groups (the *aggressive-model* condition), the confederate acted in a highly aggressive manner, "punishing" errors by the supposed victim with shocks from buttons 8, 9, or 10 on the apparatus. In the second (the *nonaggressive-model* condition), he behaved in a restrained, nonaggressive manner, administering shocks only from buttons 1, 2, and 3. Finally, in a third, *no-model* control group, the subjects served as the first teachers and were not exposed to the model's actions prior to their own opportunity to aggress.

As noted in our previous discussion of this study, exposure to the actions of the highly aggressive model strongly facilitated aggression by participants: those in the aggressive-model condition delivered stronger shocks of greater duration to the victim than those in the no-model control group. Similarly, and of greater interest in the present context, exposure to the behavior of the nonaggressive model strongly *inhibited* such behavior: subjects in the nonaggressive-model group delivered weaker and shorter shocks to the victim than did individuals in the no-model control condition (see Table 16). In view of the fact that all participants in the study were strongly provoked by the confederate prior to their opportunity to aggress (he insulted them in an obnoxious manner), these findings are quite encouraging. In particular, they suggest that exposure to the actions of restrained, nonaggressive models can often be quite effective in preventing overt aggression even on the part of individuals who have been strongly instigated to such behavior.

Encouragingly, similar findings have been obtained in several follow-up studies (Baron, 1971e, 1972b; Waldman & Baron, 1971). Further, these investigations serve to extend the results reported by Baron and Kepner by suggesting that the presence of nonaggressive models

TABLE 16

*The Aggression-Inhibiting Impact of a Nonaggressive Model*[a]

| Measure of aggression | Experimental condition[b] | |
|---|---|---|
| | No model | Nonaggressive model |
| Shock intensity | 4.74 | 2.87 |
| Shock duration (sec) | 0.72 | 0.53 |

[a]Based on data from Baron & Kepner, 1970.
[b]Subjects exposed to the actions of a restrained, nonaggressive model delivered significantly weaker and shorter shocks to an individual who had previously provoked them than subjects not exposed to such a model prior to their opportunity to aggress.

may often be quite effective in countering the aggression-enhancing impact of aggressive individuals. That is, in situations in which potential aggressors are exposed both to the actions of others who urge and demonstrate aggression *and* to the actions of others who urge and demonstrate restraint, the influence of the former may be largely "canceled" by the presence of the latter. Indeed, in one of these experiments (Baron, 1971e), the presence of a nonaggressive model was found to counteract entirely the influence of a highly aggressive model, reducing such behavior to levels virtually identical to those demonstrated in the absence of any social models. Given the prevalence of aggressive models, both in actual situations and in the mass media, and given their strong impact upon the behavior of observers, factors tending to counter their pervasive influence would seem to be of major potential importance in attempts to prevent and control human violence.

## The Impact of Nonaggressive Models: A Note on Comparative Effectiveness

The evidence we have considered so far suggests quite clearly that nonaggressive models may indeed often inhibit aggression on the part of observers. Up to this point, however, we have made no comments concerning the relative effectiveness of such procedures. Is exposure to nonaggressive models more—or less—successful in producing these effects than the other variables (e.g., threatened punishment, catharsis) we have considered? While complete information on this important issue is not yet available, a partial answer is provided by a recent study conducted by Marcia and Edward Donnerstein (1977).

In this experiment, male undergraduates were provided with an opportunity to deliver electric shocks of various intensity to a male victim under conditions in which half were led to anticipate retaliation from this individual and half were not. Before aggressing, some of the participants in each of these groups were exposed to a video tape in which another individual (a male confederate) delivered weak shocks to the victim (he used only the two lowest switches on the apparatus). In contrast, others viewed a tape in which the model's behavior was not visible.

On the basis of previous findings, it was anticipated that both retaliation and exposure to the actions of the nonaggressive model would be successful in reducing aggression, and as shown in Figure 52, both of these predictions were confirmed. Subjects led to believe that the victim would later have an opportunity to aggress against

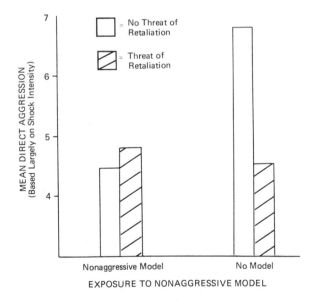

FIGURE 52. The effects of threatened retaliation and exposure to an aggressive model upon direct physical aggression. Both factors were successful in reducing such behavior. However, other findings, not shown here, indicated that threatened retaliation from the victim increased other, indirect forms of aggression; exposure to the nonaggressive model did not produce such undesirable effects. (Based on data from Donnerstein & Donnerstein, 1977.)

*them* directed weaker shocks to this person than subjects not informed that this would be the case. And participants exposed to the actions of the nonaggressive model delivered weaker shocks to the confederate than those presented with no information concerning the model's behavior.

At first glance, this pattern of findings seems to suggest that the restraining effects of nonaggressive models are roughly equal in magnitude to those of threatened retaliation. Additional results, however, point to the conclusion that modeling cues may actually be somewhat more effective in this regard. Specifically, the findings summarized above refer only to *direct* aggression against the victim, as indexed primarily by the strength of the shocks employed by subjects. In terms of inhibiting such behavior, retaliation and exposure to the actions of a nonaggressive model produced consistent results: aggression was sharply reduced by both factors. However, with respect to a more indirect and less easily recognized form of aggression—the duration of shocks employed by subjects—a sharply different pattern emerged. While exposure to a nonaggressive model produced little effect on this form of aggression, threatened retaliation actually tended to enhance its occurrence. In short, the threat of punishment from the victim seemed to produce a shift from direct, easily recognized forms of aggression to less direct, readily concealable forms; exposure to a nonaggressive model, in contrast, did not induce similar effects.

One possible explanation for this seeming advantage of modeling cues over threatened retaliation may lie in the fact that the former strategy serves to restrain aggression in two distinct ways, while the latter procedure inhibits such behavior in only one. Specifically, both threatened retaliation and exposure to the actions of a nonaggressive model may serve to strengthen subjects' restraints or inhibitions against aggressing. In addition, however, exposure to the actions of a calm, nonaggressive model may also have the effect of reducing observers' level of emotional arousal—especially following provocation—and may so tend to reduce the likelihood of aggression in this manner (cf. Buck, 1975). While these suggestions seem consistent with previous findings, they are, at present, somewhat speculative in nature. Thus, they must be subjected to further empirical tests before any firm conclusions concerning their validity can be reached. Regardless of the outcome of such research, however, existing evidence points quite convincingly to the conclusion that restraint, as well as violence, is socially "contagious" and that as a result, the presence of nonaggressive models may often prove highly effective in inhibiting the occurrence of overt aggression.

## COGNITIVE CONTROL OF AGGRESSION: THE INHIBITING EFFECT OF MITIGATING CIRCUMSTANCES

Suppose that on a trip to an expensive local store, you were confronted by an extremely rude and surly salesman. When you entered the shop, he did his best to pretend that he did not see you. And when you asked for assistance in locating a particular item, he literally told you, with obvious irritation and in a most obnoxious manner, to find it for yourself. Further, imagine that as you stormed across the shop to complain to the manager about this surly treatment, you were intercepted by another clerk, who took you aside and explained that his friend was behaving in this objectionable manner because only that afternoon he had been fired, despite long years of faithful service, to make room for the owner's young—and shiftless—nephew. Would this information have any effect upon your behavior? Common sense suggests that in many cases, it would. After learning about the stressful factors behind the salesman's actions, you might well decide to forget the incident entirely. Indeed, you might now feel more sympathy than anger toward this individual.

The occurrence of this sort of incident and many that are related points strongly to the potential importance of a specific type of cognitive factor in the control of overt aggression. In particular, such events suggest that in many cases, information concerning the causes of others' behavior plays a crucial role in determining our reactions to their words or deeds. In the presence of information suggesting that they had no grounds for behaving in a provocative manner, we may well respond aggressively to such annoyance. In the context of knowledge suggesting that they were goaded into such behavior by factors beyond their control, however, we may well "turn the other cheek" and refrain from answering their annoyance in kind.

In a sense, we have already touched upon this important topic in our earlier discussion of frustration (see Chapter 3). At that time, we noted that frustrations that are perceived as arbitrary or unjustified are much more likely to elicit overt aggression than frustrations that are not perceived in this manner. Here, we will expand upon this previous discussion by considering the aggression-inhibiting impact of information concerning *mitigating circumstances*—explanations for pro-vocative behavior on the part of another person suggesting that they were "pushed" in this direction by factors beyond their control. While a number of different experiments are indirectly related to this phe-nomenon (e.g., Burnstein & Worchel, 1962; Cohen, 1955; Rothaus & Worchel, 1960), the most revealing information regarding its occur-rence has been reported in several recent studies conducted by Zill-mann and his colleagues (Zillmann *et al.*, 1975; Zillmann & Cantor, 1976).

For example, in the experiment by Zillmann and Cantor (1976), male undergraduates participated in a study supposedly concerned with the effects of various visual stimuli upon physiological reactions. Consistent with this ostensible purpose, the heart rate, blood pres-sure, and skin temperature of each subject were assessed at several different points during the session. (The importance of these measures will soon be made apparent.) During the course of the experiment, each participant interacted with two different experimenters. The first behaved in a uniformly polite and courteous manner, while the sec-ond acted in a rude and obnoxious fashion, accusing the subject of failing to cooperate and berating the polite assistant in a highly offen-sive manner. In two experimental conditions, the polite experimenter offered a reasonable explanation for the behavior of the rude assistant, noting that he was very "uptight" about an important midterm exam. In one of these groups (the *prior-mitigation* condition), this information was provided prior to provocation from this person, while in the sec-ond (the *subsequent-mitigation* condition), it was presented only after he had provoked the subject. Finally, in a third, control group (the *no-mitigation* condition), no information regarding the reasons for the rude experimenter's harsh actions was provided at any time. In accor-dance with previous findings (e.g., Zillmann *et al.*, 1975), it was pre-dicted that mitigation would be successful in deterring later aggres-sion against the obnoxious assistant and, further, that *prior* mitigation would be more effective in this respect than subsequent mitigation.

Following his interactions with the two experimenters, each sub-ject was asked by a third individual to evaluate both. This final assis-tant explained that the subject's rating would go directly to the experi-menters' major department and would be used in the assignment of future research assistantships. Moreover, to lend credibility to these assertions, the subject's rating was placed in an envelope marked "Committee on Research Subjects" and was sealed in his presence.

TABLE 17

*The Effects of Mitigating Circumstances on Verbal Aggression[a]*

| Experimental Condition[b] | | |
| --- | --- | --- |
| Prior mitigation | Subsequent mitigation | No mitigation |
| 28[c] | −47 | −70 |

[a] Based on data from Zillmann & Cantor, 1976.
[b] Subjects informed that the person who insulted them was "uptight" about a midterm exam (i.e., those in the prior- and subsequent-mitigation groups) were more favorable toward his reappointment as a research assistant than those who did not receive such information (i.e., subjects in the no-mitigation group).
[c] Numbers refer to the subjects' recommendations concerning the experimenter's reappointment as a research assistant, along a −100 (definitely should not be reappointed) to +100 (definitely should be reappointed) scale.

Presumably, then, his ratings of the two individuals with whom he had interacted could have important consequences for them. These ratings and the physiological indices mentioned previously served as the major dependent measures of the study.

The results of the experiment were both clear and impressive in demonstrating the influence of mitigating circumstances upon the control of later aggression. First, with respect to subjects' ratings of the rude experimenter, it was found that as anticipated, both prior and subsequent mitigation reduced aggression (i.e., harsh ratings) relative to the no-mitigation control condition. Further, and also consistent with initial predictions, prior mitigation was more effective—although not significantly so—in this regard than subsequent mitigation (see Table 17). In short, learning that the obnoxious experimenter was uptight about an important exam sharply reduced subjects' tendencies to aggress against him on a later occasion, and acquiring such information *prior* to his harsh behavior produced larger reductions in aggression than acquiring it only *after* provocation.

Additional information concerning the influence of mitigation upon subjects' behavior—and one possible explanation for the inhibiting effect of this factor upon aggression—was provided by findings for the physiological measures. These indicated that subjects in the no-mitigation control group demonstrated a strong increase in arousal following provocation, which then dissipated quite slowly with the passage of time. Indeed, subjects in this group still evidenced signs of elevated arousal at the end of the session. In contrast, those in the subsequent-mitigation group demonstrated sharp reductions in arousal following their receipt of the information concerning the reasons for the assistant's rude behavior and then gradually returned to their initial level of arousal during the remainder of the session. Finally, and perhaps of greatest interest, participants in the prior-mitigation group, who received information about the experimenter's uptight frame of mind prior to their interaction with him, showed relatively little physiological response to his offensive actions when they later occurred. Moreover, even this mild level of arousal dissipated very rapidly. In short, it was as if the subjects in this group, having been warned about the experimenter's irritable mood, were somehow able to suppress or inhibit the development of anger in response to his obnoxious comments (see Figure 53). That this was indeed the case is

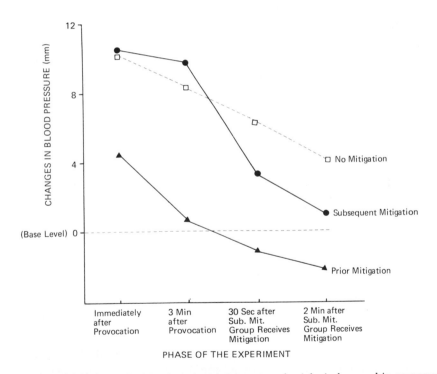

FIGURE 53. The effects of mitigating circumstances on physiological arousal in response to provocation. Subjects in the prior-mitigation group evidenced relatively little reaction to harsh treatment by the experimenter and soon returned to initial base levels of arousal. Those in the subsequent-mitigation group demonstrated sharp reductions in arousal following the receipt of mitigation and then quickly returned to base levels. Finally, those in the no-mitigation group responded strongly to the experimenter's provocation and continued to evidence signs of arousal throughout the remainder of the session. (Based on data from Zillmann & Cantor, 1976.)

suggested by the fact that while written comments supplied by subjects in the no-mitigation and subsequent-mitigation conditions were
indicative of considerable irritation (e.g., "This jackal is sure to learn
some manners soon"), those volunteered by subjects in the prior-mitigation group were much milder in tone (e.g., "Mr. Day was slightly
rude—insinuating that I was attempting to ruin his experiment").
Thus, while subsequent mitigation was effective in inhibiting overt
aggression and in reducing emotional arousal once it had developed,
prior mitigation was successful in actually *preventing* the development
of strong anger among participants.

Taken as a whole, the findings of the research conducted by Zillmann and his colleagues appear to have important implications for the
control of aggression in many situations. In particular, it is often the
case that individuals behave in a provocative manner not because of
inborn aggressive "impulses" or a sadistic desire to harm others but
rather as a result of fatigue, anxiety, discomfort, or other external circumstances. The finding that calling these factors to the attention of
the persons they offend may sharply reduce the latter's tendency to
respond in kind suggests that the provision of such information, either by the anger instigator himself or by a third party, may often be
extremely effective in preventing overt aggression. In short, knowing
*why* another person has acted in an annoying manner may frequently
serve to temper or moderate our reactions to such treatment. As noted
by Berkowitz (1974), aggression may indeed often be quite impulsive
in nature. However, there can be little doubt that it is also frequently
under the control of cognitive factors, which can be employed to moderate or inhibit its occurrence.

## THE ROLE OF INCOMPATIBLE RESPONSES: EMPATHY, LAUGHTER, AND LUST

It is a well-established principle in psychology that all organisms,
including human beings, are incapable of engaging in two incompatible responses at once. For example, it is impossible to daydream and
read at the same time, to study for an exam and watch an exciting
football game on television, or to drive a car and make passionate love
(although many people sometimes seek to combine these last two activities). Recently, attempts have been made to extend this basic prin-

ciple to the control of aggressive behavior. Specifically, it has been suggested that any conditions serving to induce responses or emotional states among aggressors that are incompatible with either anger or the performance of violent acts will often be highly effective in preventing such behavior (e.g., Baron & Byrne, 1977; Zillmann & Sapolsky, 1977). Although many different responses might prove to be

# Hi and Lois ® By Mort Walker & Dik Browne

FIGURE 54. As shown in this cartoon, mild sexual arousal is one form of incompatible response that may be used to prevent the occurrence of anger or overt aggression. (Source: King Features Syndicate, Inc.)

inconsistent with aggression in this manner, we will focus upon two that have been the subject of growing attention in this respect: *empathy* and *feelings of amusement*. In addition, a third, to which we have already directed considerable attention—*mild sexual arousal*—will also be briefly considered. (For a humorous illustration of the possible aggression-inhibiting impact of this last type of incompatible response, see Figure 54.)

## *Empathy: Reactions to the Pain and Suffering of Others*

When aggressors attack other persons in face-to-face confrontations, they are often exposed to signs of pain and suffering on the part of their victims. For example, the unfortunate target may groan, cry out, or even beg for mercy as he or she is repeatedly harmed by the aggressor. What, then, are the effects of such feedback upon the fur-

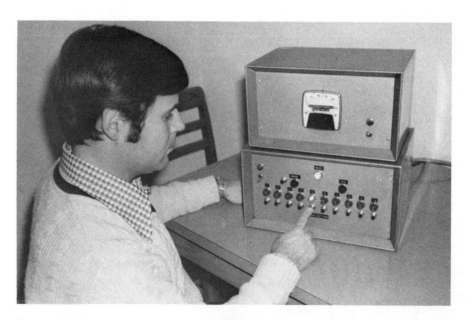

FIGURE 55. The psychoautonomic pain meter employed by the author in several investigations concerning the effects of victim's pain cues on subsequent aggression. Each time subjects deliver an electric shock to a confederate by pushing one of the buttons on the aggression machine, they receive feedback on the meter indicating the level of pain supposedly experienced by this individual. (In reality, of course, the confederate receives no shocks and experiences no discomfort.)

ther behavior of aggressors? The findings of a number of different experiments suggest that under some conditions, at least, they sharply reduce the strength or the frequency of further attacks upon the victim (e.g., Geen, 1970; Rule & Leger, 1976). For example, in a series of investigations conducted by the present author (Baron, 1971b,d; 1974a), conditions were arranged so that each time a male subject delivered a shock to a confederate within the familiar teacher–learner paradigm, he received information regarding the amount of pain supposedly experienced by this person. This information was presented by means of meter readings on the device shown in Figure 55 (known as the *psychoautonomic pain meter*) and was varied in a systematic manner across experimental conditions, so that some subjects were led to believe that the shocks they delivered caused the victim considerable pain, others that their shocks resulted in more moderate pain, and still others that these "punishments" led only to mild pain. As expected, the greater the discomfort supposedly experienced by the victim, the weaker the shocks subjects chose to deliver to him. Moreover, additional findings suggested that this was the case because under the conditions prevailing in these studies—mild or no provocation from the victim—feedback from this person tended to induce feelings of *empathy* among subjects; and such reactions, in turn, caused them to lower the strength of their assaults. In short, signs of pain and discomfort on the part of the confederate caused subjects to experience negative emotional arousal, which then proved incompatible with further, overt aggression.

While such findings are quite encouraging, further studies point to the less optimistic conclusion that pain cues from the target of aggression are not always successful in producing these effects. In particular, the findings of several recent experiments suggest that on some occasions, aggressors are relatively unaffected by such feedback and that on others, they may actually be encouraged to engage in further assaults by such feedback (e.g., Baron, 1974a; Feshbach, Stiles, & Bitter, 1967; Hartmann, 1969; Swart & Berkowitz, 1976). Basically, this appears to be the case in situations in which the aggressors have previously suffered strong provocation at the hands of their victims. Under such conditions, signs of pain and suffering fail to induce empathic arousal and may, in fact, serve as a form of reinforcement for aggressive actions. As a result, feedback from the victim may enhance rather than inhibit further attacks against this person. While such effects have often proved difficult to demonstrate in laboratory studies, they are seen quite clearly in the results of a recent investigation conducted by the present author (Baron, 1977b).

In this experiment, male college students were first angered or not angered by a male confederate and were then provided with an opportunity to aggress against this person by means of electric shock. The ostensible purpose of the study was that of investigating the effects of unpleasant stimuli upon physiological reactions, and participants were instructed to deliver any one of 10 different electric shocks to the confederate each time a red signal light was illuminated. For half of the subjects (the *pain-cues* group), each of these shocks was followed by information on the pain meter suggesting how much discomfort had been inflicted upon the victim, while for the remainder (the *no-pain-cues* group), such information was omitted.[2]

On the basis of previous research, it was predicted that under conditions in which the subjects had not been provoked by the victim, the presence of pain cues would induce empathic arousal and inhibit further aggression. However, under conditions in which the participants had previously been strongly angered by the confederate, it was anticipated that pain cues would serve as a form of reinforcement and so actually enhance such behavior. As can be seen in Figure 56, both of these predictions were confirmed. Moreover, additional findings from a postexperimental questionnaire suggested that these effects were, in turn, mediated by the subjects' emotional reactions to signs of discomfort on the part of the victim. Among the previously angered subjects, the presence of pain cues produced strong, positive shifts in subjects' reported mood (e.g., they reported feeling happier, more pleasant, and more relaxed in the presence of pain cues than in their absence). Among the subjects who had not been provoked, however, pain cues induced negative shifts in mood (e.g., they reported feeling less happy, more unpleasant, and more tense in the presence of pain cues than in their absence). Thus, as expected, the subjects reacted positively or negatively to pain cues from the victim, depending upon whether or not they had previously been angered by this person.

Taken as a whole, existing evidence concerning the impact of pain

[2] Another aspect of the study involved the race of the victim, who was either black or white. Since the influence of pain cues upon later aggression is of primary interest in the present context, however, only data for conditions in which the victim was white will be considered.

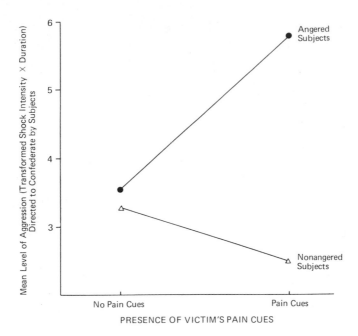

FIGURE 56. The effects of victim's pain cues and prior anger arousal upon aggression. Pain cues inhibited aggression by subjects who had not previously been angered by the victim but strongly facilitated such behavior by those who had previously been provoked. (Based on data from Baron, 1977b.)

cues suggests that this factor may sometimes be of use in controlling overt aggression. That is, victims who cry out in pain, beg for mercy, or demonstrate other signs of discomfort may often succeed in terminating assaults against them. However, such effects seem to occur only under conditions in which the aggressors have not been strongly angered. When, instead, they have previously been subjected to powerful provocation, attempts to prevent or control aggression through direct victim feedback may backfire and actually encourage the actions they are designed to deter.

## Humor and Feelings of Amusement

A second and markedly different type of reaction that also appears to be quite incompatible with aggression is that of humor or feelings of amusement. Informal observation suggests quite strongly that once angry individuals have been induced to smile, the probability that they will engage in overt acts of aggression may often be sharply reduced. Presumably, this is the case because it is difficult—if not impossible—to feel amused or to laugh and at the same time to remain enraged against others. Empirical evidence supporting such suggestions has recently been acquired in several laboratory studies (e.g., Mueller & Donnerstein, 1977; Landy & Mettee, 1969; Leak, 1974).

For example, in one of these studies (Baron & Ball, 1974), male college students were first either angered or not angered by a confederate and were then provided with an opportunity to aggress against this individual within the context of a study concerning the effects of unpleasant stimuli upon physiological reactions. Before aggressing against the victim, and while supposedly waiting for his physiological reactions to return to base level, each subject was asked to help the experimenter plan a future study by examining and rating various stimuli. Half of the participants then viewed a series of amusing cartoons (e.g., the Lone Ranger, shown wearing a ridiculous Groucho Marx mask, turns to Tonto and says, "Next time, I'll get the mask myself"; two roaches are seen strolling along a library shelf; one turns to the other and remarks, "I've always found Freud a little tough to swallow"). In contrast, the remainder of the participants examined neutral pictures of scenery, furniture, and abstract art. In accordance with the view that feelings of amusement would be incompatible with anger and overt aggression, it was predicted that the angry subjects exposed to the cartoons would direct weaker attacks against the confederate than those exposed to the neutral pictures, and as shown in Figure 57, this was actually the case. Thus, exposure to the humorous materials sharply reduced the subjects' tendencies to inflict painful shocks upon the victim.

While these findings seem consistent with the suggestion that humor and feelings of amusement are often incompatible with anger or overt aggression and may tend to deter such reactions, two notes of caution should be added. First, other findings suggest that such effects are *not* produced by all forms of humor. In fact, at least one study has reported that exposure to *hostile humor*—in which some target is harmed, attacked, or made to look foolish—may enhance rather than inhibit aggressive actions (Berkowitz, 1970). Thus, it is clear that the effects of humor upon aggression may depend quite strongly upon the content of the materials presented. And second, evidence gathered recently by Mueller and Donnerstein (1977) suggests that the inhibit-

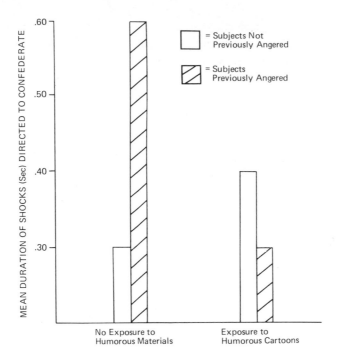

FIGURE 57. Humor as a technique for reducing aggression. Angry individuals exposed to humorous cartoons directed weaker attacks against the person who provoked them than angry individuals not exposed to such materials. (Based on data from Baron & Ball, 1974.)

ing effects of nonhostile humor upon aggression may stem from an *attentional shift*—in which subjects are distracted away from past provocation—rather than from the induction of positive emotional states incompatible with overt aggression. Specifically, these investigators found that while mildly amusing comedy routines inhibited later aggression by female subjects, more humorous routines failed to exert such effects. Since the incompatible-response hypothesis predicts that the more amusing the materials presented, the greater the reductions in aggression produced, these findings point to the possibility that other factors, such as the attentional shift mentioned above, are indeed at work.

It should be noted, however, that the attentional-shift and incompatible-response mechanisms are in no way contradictory; indeed, both may well play a role in mediating the influence of at least some types of humorous materials upon aggression, and only further systematic research can disentangle their relative contributions. Regardless of the findings of such research, however, existing evidence points to the conclusion that insofar as the prevention or the control of aggressive behavior is concerned, some kinds of humor—and the laughter they induce—may indeed prove to be one of the "best medicines."

## Incompatible Responses: A Field Study

Up to this point, all of the studies bearing on the possible aggression-inhibiting impact of incompatible responses we have considered were conducted within standard laboratory settings. In view of this fact, it seems useful to conclude our discussion of this topic by considering a recent experiment designed to examine the occurrence of such effects under more natural field conditions (Baron, 1976).

The location chosen for this study was a moderately busy intersection near a major university. Conditions were then arranged so that male drivers who happened to approach this intersection while the study was in progress would encounter a mildly frustrating or annoying situation. Specifically, they found themselves delayed by a male confederate who failed to move his car for 15 seconds after the traffic signal turned green. Since previous investigations (e.g., Doob & Gross, 1968; Turner, Layton, & Simons, 1975) had indicated that motorists frequently honk at other drivers to express irritation with them and view such behavior as aversive to the recipients, it was decided to employ horn honking as a measure of behavioral aggression in this general setting. In order to collect systematic data on this measure, two assistants were concealed in a nearby parked car. One operated a portable tape recorder and so obtained a permanent record of all horn honking, while the second observed the subjects' behavior for overt signs of anger or irritation (e.g., gestures and verbal statements).

So that it could be determined whether incompatible responses would reduce the subjects' tendencies to aggress in this situation, three experimental procedures were instituted during the period when the light was still red (i.e., prior to the annoying delay). In one of these conditions (the *empathy* group), a female confederate wearing a bandage on her leg hobbled across the street on crutches. In a second condition (the *humor* group), she crossed the street wearing an outlandish clown mask. Finally, in a third (the *mild-sexual-arousal* condition), she crossed wearing a very brief and revealing outfit. (As may be recalled from our earlier discussion in Chapter 4, mild sexual arousal has been found, in several studies, to inhibit aggression by angry individuals.)

In addition to these three experimental groups, two control conditions were also included. In one (the *distraction* group), the confederate crossed the street while dressed in normal, conservative attire. In the second, she was entirely absent from the scene. It is important to note that in the distraction group, as well as in the three experimental conditions, the confederate's walk was carefully timed so that she was completely out of sight by the time the traffic light turned green. Thus, she was no longer present on the scene at the time the subjects were exposed to frustration or annoyance. The conditions prevailing in the empathy, humor, sexual-arousal, and distraction groups are illustrated in Figure 58.

On the basis of previous laboratory research, it was predicted that exposure to the three experimental treatments would induce responses

FIGURE 58. Conditions existing in the distraction (A), empathy (B), humor (C), and mild-sexual-arousal (D) groups of the Baron (1976) study. Exposure to the treatments shown in photos B, C, and D significantly reduced the tendency of passing motorists to honk at a confederate who delayed them in traffic.

incompatible with anger or irritation among drivers and so reduce their tendencies to honk at the stalled confederate. Consistent with these predictions, results indicated that subjects in the empathy, humor, and mild-sexual-arousal groups honked significantly less frequently, as well as significantly more slowly, than those in the distraction and control groups (see Table 18). In addition, they evidenced significantly fewer overt signs of irritation than participants in these latter two groups.

That these effects were actually produced by the influence of incompatible responses is suggested by further, careful observation of the subjects' behavior during the period when the confederate was present. At this time, those in the humor group frequently laughed out loud as she passed, those in the sexual-arousal condition frequently made sexually oriented comments, and those in the empathy group often looked closely at the confederate and then quickly away, as if to avoid further exposure to the sight of another person experiencing discomfort. Thus, there was at least suggestive evidence that the subjects were, in fact, experiencing the anticipated reactions.

In sum, the findings of this study tended to confirm the results of previous laboratory experiments in suggesting that overt acts of aggression may often be inhibited through the induction of incompatible responses among potential aggressors. While further, confirming evidence regarding the influence of such effects is clearly needed, the possibilities that they (1) occur in a wide range of settings and (2) can

TABLE 18

*The Aggression-Inhibiting Influence of Incompatible Responses*[a]

| | Experimental condition[b] | | | | |
|---|---|---|---|---|---|
| | Control | Distraction | Empathy | Humor | Mild sexual arousal |
| Proportion of drivers honking | 0.90 | 0.89 | 0.57 | 0.50 | 0.47 |
| Latency of honking (sec) | 7.19 | 7.99 | 10.73 | 11.94 | 12.16 |

[a] Adapted from Baron, 1976.
[b] Male drivers exposed to experimental treatments designed to induce responses incompatible with anger or overt aggression (the empathy, humor, and mild-sexual-arousal groups) honked less frequently and more slowly at a confederate who delayed them than those not exposed to such treatment (the control and distraction groups). Only data for subjects driving non-air-conditioned cars are presented.

be induced by a variety of procedures suggest that techniques based on this general phenomenon may, with continued refinement, prove extremely useful in practical attempts to prevent or control the emergence of human violence.

## THE CONTROL OF HUMAN VIOLENCE: A POSTSCRIPT

In the 5,600 years of recorded human history, there have been more than 14,600 wars—a rate of approximately 2.6 per year. Further, of the roughly 185 generations of human beings who have been born, have lived, and have died during this same period, only 10 seem to have known the blessings of uninterrupted peace (see Montagu, 1976). Faced with this disheartening record of continued violence, one may well wonder whether it is, in fact, possible to prevent or control such behavior.

The answer I wish to propose, in closing, is a firm and resounding "YES!" As we have seen throughout the present volume, an impressive body of empirical evidence points to the conclusion that contrary to the views espoused by Freud, Lorenz, Ardrey, and others, aggression is *not* essentially innate. Rather, it seems to be a learned form of social behavior, acquired in the same manner as other types of activity and influenced by many of the same social, situational, and environmental factors. Aggression, in short, is not genetically or instinctively preordained; it arises, instead, from a complex of conditions that encourage—and stimulate—its occurrence.

As an acquired form of behavior, aggression, of course, is readily open to modification. Just as individuals can learn to behave aggressively and can be encouraged to do so by external (or even internal) conditions, so too can they be taught to behave in a nonagressive manner and to refrain from harming others. According to the perspective adopted in this text, therefore, aggression *can* be controlled, provided appropriate steps are taken to accomplish this goal.

Needless to say, it is one thing to proclaim the possibility of controlling human violence and quite another to indicate practical steps that might be taken to accomplish this end. As we have seen in earlier chapters, aggression is a highly complex phenomenon, influenced in many ways by a wide range of factors. Thus, it would be naïve to assume that it can be prevented or controlled in a simple or straightforward manner. Complex problems demand complex solutions, and aggression is no exception to this rule. Yet, despite this complexity, the social-learning perspective, as well as the research we have considered in this chapter and others, points to several practical steps that, if taken, might prove to be of considerable value in reducing the prevalence or the intensity of human violence. Among these are the following.

First, in order to control such behavior, we should make several major changes in the responses, attitudes, and values we teach to our children. At the present time, youngsters are exposed to what might reasonably be termed systematic training for violence. Through television and other mass media, they witness countless incidents of violence and, in this manner, are equipped with a wide range of techniques for harming others. Even worse, these episodes are presented in a context that often seems to imply that aggression is a perfectly acceptable and appropriate technique for handling relations with others. When it is realized that such beliefs are then strengthened and reinforced by peer groups, society at large, and even parents, it is not surprising that the incidence of violence in many societies has risen sharply in recent years. Changing the content of television shows, movies, comic books, and other widely distributed items is certainly a difficult task and one that raises many complex ethical and legal issues. Yet, existing evidence suggests that such changes, if carried out in a consistent manner, would be well worth the effort. The mass media have a distinct potential for good as well as evil, but active steps must be taken to ensure that the former predominate.

Second, we should seek to eliminate social conditions that both encourage and reward the performance of overt aggression. As noted by Buss (1971) and others, such behavior is currently rewarded in a number of different contexts. For example, young children (especially boys) are frequently praised by both peers and their parents for behaving in a tough, "macho" manner. Similarly, adults, too, are rewarded in various ways for acting aggressively in settings ranging from the athletic playing field to the executive boardroom. And finally, as noted earlier in the present chapter, the inefficiency in our existing system of criminal justice often ensures that criminals who aggress against others, and in this manner gain important material rewards, only rarely "pay" for their offenses. Again, changing these conditions and contingencies represents a mammoth and complex task. Yet, instituting such alterations wherever possible may pay handsome dividends in terms of reduced interpersonal violence.

Third, we should seek to eliminate as many of the antecedents of aggression as possible from the environment. Many of these, of course, are not amenable to direct control (e.g., uncomfortable heat, all instances of frustration). Many others, however, *are* (e.g., unpleasant noise, crowding, the presence of weapons and other aggressive cues). Thus, active steps to eliminate, or at least reduce, the prevalence of such conditions may succeed in moving us closer to the goal of human society without overt violence.

Finally, it should be noted that even in cases in which aggressive responses have already been acquired and specific individuals have been instigated to such behavior, techniques for preventing the occurrence of overt harm-doing actions still exist. As noted earlier in this chapter, such procedures as the introduction of nonaggressive models, the induction of incompatible responses among aggressors, and even threatened punishment (when employed in an appropriate manner) may be quite effective in "nipping aggression in the bud," so to speak. Thus, the further refinement of such techniques in additional research and the dissemination of information concerning their use may prove helpful in preventing overt aggression even in situations in which its occurrence seems imminent.

In sum, it is clear that at the present time, we already know a great deal about steps that could be taken to reduce the frequency of interpersonal violence—much more, in fact, than many individuals would guess. Unfortunately, there is often a considerable gap between knowledge and action, and in this particular case, the gulf seems especially wide. Little, if anything, is currently being done to implement these changes on a societal—let alone a global—scale. Despite this fact, however, I, personally, remain somewhat hopeful. Knowledge, once acquired, has a way of being used, and there is no reason to assume that information regarding the control of human aggression will represent an exception. Thus, I anticipate that in the years ahead, it, too, will gradually find its way into practical use and will benefit humanity in many ways. In any case, it is my firm conviction that the chain of violence linking us with preceding generations *can* be broken. In general terms, we already know how to accomplish this goal; what seem to be lacking are the will and the conviction to do so. We can continue to live in an increasingly violent world, or we can take steps to halt this dangerous cycle. The choice, in a very real sense, is ours.

## SUMMARY

Until quite recently, much more attention was directed to factors serving to elicit aggression than to methods for the prevention and control of such behavior. Apparently, this unsettling state of affairs stemmed, in large measure, from a widespread belief among psychologists that they already knew the most effective means of preventing such actions: *punishment* and *catharsis*. Recent studies, however, suggest that neither of these procedures is quite as effective in this respect as once believed.

Turning first to punishment, it now appears that threats of such aversive treatment are effective in reducing aggression only under conditions in which (1) the aggressors are not very angry, (2) the magnitude of punishment they anticipate is great, (3) the probability that such treatment will actually be delivered is high, and (4) they have little to gain from such actions. When such conditions do not prevail, threatened punishment may totally fail to inhibit overt aggression. The actual delivery of punishment, too, seems to be effective only under certain conditions. In particular, it is successful in inhibiting later aggression only when it is viewed as legitimate by its recipients, follows aggressive actions quite swiftly, and is administered in a sure and predictable manner. When, in contrast, such conditions do not prevail, it often "backfires" and actually enhances the occurrence of aggressive behavior.

The suggestions that providing angry individuals with an opportunity to "blow off steam" in some safe manner will (1) cause them to feel better and (2) weaken their tendencies to engage in more dangerous forms of behavior form the basis of the famous *catharsis hypothesis*. Existing evidence lends support to the first of these proposals: participation in various forms of aggression may indeed cause angry individuals to experience sharp reductions in emotional arousal. However, there does not appear to be a unique connection between aggression and such effects, and participation in almost any activity that lessens aversive treatment from others may produce similar effects.

Evidence regarding the second suggestion—that present aggression reduces the likelihood of future assaults—is less consistent. Apparently, only direct attacks against the source of one's anger or annoyance can produce such effects—a fact that reduces the usefulness of catharsis as a means of controlling overt aggression. Further, the duration of such effects, once produced, is as yet unknown. Thus, it seems reasonable to conclude that the benefits of catharsis as a technique for preventing human violence have been somewhat overstated in the past.

A third procedure that seems somewhat more useful in this regard is the introduction into tense and threatening situations of *nonaggressive models*. By both urging and demonstrating restraint, such individuals seem capable of reducing the likelihood of overt aggression. Further, they may successfully reduce or counter the influence of highly aggressive models, and in this manner, exert socially beneficial effects. Finally, nonaggressive models seem to reduce the incidence or the intensity of overt aggression without simultaneously facilitating the occurrence of more indirect forms of such behavior.

Aggression, like other forms of social interaction, is often under the control of various *cognitive factors*. One that may prove highly effective in preventing such behavior is information regarding the reasons behind provocation from another person. Recent findings suggest that when reasonable explanations for provocative actions on the part of others are provided to potential aggressors, their tendency to respond aggressively to such treatment may be sharply reduced. Further, if such information is provided *prior* to annoyance or provocation, the degree of anger induced by this aversive treatment may be held to relatively low levels.

Still another technique for the prevention or the control of aggression is based upon the well-established principle that all organisms—including human beings—are incapable of engaging in two *incompatible responses* at once. In accordance with this principle, it would be expected that the induction among aggressors of responses incompatible with anger or overt aggression will be highly effective in inhibiting overt assaults against others. While a number of different reactions might prove incompatible with aggression in this respect, most recent research has focused upon three: *empathy* toward the victim, induced through signs of discomfort on the part of this person; *feelings of amusement*, induced through exposure to various types of humorous materials; and *mild sexual arousal*, induced through exposure to mildly erotic stimuli. Evidence gathered in both laboratory and field setting suggests that all three factors are indeed successful in inducing incompatible responses among aggressors and, in this manner, sharply reducing the strength of their overt attacks against others.

# References

Altman, I. *The environment and social behavior*. Monterey, Calif.: Brooks-Cole, 1975.

American Psychological Association. *Ethical principles in the conduct of research with human participants*. Washington, D.C.: American Psychological Association, 1973.

Bandura, A. Influence of models' reinforcement contingencies on the acquisition of imitative responses. *Journal of Personality and Social Psychology*, 1965, *1*, 589–595.

Bandura, A. *Aggression: A social learning analysis*. Englewood Cliffs, N.J.: Prentice-Hall, 1973.

Bandura, A. *Social learning theory*. Englewood Cliffs, N.J.: Prentice-Hall, 1977.

Bandura, A., Ross, D., & Ross, S. A. Imitation of film-mediated aggressive models. *Journal of Abnormal and Social Psychology*, 1963a, *66*, 3–11.

Bandura, A., Ross, D., & Ross, S. A. Vicarious reinforcement and imitative learning. *Journal of Abnormal and Social Psychology*, 1963b, *67*, 601–607.

Baron, R. *The tyranny of noise*. New York: St. Martin's, 1970.

Baron, R. A. Aggression as a function of audience presence and prior anger arousal. *Journal of Experimental Social Psychology*, 1971a, *7*, 515–523.

Baron, R. A. Aggression as a function of magnitude of victim's pain cues, level of prior anger arousal, and aggressor–victim similarity. *Journal of Personality and Social Psychology*, 1971b, *18*, 48–54.

Baron, R. A. Exposure to an aggressive model and apparent probability of retaliation as determinants of adult aggressive behavior. *Journal of Experimental Social Psychology*, 1971c, *7*, 343–355.

Baron, R. A. Magnitude of victim's pain cues and level of prior anger arousal as determinants of adult aggressive behavior. *Journal of Personality and Social Psychology*, 1971d, *17*, 236–243.

Baron, R. A. Reducing the influence of an aggressive model: The restraining effects of discrepant modeling cues. *Journal of Personality and Social Psychology*, 1971e, *20*, 240–245.

Baron, R. A. Aggression as a function of ambient temperature and prior anger arousal. *Journal of Personality and Social Psychology*, 1972a, *21*, 183–189.

Baron, R. A. Reducing the influence of an aggressive model: The restraining effects of peer censure. *Journal of Experimental Social Psychology*, 1972b, *8*, 266–275.

Baron, R. A. Threatened retaliation from the victim as an inhibitor of physical aggression. *Journal of Research in Personality*, 1973, *7*, 103–115.

Baron, R. A. Aggression as a function of victim's pain cues, level of prior anger arousal, and exposure to an aggressive model. *Journal of Personality and Social Psychology*, 1974a, *29*, 117–124.

Baron, R. A. The aggression-inhibiting influence of heightened sexual arousal. *Journal of Personality and Social Psychology*, 1974b, *30*, 318–322.

Baron, R. A. Sexual arousal and physical aggression: The inhibiting influence of "cheesecake" and nudes. *Bulletin of the Psychonomic Society*, 1974c, *3*, 337–339.

Baron, R. A. Threatened retaliation as an inhibitor of human aggression: Mediating effects of the instrumental value of aggression. *Bulletin of the Psychonomic Society*, 1974d, *29*, 217–219.

Baron, R. A. The reduction of human aggression: A field study of the influence of incompatible reactions. *Journal of Applied Social Psychology*, 1976, *6*, 260–274.

Baron, R. A. Heightened sexual arousal and physical aggression: An extension to females. Unpublished manuscript, Purdue University, 1977a.

Baron, R. A. Effects of victim's pain cues, victim's race, and level of prior instigation upon physical aggression. Unpublished manuscript, Purdue University, 1977b.

Baron, R. A., & Ball, R. L. The aggression-inhibiting influence of nonhostile humor. *Journal of Experimental Social Psychology*, 1974, *10*, 23–33.

Baron, R. A., & Bell, P. A. Effects of heightened sexual arousal on physical aggression. *Proceedings of the American Psychological Association*, 81st annual convention, 1973, 171–172.

Baron, R. A., & Bell, P. A. Aggression and heat: Mediating effects of prior provocation and exposure to an aggressive model. *Journal of Personality and Social Psychology*, 1975, *31*, 825–832.

Baron, R. A., & Bell, P. A. Aggression and heat: The influence of ambient temperature, negative affect, and a cooling drink on physical aggression. *Journal of Personality and Social Psychology*, 1976, *33*, 245–255.

Baron, R. A., & Bell, P. A. Sexual arousal and aggression by males: Effects of type of erotic stimuli and prior provocation. *Journal of Personality and Social Psychology*, 1977, *35*, 79–87.

Baron, R. A., & Byrne, D. *Social psychology: Understanding human interaction*, 2nd ed. Boston: Allyn & Bacon, 1977.

Baron, R. A., & Eggleston, R. J. Performance on the "aggression machine": Motivation to help or harm? *Psychonomic Science*, 1972, *26*, 321–322.

Baron, R. A., & Kepner, C. R. Model's behavior and attraction toward the model as determinants of adult aggressive behavior. *Journal of Personality and Social Psychology*, 1970, *14*, 335–344.

Baron, R. A., & Lawton, S. F. Environmental influences on aggression: The facilitation of modeling effects by high ambient temperatures. *Psychonomic Science*, 1972, *26*, 80–83.

Baxter, G. W. Race of other player, information about other player, and cooperation in a two-person game. In L. S. Wrightsman, J. O'Conner, & N. J. Baker (Eds.), *Cooperation and competition: Readings on mixed-motive games*. Belmont, Calif.: Brooks/Cole, 1972.

Bell, P. A., & Baron, R. A. Aggression and heat: The mediating role of negative affect. *Journal of Applied Social Psychology*, 1976, *6*, 18–30.

Bell, P. A., & Baron, R. A. Aggression and ambient temperature: The inhibiting and facilitating effects of hot and cold environments. *Bulletin of the Psychonomic Society*, 1977, in press.

Bennett, R. M., Buss, A. H., & Carpenter, J. A. Alcohol and human physical aggression. *Quarterly Journal of Studies on Alcohol*, 1969, *30*, 870–877.

Berdie, R. F. Playing the dozens. *Journal of Abnormal and Social Psychology*, 1947, *42*, 120–121.

Bergmann, G. *Philosophy of science*. Madison: University of Wisconsin Press, 1966.

Berkowitz, L. Anti-Semitism and the displacement of aggression. *Journal of Abnormal and Social Psychology*, 1959, *59*, 182–187.

Berkowitz, L. *Aggression: A social psychological analysis*. New York: McGraw-Hill, 1962.

Berkowitz, L. Aggressive cues in aggressive behavior and hostility catharsis. *Psychological Review*, 1964, *71*, 104–122.

Berkowitz, L. The concept of aggressive drive: Some additional considerations. *In* L. Berkowitz (Ed.), *Advances in experimental social psychology*, Vol. 2. New York: Academic Press, 1965a.

Berkowitz, L. Some aspects of observed aggression. *Journal of Personality and Social Psychology*, 1965b, *2*, 359–369.

Berkowitz, L. Impulse, aggression, and the gun. *Psychology Today*, 1968, *2*(4), 18–22.

Berkowitz, L. The frustration–aggression hypothesis revisited. *In* L. Berkowitz (Ed.), *Roots of aggression*. New York: Atherton Press, 1969.

Berkowitz, L. Aggressive humor as a stimulus to aggressive responses. *Journal of Personality and Social Psychology*, 1970, *16*, 710–717.

Berkowitz, L. The contagion of violence: An S–R mediational analysis of some effects of observed aggression. *In* W. J. Arnold & M. M. Page (Eds.), *Nebraska symposium on motivation*. Lincoln: University of Nebraska Press, 1971. Pp. 95–135.

Berkowitz, L. Control of aggression. *In* B. M. Caldwell and H. M. Ricciutti (Eds.), *Review of child development research*. Vol. 3. Chicago: Chicago University Press, 1973.

Berkowitz, L. Some determinants of impulsive aggression: The role of mediated associations with reinforcements for aggression. *Psychological Review*, 1974, *81*, 165–176.

Berkowitz, L., & Alioto, J. T. The meaning of an observed event as a determinant of its aggressive consequences. *Journal of Personality and Social Psychology*, 1973, *28*, 206–217.

Berkowitz, L., & Geen, R. G. Film violence and the cue properties of available targets. *Journal of Personality and Social Psychology*, 1966, *3*, 525–530.

Berkowitz, L., & Geen, R. G. Stimulus qualities of the target of aggression: A further study. *Journal of Personality and Social Psychology*, 1967, *5*, 364–368.

Berkowitz, L., & Knurek, D. A. Label-mediated hostility generalization. *Journal of Personality and Social Psychology*, 1969, *13*, 200–206.

Berkowitz, L., & LePage, A. Weapons as aggression-eliciting stimuli. *Journal of Personality and Social Psychology*, 1967, *7*, 202–207.

Berkowitz, L., & Turner, C. W. Perceived anger level, instigating agent, and aggression. *In* H. London & R. E. Nisbett (Eds.), *Cognitive alteration of feeling states*. Chicago: Aldine, 1974.

Berne, E. *Games people play*. New York: Grove Press, 1964.

Blackburn, R. Personality patterns in homicide: A typological analysis of abnormal offenders. Paper presented at the Fifth International Meeting of Forensic Sciences, Toronto, Canada, June, 1969.

Borden, R. J. Witnessed aggression: Influence of an observer's sex and values on aggressive responding. *Journal of Personality and Social Psychology*, 1975, *31*, 567–573.

Borden, R. J., Bowen, R., & Taylor, S. P. Shock setting behavior as a function of physical attack and extrinsic reward. *Perceptual and Motor Skills*, 1971, *33*, 563–568.

Borden, R. J., & Taylor, S. P. The social instigation and control of physical aggression. *Journal of Applied Social Psychology*, 1973, *3*, 354–361.

Bramel, D., Taub, B., & Blum, B. An observer's reaction to the suffering of his enemy. *Journal of Personality and Social Psychology*, 1968, *8*, 384–392.

Brown, D. G., & Tyler, V. O., Jr. Time out from reinforcement: A technique for dethroning the "duke" of an institutionalized group. *Journal of Child Psychology and Psychiatry and Allied Disciplines*, 1968, *9*, 203–211.

Brown, P., & Elliott, R. Control of aggression in a nursery school class. *Journal of Experimental Child Psychology*, 1965, *2*, 103–107.

Buck, R. Nonverbal communication of affect in children. *Journal of Personality and Social Psychology*, 1975, *31*, 644–653.

Burnam, M. A., Pennebaker, J. W., & Glass, D. C. Time consciousness, achievement striving, and the type A coronary-prone behavior pattern. *Journal of Abnormal Psychology*, 1975, *84*, 76–79.

Burnstein, E., & Worchel, P. Arbitrariness of frustration and its consequences for aggression in a social situation. *Journal of Personality*, 1962, *30*, 528–540.

Buss, A. H. *The psychology of aggression*. New York: Wiley, 1961.

Buss, A. H. Physical aggression in relation to different frustrations. *Journal of Abnormal and Social Psychology*, 1963, *67*, 1–7.

Buss, A. H. The effect of harm on subsequent aggression. *Journal of Experimental Research in Personality*, 1966a, *1*, 249–255.

Buss, A. H. Instrumentality of aggression, feedback, and frustration as determinants of physical aggression. *Journal of Personality and Social Psychology*, 1966b, *3*, 153–162.

Buss, A. H. Aggression pays. *In* J. L. Singer (Ed.), *The control of aggression and violence*. New York: Academic Press, 1971.

Buss, A. H., Booker, A., & Buss, E. Firing a weapon and aggression. *Journal of Personality and Social Psychology*, 1972, *22*, 196–302.

Buvinic, M. L., & Berkowitz, L. Delayed effects of practiced versus unpracticed responses after observation of movie violence. *Journal of Experimental Social Psychology*, 1976, *12*, 283–293.

Byrne, D., & Byrne, L. *Exploring human sexuality*. New York: Crowell, 1977.

Calvert-Boyanowsky, J., Boyanowsky, E. O., Atkinson, M., Goduto, D., & Reeves, J. Patterns of passion: Temperature and human emotion. *In* D. Krebs (Ed.), *Readings in social psychology: A contemporary perspective*. New York: Harper & Row, 1976.

Carver, C. S. Facilitation of physical aggression through objective self-awareness. *Journal of Experimental Social Psychology*, 1974, *10*, 365–370.

Carver, C. S. The facilitation of aggression as a function of objective self-awareness and attitudes toward punishment. *Journal of Experimental Social Psychology*, 1975, *11*, 510–519.

Carver, C. S., Coleman, A. E., & Glass, D. C. The coronary-prone behavior pattern and the suppression of fatigue on a treadmill test. *Journal of Personality and Social Psychology*, 1976, *33*, 460–466.

Carver, C. S., & Glass, D. C. The coronary prone behavior pattern and interpersonal aggression. Unpublished manuscript, University of Texas, 1977.

Chaikin, A. L., Sigler, E., & Derlega, V. J. Nonverbal mediators of teacher expectancy effects. *Journal of Personality and Social Psychology*, 1974, *30*, 144–149.

Cherry, F., Mitchell, H. E., & Nelson, D. A. Helping or hurting? The aggression paradigm. *Proceedings of the 81st Annual Convention*, American Psychological Association, 1973. Pp. 117–118.

Christy, P. R., Gelfand, D. M., & Hartmann, D. P. Effects of competition-induced frustration on two classes of modeled behavior. *Developmental Psychology*, 1971, *5*, 104–111.

Church, R. M. Response suppression. *In* B. A. Campbell & R. M. Church (Eds.), *Punishment and aversive behavior*. New York: Appleton-Century-Crofts, 1969.

Cline, V. B., Croft, R. G., & Courrier, S. Desensitization of children to television violence. *Journal of Personality and Social Psychology*, 1973, 27, 360–365.

Cohen, A. R. Social norms, arbitrariness of frustration, and status of the agent of frustration in the frustration–aggression hypothesis. *Journal of Abnormal and Social Psychology*, 1955, 51, 222–226.

Comstock, G. *Television and human behavior: The key studies*. Santa Monica, Calif.: Rand Corp, 1975.

Conn. L. K., & Crowne, D. P. Instigation to aggression, emotional arousal, and defensive emulation. *Journal of Personality*, 1964, 32, 163–179.

Conot, R. *Rivers of blood, years of darkness*. New York: Bantam, 1967.

Davitz, J. R. The effects of previous training on postfrustration behavior. *Journal of Abnormal and Social Psychology*, 1952, 47, 309–315.

Deaux, K. Honking at the intersection: A replication and extension. *Journal of Social Psychology*, 1971, 84, 159–160.

Deaux, K. *The behavior of women and men*. Monterey, Calif.: Brooks/Cole, 1976.

DeCharms, R., & Wilkins, E. J. Some effects of verbal expression of hostility. *Journal of Abnormal and Social Psychology*, 1963, 66, 462–470.

Dengerink, H. A. Aggression, anxiety, and physiological arousal. *Journal of Experimental Research in Personality*, 1971, 5, 223–232.

Dengerink, H. A. Personality variables as mediators of attack-instigated aggression. *In* R. G. Geen & E. C. O'Neal (Eds.), *Perspectives on aggression*. New York: Academic Press, 1976.

Dengerink, H. A., & Bertilson, H. S. The reduction of attack instigated aggression. *Journal of Research in Personality*, 1974, 8, 254–262.

Dengerink, H. A., & Myers, J. D. The effects of failure and depression on subsequent aggression. *Journal of Personality and Social Psychology*, 1977, 35, 88–96.

Dengerink, H. A., O'Leary, M. R., & Kasner, K. H. Individual differences in aggressive responses to attack: Internal–external locus of control and field dependence–independence. *Journal of Research in Personality*, 1975, 9, 191–199.

Deur, J. D., & Parke, R. D. Effects of inconsistent punishment on aggression in children. *Developmental Psychology*, 1970, 2, 401–411.

Dey, F. Auditory fatigue and predicted permanent hearing defects from rock-and-roll music. *The New England Journal of Medicine*, 1970, 282, 467–469.

Diener, E. Effects of prior destructive behavior, anonymity, and group presence on deindividuation and aggression. *Journal of Personality and Social Psychology*, 1976, 33, 497–507.

Diener, E., Dineen, J., & Endresen, K. Effects of altered responsibility, cognitive set, and modeling on physical aggression and deindividuation. *Journal of Personality and Social Psychology*, 1975, 31, 328–337.

Dollard, J., Doob, L., Miller, N., Mowrer, O. H., & Sears, R. R. *Frustration and aggression*. New Haven, Conn.: Yale University Press, 1939.

Donnerstein, E., & Donnerstein, M. Variables in interracial aggression: Potential ingroup censure. *Journal of Personality and Social Psychology*, 1973, 27, 143–150.

Donnerstein, E., & Donnerstein, M. The effect of attitudinal similarity on interracial aggression. *Journal of Personality*, 1975, 43, 485–502.

Donnerstein, E., & Donnerstein, M. Research in the control of interracial aggression. *In* R. G. Geen & E. C. O'Neal (Eds.), *Perspectives on aggression*. New York: Academic Press, 1976.

Donnerstein, E., Donnerstein, M., & Barrett, G. Where is the facilitation of media violence: The effects of nonexposure and placement of anger arousal. *Journal of Research in Personality*, 1976, 10, 386–398.

Donnerstein, E., Donnerstein, M., & Evans, R. Erotic stimuli and aggression: Facilitation or inhibition. *Journal of Personality and Social Psychology*, 1975, 32, 237–244.

Donnerstein, E., Donnerstein, M., Simon, S., & Ditrichs, R. Variables in interracial aggression: Anonymity, expected retaliation, and a riot. *Journal of Personality and Social Psychology*, 1972, 22, 236–245.

Donnerstein, E., & Wilson, D. W. The effects of noise and perceived control upon ongoing and subsequent aggressive behavior. *Journal of Personality and Social Psychology*, 1976, 34, 774–781.

Donnerstein, M., & Donnerstein, E. Modeling in the control of interracial aggression: The problem of generality. *Journal of Personality*, 1977, 45, in press.

Doob, A. N. Catharsis and aggression: The effect of hurting one's enemy. *Journal of Experimental Research in Personality*, 1970, 4, 291–296.

Doob, A. N., & Climie, R. J. Delay of measurement and the effects of film violence. *Journal of Experimental Social Psychology*, 1972, 8, 136–142.

Doob, A. N., & Gross, A. E. Status of frustrator as an inhibitor of horn-honking responses. *Journal of Social Psychology*, 1968, 76, 213–218.

Doob, A. N., & Wood, L. Catharsis and aggression: The effects of annoyance and retaliation on aggressive behavior. *Journal of Personality and Social Psychology*, 1972, 22, 156–162.

Doob, L. W., & Sears, R. R. Factors determining substitute behavior and the overt expression of aggression. *Journal of Abnormal and Social Psychology*, 1939, 34, 293–313.

Dorsky, F. S., & Taylor, S. P. Physical aggression as a function of manifest anxiety. *Psychonomic Science*, 1972, 27, 103–104.

Duval, S., & Wicklund, R. A. *A theory of objective self awareness.* New York: Academic Press, 1972.

Eaton, W. O., & Clore, G. L. Interracial imitation at a summer camp. *Journal of Personality and Social Psychology*, 1975, 32, 1099–1105.

Ebbesen, E. B., Duncan, B., & Konečni, V. J. Effects of content of verbal aggression on future verbal aggression: A field experiment. *Journal of Experimental Social Psychology*, 1975, 11, 192–204.

Eleftheriou, B. E., & Scott, J. P. (Eds.). *The physiology of aggression and defeat.* New York: Plenum Press, 1971.

Elms, A. C. *Social psychology and social relevance.* Boston: Little, Brown, 1972.

Elms, A. M., & Milgram, S. Personality characteristics associated with obedience and defiance toward authoritative command. *Journal of Experimental Research in Personality*, 1966, 1, 282–289.

Estes, W. K. An experimental study of punishment. *Psychological Monographs*, 1944, 57 (Whole No. 263).

Evans, R. I. Lorenz warns: "Man must know that the horse he is riding may be wild and should be bridled." *Psychology Today*, 1974, 8, 82–93.

Fantino, E. Aversive control. *In* T. A. Nevin & C. S. Reynolds (Eds), *The study of behavior: Learning, motivation, emotion, and instinct.* Glenview, Ill.: Scott, Foresman, 1973.

Fenigstein, A., & Buss, A. H. Association and affect as determinants of displaced aggression. *Journal of Research in Personality*, 1974, 7, 306–313.

Ferson, J. E. The displacement of hostility. *Dissertation Abstracts*, 1959, 19, 2386–2387.

Feshbach, S. The function of aggression and the regulation of aggressive drive. *Psychological Review*, 1964, 71, 257–272.

Feshbach, S. Aggression. *In* P. H. Mussen (Ed.), *Carmichael's manual of child psychology.* New York: Wiley, 1970. Pp. 159–259.

Feshbach, S., & Singer, R. D. *Television and aggression.* San Francisco: Jossey-Bass, 1971.

Feshbach, S., Stiles, W. B., & Bitter, E. The reinforcing effect of witnessing aggression. *Journal of Experimental Research in Personality,* 1967, *2,* 133–139.

Fishman, C. G. Need for approval and the expression of aggression under varying conditions of frustration. *Journal of Personality and Social Psychology,* 1965, *2,* 809–816.

Fitz, D. A renewed look at Miller's conflict theory of aggression displacement. *Journal of Personality and Social Psychology,* 1976, *33,* 725–732.

Freedman, J. L. *Crowding and behavior.* San Francisco: Freeman, 1975.

Freedman, J. L., Heshka, S., & Levy, A. Population density and pathology: Is there a relationship? *Journal of Experimental Social Psychology,* 1975, *11,* 539–552.

Freedman, J. L., Levy, A. S., Buchanan, R. W., & Price, J. Crowding and human aggressiveness. *Journal of Experimental Social Psychology,* 1972, *8,* 528–548.

Freud, S. *A general introduction to psycho-analysis.* New York: Boni & Liveright, 1920.

Freud, S. *New introductory lectures on psycho-analysis.* New York: Norton, 1933.

Frodi, A. The effect of exposure to weapons on aggressive behavior from a cross-cultural perspective. *International Journal of Psychology,* 1975, *10,* 283–292.

Frodi, A. Sexual arousal, situational restrictiveness, and aggressive behavior. *Journal of Research in Personality,* 1977a, *11,* 48–58.

Frodi, A. Sex differences in perception of a provocation, a survey. *Perceptual and Motor Skills,* 1977b, *44,* 113–114.

Frodi, A., Macaulay, J., & Thome, P. R. Are women always less aggressive than men? A review of the experimental literature. *Psychological Bulletin,* 1977, in press.

Gaebelein, J. W. Third-party instigation of aggression: An experimental approach. *Journal of Personality and Social Psychology,* 1973, *27,* 389–395.

Gambaro, S., & Rabin, A. K. Diastolic blood pressure responses following direct and displaced aggression after anger arousal in high- and low-guilt subjects. *Journal of Personality and Social Psychology,* 1969, *12,* 87–94.

Geen, R. G. Effects of frustration, attack, and prior training in aggressiveness upon aggressive behavior. *Journal of Personality and Social Psychology,* 1968, *9,* 316–321.

Geen, R. G. Perceived suffering of the victim as an inhibitor of attack-induced aggression. *Journal of Social Psychology,* 1970, *81,* 209–215.

Geen, R. G. Observing violence in the mass media: Implications of basic research. *In* R. G. Geen & E. C. O'Neal (Eds.), *Perspectives on aggression.* New York: Academic Press, 1976.

Geen, R. G., & Berkowitz, L. Name-mediated aggressive cue properties. *Journal of Personality,* 1966, *34,* 456–465.

Geen, R. G., & Berkowitz, L. Some conditions facilitating the occurrence of aggression after the observation of violence. *Journal of Personality,* 1967, *35,* 666–676.

Geen, R. G., & O'Neal, E. C. Activation of cue-elicited aggression by general arousal. *Journal of Personality and Social Psychology,* 1969, *11,* 289–292.

Geen, R. G., & O'Neal, E. C. (Eds.). *Perspectives on aggression.* New York: Academic Press, 1976.

Geen, R. G., & Stonner, D. Effects of aggressiveness habit strength on behavior in the presence of aggression-related stimuli. *Journal of Personality and Social Psychology,* 1971, *17,* 149–153.

Geen, R. G., & Stonner, D. Context effects in observed violence. *Journal of Personality and Social Psychology,* 1972, *25,* 145–150.

Geen, R. G., Stonner, D., & Shope, G. L. The facilitation of aggression by aggression:

Evidence against the catharsis hypothesis. *Journal of Personality and Social Psychology*, 1975, *31*, 721–726.

Genthner, R. W., & Taylor, S. P. Physical aggression as a function of racial prejudice and the race of the target. *Journal of Personality and Social Psychology*, 1973, *27*, 207–210.

Gentry, W. D. Effects of frustration, attack, and prior aggressive training on overt aggression and vascular processes. *Journal of Personality and Social Psychology*, 1970a, *16*, 718–725.

Gentry, W. D. Sex differences in the effects of frustration and attack on emotion and vascular processes. *Psychological Reports*, 1970b, *27*, 383–390.

Glass, D. C. *Stress and coronary prone behavior*. Hillsdale, N.J.: Lawrence Erlbaum Associates, 1977.

Glass, D. C., & Krantz, D. S. Noise and behavior. In B. B. Wolman (Ed.), *International encyclopedia of neurology, psychiatry, psychoanalysis, and psychology*. New York: Springer, 1975.

Glass, D. C., & Singer, J. E. *Urban stress: Experiments on noise and social stressors*. New York: Academic Press, 1972.

Goldstein, J. H. *Aggression and crimes of violence*. New York: Oxford University Press, 1975.

Goldstein, J. H., & Arms, R. L. Effects of observing athletic contests on hostility. *Sociometry*, 1971, *34*, 93–90.

Goranson, R. E. Media violence and aggressive behavior: A review of experimental research. In L. Berkowitz (Ed.), *Advances in experimental social psychology*, Vol. 5. New York: Academic Press, 1970.

Goranson, R. E., & King, D. Rioting and daily temperature: Analysis of the U.S. riots in 1967. Unpublished manuscript, York University, 1970.

Graham, F. K., Charwat, W. A., Honig, A. S., & Weltz, P. C. Aggression as a function of the attack and the attacker. *Journal of Abnormal and Social Psychology*, 1951, *46*, 512–520.

Greenwell, J., & Dengerink, H. A. The role of perceived versus actual attack in human physical aggression. *Journal of Personality and Social Psychology*, 1973, *26*, 66–71.

Griffin, B. Q., & Rogers, R. W. Reducing interracial aggression: Inhibiting effects of victim's suffering and power to retaliate. *Journal of Psychology*, 1977, *95*, 151–157.

Griffitt, W. Environmental effects on interpersonal affective behavior: Ambient effective temperature and attraction. *Journal of Personality and Social Psychology*, 1970, *15*, 240–244.

Griffitt, W., & Veitch, R. Hot and crowded: Influence of population density and temperature on interpersonal affective behavior. *Journal of Personality and Social Psychology*, 1971, *17*, 92–98.

Grusec, J. E. Demand characteristics of the modeling experiment: Altruism as a function of age and aggression. *Journal of Personality and Social Psychology*, 1972, *22*, 139–148.

Guthrie, R. V. *Even the rat was white*. New York: Harper & Row, 1976.

Haner, C. E., & Brown, P. A. Clarification of the instigation to action concept in the frustration–aggression hypothesis. *Journal of Abnormal and Social Psychology*, 1955, *51*, 204–206.

Hanratty, M. A., O'Neal, E., & Sulzer, J. L. Effect of frustration upon imitation and aggression. *Journal of Personality and Social Psychology*, 1972, *21*, 30–34.

Harris, M. B. Field studies of modeled aggression. *Journal of Social Psychology*, 1973, *89*, 131–139.

Harris, M. B. Instigators and inhibitors of aggression in a field experiment. Unpublished manuscript, University of New Mexico, 1974a.

Harris, M. B. Mediators between frustration and aggression in a field experiment. *Journal of Experimental Social Psychology*, 1974b, *10*, 561–571.

Harris, M. B., & Samerotte, G. The effects of aggressive and altruistic modeling on subsequent behavior. *Journal of Social Psychology*, 1975, *95*, 173–182.

Hartmann, D. P. Influence of symbolically modeled instrumental aggression and pain cues on aggressive behavior. *Journal of Personality and Social Psychology*, 1969, *11*, 280–288.

Hartmann, H., Kris, E., & Loewenstein, R. M. *Notes on the theory of aggression: The psychoanalytic study of the child*. New York: International Universities Press, 1949.

Hendrick, C., & Taylor, S. P. Effects of belief similarity and aggression on attraction and counteraggression. *Journal of Personality and Social Psychology*, 1971, *17*, 342–349.

Hokanson, J. E. Psychophysiological evaluation of the catharsis hypothesis. In E. I. Megargee and J. E. Hokanson (Eds.), *The dynamics of aggression*. New York: Harper & Row, 1970.

Hokanson, J. E., & Burgess, M. The effects of status, type of frustration, and aggression on vascular processes. *Journal of Abnormal and Social Psychology*, 1962a, *65*, 232–237.

Hokanson, J. E., & Burgess, M. The effects of three types of aggression on vascular processes. *Journal of Abnormal and Social Psychology*, 1962b, *64*, 446–449.

Hokanson, J. E., Burgess, M., & Cohen, M. E. Effects of displaced aggression on systolic blood pressure. *Journal of Abnormal and Social Psychology*, 1963, *67*, 214–218.

Hokanson, J. E., & Edelman, R. Effects of three social responses on vascular processes. *Journal of Personality and Social Psychology*, 1966, *3*, 442–447.

Hokanson, J. E., & Shetler, S. The effect of overt aggression on physiological arousal. *Journal of Abnormal and Social Psychology*, 1961, *63*, 446–448.

Hokanson, J. E., Willers, K. R., & Koropsak, E. The modification of autonomic responses during aggressive interchanges. *Journal of Personality*, 1968, *36*, 386–404.

Hollenberg, E., & Sperry, M. Some antecedents of aggression and effects of frustration in doll play. *Personality*, 1951, *1*, 34–43.

Hutchinson, R. R. The environmental causes of aggression. In J. K. Cole & D. D. Jensen (Eds.), *Nebraska symposium on motivation*. Lincoln: University of Nebraska Press, 1972.

Hutt, C., & Vaizey, M. J. Differential effects of group density on social behavior. *Nature*, 1966, *209*, 1371–1372.

Jacobs, P. A., Brunton, M., & Melville, M. M. Aggressive behavior, mental subnormality, and the XYY male. *Nature*, 1965, *208*, 1351–1352.

Jaffe, Y., Malamuth, N., Feingold, J., & Feshbach, S. Sexual arousal and behavioral aggression. *Journal of Personality and Social Psychology*, 1974, *30*, 759–764.

Jarvik, L. F., Klodin, V., & Matsuyama, S. S. Human aggression and the extra Y chromosome: Fact or fantasy? *American Psychologist*, 1973, *28*, 674–682.

Jenkins, C. D., Rosenman, R. H., and Zyzanski, S. J. The Jenkins activity survey for health prediction, Form B. Boston: Authors, 1972.

Johnston, A., DeLuca, D., Murtaugh, K., & Diener, E. Validation of a laboratory play measure of child aggression. *Child Development*, 1977, *48*, 324–327.

Jones, J. M. *Prejudice and racism*. Reading, Mass.: Addison-Wesley, 1972.

Kahn, M. The physiology of catharsis. *Journal of Personality and Social Psychology*, 1966, *3*, 278–286.

Kaleta, R. J., & Buss, A. H. Aggression intensity and femininity of the victim. Paper presented at the meeting of the Eastern Psychological Association, May 1973.

Kaufmann, H. *Aggression and altruism*. New York: Holt, 1970.

Kelley, K., & Byrne, D. Strength of instigation as a determinant of the aggression–attraction relationship. *Motivation and Emotion*, 1977, *1*, 29–38.

Kilham, W., & Mann, L. Level of destructive obedience as a function of transmitter and executant roles in the Milgram obedience paradigm. *Journal of Personality and Social Psychology*, 1974, *29*, 696–702.

Kimble, C. E., Fitz, D., & Onorad, J. The effectiveness of counteraggression strategies in reducing interactive aggression by males. *Journal of Personality and Social Psychology*, 1977, *35*, 272–278.

Klapper, J. T. The impact of viewing "aggression": Studies and problems of extrapolation. *In* O. N. Larsen (Ed.), *Violence and the mass media*. New York: Harper & Row, 1968.

Knott, P. D., & Drost, B. A. Effects of status of attacker and intensity of attack on the intensity of counter-aggression. *Journal of Personality*, 1972a, *40*, 450–459.

Knott, P. D., & Drost, B. Effects of varying intensity of attack and fear arousal on the intensity of counter aggression. *Journal of Personality*, 1972b, *40*, 27–37.

Knott, P. D., Lasater, L., & Shuman, R. Aggression-guilt and conditionability for aggressiveness. *Journal of Personality*, 1974, *42*, 332–344.

Konečni, V. J. Annoyance, type and duration of postannoyance activity, and aggression: The "cathartic effect." *Journal of Experimental Psychology: General*, 1975a, *104*, 76–102.

Konečni, V. J. The mediation of aggressive behavior: Arousal level versus anger and cognitive labeling. *Journal of Personality and Social Psychology*, 1975b, *32*, 706–712.

Konečni, V. J., & Doob, A. N. Catharsis through displacement of aggression. *Journal of Personality and Social Psychology*, 1972, *23*, 379–387.

Konečni, V. J., & Ebbesen, E. B. Disinhibition versus the cathartic effect: Artifact and substance. *Journal of Personality and Social Psychology*, 1976, *34*, 352–365.

Kryter, K. D. *The effects of noise on man*. New York: Academic Press, 1970.

Kuhn, D. Z., Madsen, C. H., & Becker, W. C. Effects of exposure to an aggressive model and "frustration" on children's aggressive behavior. *Child Development*, 1967, *38*, 739–745.

Landy, D., & Mettee, D. Evaluation of an aggressor as a function of exposure to cartoon humor. *Journal of Personality and Social Psychology*, 1969, *12*, 66–71.

Larsen, K. S., Coleman, D., Forbes, J., & Johnson, R. Is the subject's personality or the experimental situation a better predictor of a subject's willingness to administer shock to a victim? *Journal of Personality and Social Psychology*, 1972, *22*, 287–295.

Leak, G. K. Effects of hostility arousal and aggressive humor on catharsis and humor preference. *Journal of Personality and Social Psychology*, 1974, *30*, 736–740.

Leamer, L. Bangladesh in morning. *Harper's Magazine*, August 1972, 84–98.

Leavitt, F. *Drugs and behavior*. Philadelphia: Saunders, 1974.

Leyens, J. P., Camino, L., Parke, R. D., & Berkowitz, L. Effects of movie violence on aggression in a field setting as a function of group dominance and cohesion. *Journal of Personality and Social Psychology*, 1975, *32*, 346–360.

Leyens, J. P., & Parke, R. E. Aggressive slides can induce a weapons effect. *European Journal of Social Psychology*, 1975, *5*, 229–236.

Lieber, A. L., & Sherin, C. R. Homicides and the lunar cycle: Toward a theory of lunar influence on human emotional disturbance. *Journal of Psychiatry*, 1972, *129*, 69–74.

Lieberson, S., & Silverman, A. R. The precipitants and underlying conditions of race riots. *American Sociological Review*, 1965, *30*, 887–898.

Liebert, R. M., & Baron, R. A. Some immediate effects of televised violence on childrens' behavior. *Developmental Psychology*, 1972, *6*, 469–475.

Longstreth, L. E. Distance to goal and reinforcement schedule as determinants of human instrumental behavior. *Proceedings of the 74th Annual Convention of the American Psychological Association*, 1966, 39–40.

Loo, C. M. The effects of spatial density on the social behavior of children. *Journal of Applied Social Psychology*, 1972, 2, 372–381.

Lorenz, K. *On aggression*: New York: Harcourt, Brace, & World, 1966.

Lorenz, K. *Civilized man's eight deadly sins*. New York: Harcourt Brace Jovanovich, 1974.

Ludwig, A. M., Marx, A. J., Hill, P. A., & Browning, R. M. The control of violent behavior through faradic shock. *Journal of Nervous and Mental Disease*, 1969, 148, 624–637.

Lykken, D. T. A study of anxiety in the sociopathic personality. *Journal of Abnormal and Social Psychology*, 1957, 55, 6–10.

Maier, S. F., & Seligman, M. E. P. Learned helplessness: Theory and evidence. *Journal of Experimental Psychology: General*, 1976, 105, 3–45.

Mallick, S. K., & McCandless, B. R. A study of catharsis of aggression. *Journal of Personality and Social Psychology*, 1966, 4, 591–596.

Manning, S. A., & Taylor, D. A. Effects of viewed violence and aggression: Stimulation and catharsis. *Journal of Personality and Social Psychology*, 1975, 31, 180–188.

McClelland, D. C., & Apicella, F. S. A functional classification of verbal reactions to experimentally induced failure. *Journal of Abnormal and Social Psychology*, 1945, 46, 376–390.

Megargee, E. I. Undercontrolled and overcontrolled personality types in extreme antisocial aggression. *Psychological Monographs*, 1966, 80 (Whole No. 611).

Megargee, E. I. The role of inhibition in the assessment and understanding of violence. In J. L. Singer (Ed.), *The control of aggression and violence*. New York: Academic Press, 1971.

Megargee, E. I., Cook, P. E., & Mendelsohn, G. A. Development and evaluation of an MMPI scale of assaultiveness in overcontrolled individuals. *Journal of Abnormal Psychology*, 1967, 72, 519–528.

Meyer, R. G. The relationship of blood pressure levels to the chronic inhibition of aggression. *Dissertation Abstracts*, 1967, 28, 2099.

Meyer, T. P. The effects of sexually arousing and violent films on aggressive behavior. *Journal of Sex Research*, 1972, 8, 324–333.

Milgram, S. Behavioral study of obedience. *Journal of Abnormal and Social Psychology*, 1963, 67, 371–378.

Milgram, S. Group pressure and action against a person. *Journal of Abnormal and Social Psychology*, 1964, 69, 137–143.

Milgram, S. Liberating effects of group pressure. *Journal of Personality and Social Psychology*, 1965a, 1, 127–134.

Milgram, S. Some conditions of obedience and disobedience to authority. *Human Relations*, 1965b, 18, 57–76.

Milgram, S. *Obedience to authority*. New York: Harper & Row, 1974.

Milgram, S., & Shotland, R. L. *Television and antisocial behavior: Field experiments*. New York: Academic Press, 1973.

Miller, N. E. The frustration–aggression hypothesis. *Psychological Review*, 1941, 48, 337–342.

Miller, N. E. Theory and experiment relating psychoanalytic displacement to stimulus–response generalization. *Journal of Abnormal and Social Psychology*, 1948, 43, 155–178.

Momboisse, R. M. *Riots, revolts, and insurrections*. Springfield, Ill.: Charles C Thomas, 1967.

Montagu, A. *The nature of human aggression*. New York: Oxford University Press, 1976.

Mosher, D. L. The development and validation of a sentence completion measure of guilt. *Dissertation Abstracts*, 1962, 22, 2468–2469.

Mueller, C., & Donnerstein, E. The effects of humor-induced arousal upon aggressive behavior. *Journal of Research in Personality*, 1977, *11*, 73–82.

Murray, E. J., & Berkun, M. M. Displacement as a function of conflict. *Journal of Abnormal and Social Psychology*, 1955, *51*, 47–56.

O'Leary, M. R., & Dengerink, H. A. Aggression as a function of the intensity and pattern of attack. *Journal of Experimental Research in Personality*, 1973, *7*, 61–70.

O'Neal, E. C., & Kaufman, L. The influence of attack, arousal, and information about one's arousal upon interpersonal aggression. *Psychonomic Science*, 1972, *26*, 211–214.

O'Neal, E. C., & McDonald, P. J. The environmental psychology of aggression. *In* R. G. Geen & E. C. O'Neal (Eds.), *Perspectives on aggression*. New York: Academic Press, 1976.

Page, M. P., & Scheidt, R. J. The elusive weapons effect: Demand awareness, evaluation apprehension, and slightly sophisticated subjects. *Journal of Personality and Social Psychology*, 1971, *20*, 304–318.

Page, R. A., & Moss, M. K. Environmental influences on aggression: The effects of darkness and proximity of victim. *Journal of Applied Social Psychology*, 1976, *6*, 126–133.

Parke, R. D., Berkowitz, L., Leyens, J. P., & Sebastian, R. The effects of repeated exposure to movie violence on aggressive behavior in juvenile delinquent boys: Field experimental studies. *In* L. Berkowitz (Ed.), *Advances in experimental social psychology*, Vol. 8. New York: Academic Press, 1975.

Pastore, N. The role of arbitrariness in the frustration–aggression hypothesis. *Journal of Abnormal and Social Psychology*, 1952, *47*, 728–731.

Patterson, G. R., Littman, R. A., & Bricker, W. Assertive behavior in children: A step toward a theory of aggression. *Monographs of the Society for Research in Child Development*, 1967, *32*, No. 5 (Serial No. 113).

Pisano, R., & Taylor, S. P. Reduction of physical aggression: The effects of four strategies. *Journal of Personality and Social Psychology*, 1971, *19*, 237–242.

Powers, P. C., & Geen, R. G. Effects of the behavior and the perceived arousal of a model on instrumental aggression. *Journal of Personality and Social Psychology*, 1972, *23*, 175–184.

Price, W. H., & Whatmore, P. B. Behavior disorders and pattern of crime among XYY males identified at a maximum security hospital. *British Medical Journal*, 1967, *1*, 533–536.

Proshansky, H. M., Ittelson, W., & Rivlin, L. (Eds.), *Environmental psychology: People and their physical settings*. New York: Holt, Rinehart, & Winston, 1976.

Provins, K. A., & Bell, C. R. Effects of heat stress on the performance of two tasks running concurrently. *Journal of Experimental Psychology*, 1970, *85*, 40–44.

Quanty, M. Aggression catharsis. *In* R. G. Geen & E. C. O'Neal (Eds.), *Perspectives on aggression*. New York: Academic Press, 1976.

Rice, M. E., & Grusec, J. E. Saying and doing: Effects on observer performance. *Journal of Personality and Social Psychology*, 1975, *32*, 584–593.

Rosenbaum, M. E., & DeCharms, R. Direct and vicarious reduction of hostility. *Journal of Abnormal and Social Psychology*, 1960, *60*, 105–111.

Rothaus, P., & Worchel, P. The inhibition of aggression under nonarbitrary frustration. *Journal of Personality*, 1960, *28*, 108–117.

Rotter, J. B. Generalized expectancies for internal versus external control of reinforcement. *Psychological Monographs*, 1966, *80* (Whole No. 609).

Rotter, J. B. An introduction to social learning theory. *In* J. B. Rotter, J. E. Chance, & E. J. Phares (Eds.), *Applications of a social learning theory of personality*. New York: Holt, 1972. Pp. 1–44.

Rotton, J., Frey, J., Barry, T., Milligan, M., & Fitzpatrick, M. Modeling, malodorous air pollution, and interpersonal aggression. Paper presented at the meeting of the Midwestern Psychological Association, Chicago, May, 1977.

Rule, B. G., & Hewitt, L. S. Effects of thwarting on cardiac response and physical aggression. *Journal of Personality and Social Psychology*, 1971, *19*, 181–187.

Rule, B. G., & Leger, G. J. Pain cues and differing functions of aggression. *Canadian Journal of Behavioral Science*, 1976, *8*, 213–222.

Rule, B. G., & Nesdale, A. R. Emotional arousal and aggressive behavior. *Psychological Bulletin*, 1976a, *83*, 851–863.

Rule, B. G., & Nesdale, A. R. Moral judgment of aggressive behavior. *In* R. G. Geen & E. C. O'Neal (Eds.), *Perspectives on aggression*. New York: Academic Press, 1976b.

Rule, B. G., Nesdale, A. R., & Dyck, R. Objective self-awareness and differing standards of aggression. *Representative Research in Social Psychology*, 1977, in press.

Scheier, M. F. Self-awareness, self-consciousness, and angry aggression. *Journal of Personality*, 1977, in press.

Scheier, M. F., Fenigstein, A., & Buss, A. H. Self-awareness and physical aggression. *Journal of Experimental Social Psychology*, 1974, *10*, 264–273.

Schuck, J., & Pisor, K. Evaluating an aggression experiment by the use of simulating subjects. *Journal of Personality and Social Psychology*, 1974, *29*, 181–186.

Schultz, L. G. The wife assaulter. *Journal of Social Therapy*, 1960, *6*, 103–111.

Scott, J. P. Hostility and aggression. *In* B. Wolman (Ed.), *Handbook of general psychology*. Englewood Cliffs, N.J.: Prentice-Hall, 1973.

Seligman, M. E. P. *Helplessness*. San Francisco: Freeman, 1975.

Shaw, M. E., & Costanzo, P. R. *Theories of social psychology*. New York: McGraw-Hill, 1970.

Shemberg, K. M., Leventhal, D. B., & Allman, L. Aggression machine performance and rated aggression. *Journal of Experimental Research in Personality*, 1968, *3*, 117–119.

Shortell, J., Epstein, S., & Taylor, S. P. Instigation to aggression as a function of degree of defeat and the capacity for massive retaliation. *Journal of Personality*, 1970, *38*, 313–328.

Sigall, H., Aronson, E., & Van Hoose, T. The cooperative subject: Myth or reality? *Journal of Experimental Social Psychology*, 1970, *6*, 1–10.

Skinner, B. F. *The behavior of organisms*. New York: Appleton-Century-Crofts, 1938.

Skinner, B. F. *Beyond freedom and dignity*. New York: Knopf, 1971.

Sosa, J. N. Vascular effects of aggression and passivity in a prison population. Unpublished master's thesis, Florida State University, 1968.

Stevens, S. The "rat packs" of New York. *New York Times*, November 28, 1971.

Stone, L. J., & Hokanson, J. E. Arousal reduction via self-punitive behavior. *Journal of Personality and Social Psychology*, 1969, *12*, 72–79.

Swart, C., & Berkowitz, L. Effects of a stimulus associated with a victim's pain on later aggression. *Journal of Personality and Social Psychology*, 1976, *33*, 623–631.

Tannenbaum, P. H., & Zillmann, D. Emotional arousal in the facilitation of aggression through communication. *In* L. Berkowitz (Ed.), *Advances in experimental social psychology*, Vol. 8. New York: Academic Press, 1975.

Taylor, D. Should we integrate organizations? *In* H. Fromkin & J. Sherwood (Eds.), *Integrating the organization*. New York: Free Press, 1974.

Taylor, S. P. Aggressive behavior and physiological arousal as a function of provocation and the tendency to inhibit aggression. *Journal of Personality*, 1967, *35*, 297–310.

Taylor, S. P. Aggressive behavior as a function of approval motivation and physical attack. *Psychonomic Science*, 1970, *18*, 195–196.

Taylor, S. P., & Epstein, S. Aggression as a function of the interaction of the sex of the aggressor and the sex of the victim. *Journal of Personality*, 1967, *35*, 474–486.

Taylor, S. P., & Gammon, C. B. Effects of type and dose of alcohol on human physical aggression. *Journal of Personality and Social Psychology*, 1975, *32*, 169–175.

Taylor, S. P., & Pisano, R. Physical aggression as a function of frustration and physical attack. *Journal of Social Psychology*, 1971, *84*, 261–267.

Taylor, S. P., Gammon, C. B., & Capasso, D. R. Aggression as a function of the interaction of alcohol and threat. *Journal of Personality and Social Psychology*, 1976a, *34*, 938–941.

Taylor, S. P., Vardaris, R. M., Rawitch, A. B., Gammon, C. B., Cranston, J. W., & Lubetkin, A. I. The effects of alcohol and delta-9-tetrahydrocannabinol on human physical aggression. *Aggressive Behavior*, 1976b, *2*, 153–161.

Tedeschi, J. T., Smith, R. B., III, & Brown, R. C., Jr. A reinterpretation of research on aggression. *Psychological Bulletin*, 1974, *81*, 540–563.

Thibaut, J. W., & Coules, J. The role of communication in the reduction of interpersonal hostility. *Journal of Abnormal and Social Psychology*, 1952, *47*, 770–777.

Thibaut, J. W., & Riecken, H. W. Some determinants and consequences of the perception of social causality. *Journal of Personality*, 1955, *24*, 113–133.

Thomas, M. H., Horton, R. W., Lippincott, E. C., & Drabman, R. S. Desensitization to portrayals of real-life aggression as a function of exposure to television violence. *Journal of Personality and Social Psychology*, 1977, in press.

Thorndike, E. L. *Animal intelligence*. New York: Macmillan, 1911.

Tilker, H. A. Socially responsible behavior as a function of observer responsibility and victim feedback. *Journal of Personality and Social Psychology*, 1970, *14*, 95–100.

Toch, H. *Violent men*. Chicago: Aldine, 1969.

Toch, H. *Men in crisis: Human breakdowns in prison*. Chicago: Aldine, 1975.

Turner, C. W., Layton, J. F., & Simons, L. S. Naturalistic studies of aggressive behavior: Aggressive stimuli, victim visibility, and horn honking. *Journal of Personality and Social Psychology*, 1975, *31*, 1098–1107.

Turner, C. W., & Simons, L. S. Effects of subject sophistication and evaluation apprehension on aggressive responses to weapons. *Journal of Personality and Social Psychology*, 1974, *30*, 341–348.

Tyler, V. O., Jr., & Brown, G. D. The use of swift, brief isolation as a group control device for institutionalized delinquents. *Behavior Research and Therapy*, 1967, *5*, 1–9.

Ulrich, R. E., Johnston, M., Richardson, J., & Wolff, P. The operant conditioning of fighting behavior in rats. *Psychological Record*, 1963, *13*, 465–470.

U.S. Riot Commission. *Report of the National Advisory Commission on Civil Disorders*. New York: Bantam Books, 1968.

Waldman, D. M., & Baron, R. A. Aggression as a function of exposure and similarity to a nonaggressive model. *Psychonomic Science*, 1971, *23*, 381–383.

Walters, R. H. Implications of laboratory studies of aggression for the control and regulation of violence. *Annals of the American Academy of Political and Social Science*, 1966, *364*, 60–72.

Walters, R. H., & Brown, M. Studies of reinforcement of aggression: III. Transfer of responses to an interpersonal situation. *Child Development*, 1963, *34*, 536–571.

Weiss, W. Effects of the mass media of communication. *In* G. Lindzey & E. Aronson (Eds.), *The handbook of social psychology*, Vol. 5. Reading, Mass.: Addison-Wesley, 1969.

Wheeler, L., & Caggiula, A. R. *Journal of Experimental Social Psychology*, 1966, *2*, 1–10.

Wicklund, R. A. Objective self awareness. *In* L. Berkowitz (Ed.), *Advances in experimental social psychology*, Vol. 8. New York: Academic Press, 1975.

Wilkins, J. L., Scharff, W. H., & Schlottmann, R. S. Personality type, reports of violence, and aggressive behavior. *Journal of Personality and Social Psychology*, 1974, *30*, 243–247.

Wilson, L., & Rogers, R. W. The fire this time: Effects of race of target, insult, and potential retaliation on black aggression. *Journal of Personality and Social Psychology*, 1975, *32*, 857–864.

Witkin, H. A., Mednick, S. A., Schulsinger, F., Bakkestrom, E., Christiansen, K. O., Goodenough, D. R., Hirschhorn, K., Lundsteen, C., Owen, D. R., Philip, J., Rubin, D. B., & Stocking, M. Criminality in XYY and XXY men. *Science*, 1976, *196*, 547–555.

Wolfe, B. M., & Baron, R. A. Laboratory aggression related to aggression in naturalistic social situations: Effects of an aggressive model on the behavior of college student and prisoner observers. *Psychonomic Science*, 1971, *24*, 193–194.

Worchel, P. Catharsis and the relief of hostility. *Journal of Abnormal and Social Psychology*, 1957, *55*, 238–243.

Worchel, S. The effect of three types of arbitrary thwarting on the instigation to aggression. *Journal of Personality*, 1974, *42*, 301–318.

Zillmann, D. Excitation transfer in communication-mediated aggressive behavior. *Journal of Experimental Social Psychology*, 1971, *7*, 419–434.

Zillmann, D. *Hostility and aggression*. Hillsdale, N.J.: Lawrence Earlbaum Associates, 1978.

Zillmann, D., & Bryant, J. Effects of residual excitation on the emotional response to provocation and delayed aggressive behavior. *Journal of Personality and Social Psychology*, 1974, *30*, 782–791.

Zillmann, D., Bryant, J., Cantor, J. R., & Day, K. D. Irrelevance of mitigating circumstances in retaliatory behavior at high levels of excitation. *Journal of Research in Personality*, 1975, *9*, 282–293.

Zillmann, D., & Cantor, J. R. Effect of timing of information about mitigating circumstances on emotional responses to provocation and retaliatory behavior. *Journal of Experimental Social Psychology*, 1976, *12*, 38–55.

Zillmann, D., & Johnson, R. C. Motivated aggressiveness perpetuated by exposure to aggressive films and reduced by exposure to nonaggressive films. *Journal of Research in Personality*, 1973, *7*, 261–276.

Zillmann, D., Johnson, R. C., & Day, K. D. Attribution of apparent arousal and proficiency of recovery from sympathetic activation affecting activation transfer to aggressive behavior. *Journal of Experimental Social Psychology*, 1974, *10*, 503–515.

Zillmann, D., Katcher, A. H., & Milavsky, B. Excitation transfer from physical exercise to subsequent aggressive behavior. *Journal of Experimental Social Psychology*, 1972, *8*, 247–259.

Zillmann, D., & Sapolsky, B. S. What mediates the effect of mild erotica on hostile behavior by males? *Journal of Personality and Social Psychology*, 1977, in press.

# Author Index

# Subject Index

Incentive-motivated aggression, 15
Incompatible responses, and the reduction of aggression, 258–272
  field study of, 266–269
  laboratory studies of, 260–266
Individual determinants of aggression, 173–222
Informed consent, in laboratory studies of aggression, 42
Instigation toward aggression, 22
Instinct theories of aggression, 16–21
  ethological approach, 18–20
  implications of, 20–21
  psychoanalytic approach, 16–18
Instrumental aggression, 13–15
Intensification of behavior, by crowding, 136–137
Intention to harm, role of in aggression, 8–10
Internal standards, and aggression, 208–212
Internals and externals, differences in aggression by, 184–187
Interracial aggression, 203–208

Laboratory methods for the study of aggression, 42–69
  Berkowitz procedure, 62–65
  Buss technique, 54–62
  Diener paradigm, 51–54
  play measures of aggression, 47–51
  Taylor procedure, 66–68
  verbal measures of aggression, 43–47
Learning-performance distinction, 48–50
Locus of control, and aggression, 184–187
"Long, hot summer" effect, evidence regarding, 137–149

Magnitude of frustration, and aggression, 87–90
Maintenance of aggressive behavior, 35–36
Male–female differences in aggression, 218–222
Marijuana, effects of upon aggression, 167–169
Mitigating circumstances, effects of in reducing aggression, 254–258
  timing of, 255–258
Modeling, and aggression, 34, 98–111,

249–254 (see also Televised violence)
Models, and the control of aggression, 249–254
Motive to avoid harm, and aggression, 12

Need for social approval, and aggression, 180–181
Negative affect, and aggression, 145–148
Noise, effects of upon aggression, 128–132
  psychological mechanisms underlying, 132
Nonaggressive models, effects of, 249–254
  effectiveness in reducing aggression, 251–253
Noninjurious physical aggression, 51–53

Obedience, and aggression, 111–117
Obedience, counteraction of, 116–117
Objective self-awareness, and aggression, 208–212
Objects, as elicitors of aggression, 163–166
Observational learning, role of in effects of televised violence, 109
Orders, as an antecedent of aggression, 111–117
Overcontrolled aggressors, 197 201
Overcontrolled Hostility Scale, 201

Pain cues, effects of upon aggression, 260–263
Passive versus active aggression, 10
Personal confrontations, as context for the study of aggression, 71–74
  cost–benefit ratio of, 73–74
  ethical issues in, 72–74
  validity of, 73
Personality, and aggression, 175–202
Personality traits, of "normal" aggressors, 176–191
Personality versus situational determinants of aggression, 190–191
Physical provocation, and aggression, 92–97
Physical versus verbal aggression, 10
Play measures of aggression, 47–51
  validity of, 51
Prejudice, and interracial aggression, 203–208
Prevention of aggression, 225–272
Psychoanalytic theory of aggression, 16–18

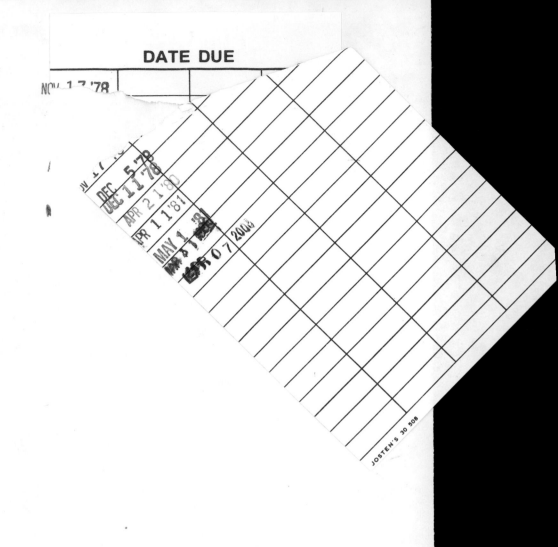